D0098939

The baddest bitch in the room: a memoir

Praise for

The Baddest Bitch in the Room

"Sophia Chang is one of the bravest, most uncompromising people I know. Her life story is filled with all the triumph and pain you'd expect from an industry legend. But it's also secretly a how-to guide. How to value yourself, how to demand what you deserve, and how to remain generously, stubbornly true to yourself the whole way through."

—HUA HSU, author of *A Floating Chinaman*

"Sophia Chang and I are not blood-related, but I will always claim her as my Asian American sister and my hip-hop hero. When the obstacle was too high, she got over it. When it was too wide, she got around it. She blazed the trail so the rest of us could find our way. A courageous pioneer, a fearless advocate, and a true original, her story will shock, amaze, and inspire." —JEFF CHANG, author of *Can't Stop Won't Stop*, *Who We Be*, and *We Gon' Be Alright*

"Sophia Chang is a smart, kind, funny, badass trailblazer with a heart of fire. She's fully living her bold truth as a woman of color in today's world, and we all should be paying attention."

—IJEOMA OLUO, author of the *New York Times* bestselling *So You Want to Talk About Race*

"As hip-hop continues to evolve and stretch into a new decade of its still-young life, it becomes vital to have an archive of stories, told by the people who lived through its most vital eras. I'm thankful for this book and for Sophia Chang's incisive wit and gift of narrative flourish. This book overflows with gems—a tribute to not just the music, but also to the many people who have had their lives moved by it."

—HANIF ABDURRAQIB, author of
They Can't Kill Us Until They Kill Us and
Go Ahead in the Rain

THE BADDEST BITCH IN THE ROOM

THE
BADDEST
BITCH
IN THE ROOM

A MEMOIR

SOPHIA CHANG

CATAPULT
NEW YORK

For my father, Bomshik Chang (God rest his soul),
who taught me justice, fairness, empathy, open-mindedness,
and to defend others.

And my mother, Tongsook Chang,
the strongest person I know.

And my brother, Heesok Chang,
the ten smartest people I know.

And above all, for my extraordinary children,
Jin Long and Jian Hong,
who are so much better than their mother in every way.

Everything I do is for you. I love you so much it hurts.

CONTENTS

1: Where Are You From?   3

2: New York State of Grind   33

3: Enter the Wu-Tang   71

4: When the Student Is Ready   93

5: The Shaolin and the Wu-Tang Could Be Dangerous   115

6: Everything You Need to Know Is Never Enough   133

7: I Want Me Back   149

8: Things Fall Apart   167

9: The Juggling Act   193

10: Blindsided   225

11: Doors Open   245

12: Letting Go   271

13: A Coming-of-Age Story   289

Acknowledgments   305

GZA Sophia and I are very close. We met in the early nineties before the first Clan album came out, and we are still just as close today. Sophia is bright and articulate and an awesome judge of character.

Sophia managed me for a few years and has been involved with some of my greatest accomplishments. She was the person who pushed me to lecture. She believed so deeply in me. Though there were times when I moved at a snail's pace, she had the patience to watch a flower grow, and I am very grateful for that. As a manager, she was always concerned with the heath and well-being of her artists. All advice and constructive criticism always came from a place of love. As a friend, she is loyal and solid as a rock.

Sophia's relationship with the Clan is one that has existed since the beginning of our career. Her photos alone are documented proof of that. She's personally witnessed the ups and downs, the good and bad, the ins and outs, the accomplishments and failures, the growth and development.

It's important for Sophia to tell her story because her journey is a long and very interesting one. I am sure that the readers will be inspired, moved, and motivated by it, and I am proud and happy for her.

GHOSTFACE   Sometimes things just happen, I just put it in the Most High's hands. It just clicks and boom, it's like you're home. Once we connected spiritually, it's like you were right there. Other motherfuckas might not have got that far, even though we knew them. I met motherfuckas twenty-five, twenty-six years ago but you right here. Most of those other motherfuckas, I don't even talk to a lot, but it seems like we stay together out of these twenty-five. It's like no questions asked, it's like you're family. And when you feel like family, you automatically look out for each other. It went like that, and after the first time, you were just there all the time. Like, shit, we here twenty-six years later on a couch. And everybody don't get that. From everybody back then, I don't think there's another person around that's like you that like we close to like that. You never change. You come in one way and leave that way. You're like sunshine, I never see you go nowhere with an attitude, never super down, your energy's always the same. That's why we love you so much. You only show us one side: the sunshine side. If you ever show us another side, then I know something's wrong. I will always be here for you. You've always been here for me—since day one. Any way I can give that same energy back. It's whatever. When you're friends, you do things without thinking. Soph, you know how it is. We love you. It's just real shit.

CHAPTER 1
WHERE ARE YOU FROM?

We never said "I love you" like the white families. Did my parents love me? Didn't even think about it. We were family. The love my parents had for my brother and me far preceded our births, before they even met. It accrued with every step they took from childhood that eventually led them from Korea to a foreign land. In that single act, they had left behind the comfort of everything they knew: their families, their language, their culture. All in pursuit of a better life for themselves, but more importantly, for their children to come: Heesok, number one son, golden boy, top of every class, good at every fucking thing; and me, a bullheaded ill-tempered Taurus, fair-to-middling student.

My mother, Tongsook Park, was born in 1932 on May 17, in Kiyang, North Korea, the fourth of nine children. Her father, Jaebok Young, owned Hwashin, the largest department store in their town, so they were "well-to-do," as my mother calls it. Like most of the other families in the town, hers was a Christian household. Her father was an incredibly generous person who liked to help others. Under the Japanese annexation, many Koreans were very poor and weren't able to eat three meals a day. Much of the rice they grew was sent to Japan. There was a Mitsubishi factory in her hometown, and people from nearby Jeollado, the poorest town in Korea, would travel over every morning to try to get work as day laborers. My grandfather would go for a walk every morning and, because they lived close to the train station, often encountered young mothers and their babies who had come to Kiyang to find their husbands. He would inevitably bring them home, feed them, and help them find their spouses.

My mother's mother, Seungyu Park, was a fighter with a keen business mind and knew exactly how to handle people. My mother laughs when she tells me that I am exactly like my grandmother. My grandmother used to get angry with her father because he let her three older sisters marry poor men. Every autumn, she had her sisters come visit for a few weeks and paid them to do some household chores. When they left, she sent them home with big bundles of food. My grandmother had no trouble confronting people and made sure everyone was doing what they were supposed to be doing. When she heard that the people working at her brother's orchard were being lazy, she called them all to her house and read them the riot act. Both my mother and I inherited her sartorial sense. She loved clothes and delighted in going to church every Sunday to show them off. As a mother she had to be very strict because she had so many children, but she was very kind and, like her husband, liked to take care of people.

My mother is no impresario, but she is an unbroken warrior. After the Japanese surrendered at the end of the Second World War in August 1945, the Korean peninsula was divided into North and South at the thirty-eighth parallel, with Russia occupying the former, the United States the latter. Anyone with money in the North wanted to flee the pending Communist rule because they knew that they would be stripped of their wealth and property. My mother said they'd heard that the Russians were raping the women and pillaging the towns as soon as they landed. Luckily, they started in the big cities and hadn't reached her small town before her father arranged for my mother, then fourteen, and her sixteen-year-old sister, Tongnam, to follow their two older brothers to the South. He paid a hotelier who had been sneaking people out of the North on boats. They dressed down like locals so as not to stand out. They boarded a train and, when they arrived at their station, were elated to be one step closer to freedom and reuniting with their older brothers. The joy would be short-lived.

They had gotten off a stop too early. The police were at the station, on the lookout for people trying to escape the North. Despite their disguises, my mother and her sister were detected immediately and taken to the police station, where they were separated and questioned. Not having anticipated this, they gave conflicting stories. Seeing as the next train was in the morning, they would spend the night at a police-sanctioned hotel and be escorted back to the station.

Serendipitously, a man standing nearby at the police

station, not an officer but someone with great authority, over-heard the entire exchange. I don't think he was a man, rather a bodhisattva. This is a being in Buddhism who has reached nirvana but chooses to stay on earth to alleviate the suffering of others. He took pity on my mother and aunt and offered to take them on a tour of the town before delivering them to the hotel the police had checked them into for the night. Miracu-lously, as they were walking about, the sisters spotted another hotel, branded with the name of the hotelier whom they were supposed to meet to take them across the border! They made a mental note, desperate to get back to it somehow.

My aunt fell very ill overnight, and when the police came to pick the girls up the next morning, they decided to let her rest another day. The sisters saw their opening. The other ho-tel wasn't far, but the town was small and they were terrified of being spotted and apprehended again. Happily, they made it there without incident, and the man they were supposed to meet was there. He arranged for someone to sneak them out in the dead of night. At around 1:00 a.m., another man picked them up at the hotel; he didn't have any lights—no lamp, no flashlight, nothing. And there were no streetlights. My mother and aunt stumbled in the pitch-black night until they got to the beach, where they were handed off to a third man with a boat.

Even the beach was in utter darkness. They saw nothing, heard nothing. The sisters were silently herded onto a small boat with about thirty other people. The boat was probably built to hold a third of that number. No one said a word as they held their breath in fear. The ride lasted only about thirty

minutes but felt interminable. The fear of capture was exac-
erbated by the rough waves; the boat took on so much water
that my mother and aunt were sure they were going to die.
To this day my mother has a morbid fear of rough waters and
airplane turbulence.

When they finally reached the shores of South Korea,
there were makeshift huts on the beach directly in front of
them. Everyone crowded into the huts and sat on the cold
ground, awaiting daybreak. The next morning, huge U.S.
Army trucks arrived to transport the refugees to Seoul. Once
in Seoul, the sisters took a bus to meet their older brothers,
Tongchun and Tongsup, who had rented space in a small,
two-family house.

My aunt cried nonstop for days and weeks and months,
but my mother didn't shed one tear. Perhaps watching her sister prompted her to stay strong for both of them. My mother
recounted this story to me when I was around ten, in much
less detail, in a matter-of-fact manner, as if she were reciting
a recipe. I was sitting on the corner of my parents' bed, not
quite facing her. As she continued sharing the details, I felt
my body shrinking in anguish, and I bowed my head to look
at the pink polyester quilted bedding, fidgeting with a non-
existent loose thread. I watched as the tears, slowly at first,
dropped onto the quilt, darkening it with each drop. By the
time she was done, I turned to her, tears streaming down my
face. She was surprised. She didn't comfort me and I didn't
expect her to. I asked if she could contact her family. She
hadn't seen or spoken to her parents or her five younger siblings since she'd sneaked out that night. She explained that

the government makes it very difficult for them to have any contact.

Five short years after the end of the Second World War, the Korean War broke out between the North and South, each declaring itself the single legitimate government of Korea. During the Korean War, Tongsup joined a makeshift army that fought with the Americans, who were advancing against the North. There, he reconnected with the family. Then the Chinese army intervened on behalf of North Korea and pushed the South Korean army back. There were a number of U.S. ships taking people from the North to the South. By the time my uncle had gathered the family, the last ship was loading. Because they had to get there by foot, my grandmother determined that they wouldn't make it because of the children, so she sent my uncle ahead without them. When he got back to the South, he was so distraught that he was unable to speak about what had happened for a long time. Later, they heard my grandfather was killed during the Korean War, but they had no way of verifying it. My mother thinks that if any of her brothers and sisters survived, they are currently in labor camps.

When my mother and aunt left that day in 1946, they never imagined that it would be the last time they would see their parents and younger siblings. They expected that their remaining family would follow and be reunited in the South. I couldn't fathom never seeing my parents and brother again. More painful, still, to imagine is the thought of never seeing my children again and them not seeing each other. My son and daughter are both older now than my mother was when she escaped North Korea. It means that every moment I've enjoyed, endured, and engineered with my children over the past few years would never have happened if I had been in the position of my grandparents, who had to send their children away in order to save them. As a parent, even the shitty moments are moments—opportunities to learn from and work through, all while loving your children.

My mother finished high school in Inchon, South Korea, strong in English and German. Like her, my strength was languages, and we both hated math. From there, she attended So-ul dae-hak, or Seoul National University, where she met my father, Bomshik Chang, who was born in Inchon a year before her. His father was the head of the Korean Rice Granary Company. My dad was a smart, highly competitive boy with a healthy ego—all traits he would pass on to me. He liked to make things with his hands, draw, and play harmonica, but mathematics was his true gift and passion. As a teen, the first word he wrote in his notebook with a new pen he had bought was *mathematics*. Well-known in Inchon for his intelligence, my father earned the nickname "The Razor." He was named not only for his incredible intellectual capacity, but also for his appearance. He had beautiful high cheekbones and was as sharp a dresser as there ever was. He and my mother made an exceptionally good-looking couple.

The Japanese had annexed Korea in 1910 and continued their occupation until the end of World War II. Koreans were marginalized and forced to learn Japanese. If they were caught speaking Korean in school, they were beaten. The Japanese created schools that were exclusively intended to educate Japanese children, because they didn't want their kids mixing with the Koreans. Because my father was so smart, he was one of only a few Koreans permitted to attend one of the exclusively Japanese schools. He even skipped a grade and started a year early. His mathematics teacher initially favored him because of his talent but erupted in anger when the teacher discovered my father was Korean. (My father spoke impeccable Japanese.) The teacher would put a problem on the chalkboard and ask if anyone could solve it. Often, no one but my father knew how to do it. He approached the board and solved the problem correctly. When he was done, the teacher beat him with a ruler. This would happen a couple more times before my father stopped volunteering.

But the teacher found another way to humiliate my father. All the Japanese students would come to school with their lunches packed in bento boxes. My father was too poor to bring one. The teacher said that someone had been stealing lunch boxes and wanted to discover who the culprit was. He asked everyone to place their boxes on the table, and when my father was the only student without one, the teacher announced that he must be the bento box thief. He proceeded to beat my father again. Decades later, my mother and father went to Japan for a school reunion. My father told my mother that if he saw that teacher again, he would punch him in the face. Unfortunately, he didn't have the opportunity.

When the Japanese occupation ended after the war, my father was in tenth grade. The principal of my father's school told him to sit in the front of class every time a new math teacher was hired. He was to ask the teacher questions in order to vet him. He was recognized as a genius. My father was eighteen when the Korean War broke out and the North Korean army marched into Inchon. One day, he was summoned to a meeting at the local ward office, at which all the unsuspecting attendees were forced to join the South Korean Volunteer Army on the spot. None of them returned home from the meeting. They were made to travel by foot to an unknown destination in North Korea. At some point north of Seoul, my father began to slow down, moving farther and farther away from his group and eventually turning back without being noticed. By dint of sheer will and a little luck, he escaped and made it back home.

He did his first two years of graduate school at Seoul National University and finished his studies at the University of British Columbia in 1956, after being invited there by one of his colleagues. He returned to Korea to teach mathematics at his alma mater.

My parents married on November 15, 1960, and my brother, Heesok, was born March 13, 1962. A few months after he was born, my father came to Vancouver to teach at the University of British Columbia. He told my mother that he cried every time he saw babies because he missed his son so much. My mother followed in the fall of 1963, leaving Heesok behind. My father's mother was worried that if the whole family left, they would never return to Korea, so she promised to raise Heesok while they were gone. This is a common practice for migrants that allows the parents to establish themselves financially and settle in before having the children come over. She brought Heesok to Vancouver in early 1964.

The next year, I was the first in my family to be born outside of Korea, and the only one to be named in English. My father named me after a Polish mathematician. *Sophia* is the Latin word for wisdom.

According to my family, I was independent from the gate. My earliest memories are from 1968, when my father taught at the University of Michigan for a year. We lived in one of four units within a campus housing apartment complex. The most striking thing about our community was its diversity: There was another Korean family, a Japanese family, an Indian family. My brother became close with a black neighbor named Robert Brae, whose older brother wore Malcolm X frames, very much of the era. Another neighbor we talked about and, frankly, made fun of, was Lubo, a recent Polish immigrant. Lubo was an adolescent who used to rummage through the dumpsters, not because he was poor, but because he couldn't believe what Americans threw away. He found toys that were practically new and other random household items.

While Heesok was at school at Northside Elementary, just outside of campus, I would spend all day in the sandbox, mostly playing alone. One day, I got it into my head that I wanted to go for a spin around the grounds on the campus bus and took it upon myself to do so. The stop was right outside our apartment building. I rode the perimeter of the campus and got off back at home. I was three. There are so many things wrong with this picture: How did I get out of the house, into the streets, and find the bus stop? How did the bus driver allow an unattended toddler to board without any questions asked? What were the other passengers thinking? The parent in me now would shame the shit out of those parents, but I've got nathan. It was 1968 and things were much different back then. Perhaps not so much so that a toddler could ride semiprivate transportation alone with ease, but certainly parenting in the late 1960s did not involve the constant hovering that it does now. All things considered, my parents did a remarkable job.

In addition to riding the bus, I have a couple of clear memories of my father's tenure teaching in Ann Arbor. I distinctly remember learning to read. My father had written a bunch of words on index cards and was teaching Heesok to read. Three years old and already extremely competitive with my brother, I was fiending to catch up. The first word I read was *butterfly*. Until this moment, I had been fastidiously but silently studying as well. When my father held up the card, I blurted it out before Heesok could.

The intellectual sibling rivalry between my brother and me was, in fact, no contest whatsoever. Heesok is exponentially smarter than me and everyone else I know combined. It was intimidating to walk in the oversize footsteps of my brother, a challenge for someone as competitive as I am. We went to a small elementary school, an even smaller high school, and we took many of the same classes in college. Every first day of class throughout my underwhelming academic career, when I raised my hand for roll call, the teacher would lower their glasses, raise their eyebrows at me, and say, "Oh, so you're Heesok's sister."

Heesok also teased me to no end. Like my father, I had a mean, unpredictable temper and seemingly had a large button on my back stating PUSH HERE that my brother activated frequently. He knew precisely how to get under my skin. I remember screaming and chasing him around my uncle's house with a boot, while my mother and aunt sat calmly talking and drinking tea, as if nothing were going on. There was another incident at our home that involved me wielding a steak knife screaming "I hate you!" and Heesok laughing his ass off. Our tube-socked feet ran laps from the slippery linoleum kitchen floor over the clear vinyl multi-gripped protectors to the wall-to-wall carpet of the living room and dining room that was a slightly graying pale yellow except for under the vinyl mats. He dipped and dodged around the new off-white matching love seat and sofa, the low walnut coffee table, the two chartreuse faux velvet rocking chairs, and the teak dining room table that my father built. In a quieter moment, one summer day we were examining ourselves in the mirror and I said proudly, "I'm more tanned than you." And I was. Finally, a win. "Yeah, but you're shit brown and I'm golden brown," he replied.

Heesok's excellence was not limited to academia; he was also a phenomenal athlete. That motherfucker could play any sport. He taught me to spiral a pigskin, shoot a three, slap a puck, and throw a curve, but I was never very physically gifted. This shortcoming was impossible to hide and very humiliating. Back in the day, the phys ed teachers would elect two captains—always the jocks—who would stand at the front of the classroom to choose their teammates, excruciatingly peeling off one person at a time from best to worst. I was almost always last to be chosen. Then there were physical endurance challenges that we had to do with the whole class watching: the flexed arm hang or running laps or climbing a rope. I couldn't do any of it. I had neither stamina nor strength.

But I could dance my bony ass off. The first time, I was on the couch boogying with abandon, and my father exclaimed, "Where did you learn to dance?" I don't know what music was playing, but I recall how moving my body in rhythm with the beat felt free. When disco hit, I was engrossed. I watched *American Bandstand* every Saturday and went to see *Saturday Night Fever* and *Thank God It's Friday* multiple times. I taught myself the hustle, the bump, and how to spell out *YMCA* with my body, and I created routines in my bedroom. I helped plan dances at friends' houses as well as the ones at school.

I was a natural-born leader and extremely social. I worked hard to be the most popular, smartest, best dressed, and teacher's pet. And I could be a cruel ruler. In fifth grade, there was one particular girl, Janet, who was my best friend, until I felt like she was getting too close to some of my other friends and copying everything I was doing, particularly my style. Once I decided I didn't want to be friends with her anymore, I ostracized her. One day my teacher, Mrs. Elden, asked me to stay after school. As her favorite, I was sure she was going to laud me for my scholastic achievements. Once the classroom had cleared out, I slid into an orange plastic seat and crossed my hands atop the attached fiberboard desk that had initials carved into it just under the groove intended for holding our 2B pencils. I studied her slightly pockmarked face and thin lips as I sat across from her, beaming, smugly waiting to hear how amazing I was.

"You know, Sophia, there are a group of parents who have come together against . . ." For some reason I was convinced the next word out of her mouth was going to be *Asians*, but instead she said, "people who don't let others be friends with certain students. Do you know what I'm talking about?"

I feigned innocence, but she knew that I knew that she knew. I left the classroom and walked out the double doors, Mrs. Elden's words ringing in my ears. I swatted at the dingy tetherball hanging off the end of a gray fraying rope. As I heard it swinging around the cold metal pole behind me, I thought that the girl's parents must have said something. I felt a mix of indignance, guilt, and humiliation. The next day the desks were moved, and I was forced to sit next to Janet. It was just the two of us, whereas the other desks were clustered into groups of four or six. It worked—we ended up becoming friends again.

When I look back on that incident, it's amazing that despite being the queen of my school, I thought Mrs. Elden was going to tell me that a group of parents was conspiring against Asian students. I still felt "other." And surely my overachieving ambitions were in response to feeling marginalized. Having been called racist names, I understood on some level that a lot of the prejudices propagated by the children were passed down to them by their folks. There was racism lurking in the tidy stucco homes behind the white picket fences.

One sunny spring day as I walked alone across Balaclava Park, one of Vancouver's many massive public greenspaces, I was suddenly struck by how empty it was. Typically, there would be people playing rugby in the giant field or running track and kids lolling about in the sandbox. The sprawling emerald meadow meant fun and freedom under open skies, but it was about to become a battleground. I sensed a presence behind me.

"Where are you from?"

Ruben, the class bully—a big, lurching white boy with dirty blond hair and a dull rage in his eyes—circled me slowly on his blue Schwinn Chopper. He stopped right in front of me, shifting from cheek to cheek on his vinyl banana seat, cutting me off in my tracks. I looked at him and didn't answer. I was caught off guard by his overt hostility.

"I said, where are you from: China or Japan?"

I was only nine and had already felt the demeaning sting of thoughtless, racist barbs for years. Sometimes, if I was lucky, I would be serenaded with this charming little ditty: "Chinese, Japanese, dirty knees, look at these," the kids would sing, using their fingers to slant their eyes up, indicating Chinese, then down, indicating Japanese, putting their hands on their knees, and then, for the roaring finale, pulling their shirts out to mimic a big chest. In addition to being made acutely aware of my difference in ethnicity, I was also constantly reminded of my size. I was short to medium height, but really skinny. The older boys in school used to literally toss me from one to the other like a ball. It was all in fun, but in retrospect, it was still a clear assertion of physical dominance. People would also hold my arm up in midair and say loudly, "Look how skinny she is! Look how small her wrists are!"

In the past, I had kept quiet or responded feebly. Only days before, I had stood silent and helpless while a greasy white teen passed by our house, yelling, "Hey, chink, go back to your country!" at my dad's back as he tended to the peonies in our garden. I watched as my father ignored the bait and clenched the wooden handle of the spade in his gloved hand. My mercury rose in a tide of rage, while my heart sank in a pit of humiliation and heartache. All the *chink*s, *jap*s, and *gook*s carelessly hurtled my way were an indignity, but watching my father be the recipient of such bile irreversibly activated something in me.

The difference between my father and me was that I had the most lethal weapon at my disposal: the English language. And this brilliant, sunny afternoon in the park was the day I would unlock the safety. Truth is, in a battle of wits, me against Ruben was like bringing an AK to a plastic knife fight. But I held back on unleashing an automatic, choosing to fire only a couple of choice shots instead.

"I'm from Korea," I rallied back.

"What?"

"Korea. Your geography is pretty bad if the only countries you know in Asia are China and Japan. Maybe you should study harder in school, Ruben!" I could taste the rage in my saliva.

He grunted in response. When he realized that he hadn't succeeded in terrorizing me, he got back on his bike and trundled away. I saw Ruben again in school, but there were no more confrontations.

Walking home, I was high on victory. I felt indomitable. From this day forward, I felt prepared for any verbal jousting match. My life wasn't a horror show of constant racist attacks and threats, but growing up the child of Asian immigrants in a white world made it a challenge to establish my identity. My birth certificate says I'm a citizen of Canada, but I didn't feel fully Canadian because I wasn't white. Nor was I totally Korean because I had lost the language, a common experience among first-generation immigrants. Heesok, too, had lost Korean.

In an effort to get back the language, Heesok and I studied Korean at the Korean United Church, which my father had been instrumental in starting, despite being an atheist. He had helped Rev. Lee, who founded the church, stay in Vancouver rather than going back to Korea. My mother attended services on Christmas, but we never went with her. We were brought up broadly, like many in the West, in the Christian ethic, and my father used to say that all Asians were raised with an organic blend of Buddhism, Taoism, and Confucianism. Heesok and I recited the Lord's Prayer for the first several years of school. To this day, I remember the first several lines. When I was nine, one of my classmates took me to her church with her family. My father was not happy about it at all. He didn't say anything but grunted his disapproval. He loved the poetry of the Bible, as he did of opera, but he was not a believer.

I rejected not only the Korean language, but also the culture and cuisine. When I was around age ten, my mother had to make me cheeseburgers for a few months, while the rest of the family ate robustly textured and complexly flavored Korean meals. My mother thought I was a picky eater, so she did what she thought any mother should: feed her child, even if it meant preparing a separate meal. But it wasn't my palate, it was my pride—I was embarrassed by and ashamed of our food, which kids made fun of because it looked and smelled different. Part of my rejection of Korean culture was witnessing it being rejected by our adopted country. Despite my desperate measures to assimilate, my world continued to remind me in no uncertain terms that I was other, lesser, and an outsider.

Assimilation meant, quite simply, trying to be white. Everyone I saw as I pored through the pages of fashion magazines, flipped through the TV channels, or sat in movie theaters was white. The only time I saw characters who looked like me were the extras in *M*A*S*H*, *Hawaii Five-O*, and *Kung Fu*. I was blissfully unaware that I didn't see myself. It didn't even cross my mind that David Carradine was a white man playing an Asian character!

One of my favorite shows in the 1970s was *The Partridge Family*, about a widowed mother who forms a band with her five children. Like millions of other girls across North America, I was infatuated with the eldest son, Keith, played by David Cassidy—with his soft brown eyes, perfectly feathered hair, and signature puka shells that glowed beneath his large-collared polyester shirts. If David Cassidy was my first puppy love, then Susan Dey, who played his sister Laurie, was my first girl crush: she had big green eyes, long thick eyelashes, and flawlessly curled hair.

Little did I know that this bubble gum reverie would slap me in the face. One afternoon, alone in my room, I was pretending to be Laurie Partridge, singing and playing keyboards on my bed. I lost myself in the performance. When I reached the chorus of "I Think I Love You," I turned and looked in the mirror, and to my shock, saw an Asian face. I had convinced myself that I was white. As someone who has complained about feeling invisible her whole life, I now recognize that in that moment, I had erased myself.

The other show I watched without fail was *The Brady Bunch*. I thought they were the perfect family, never mind that they were the result of two divorced parents coming together, each with their three children from previous spouses. All I saw was Hollywood happiness in the home. A beautiful blond mother with three blond daughters. My family looked different and talked different. One night after dinner I got up and said, "Thanks, Mom, that was a delicious dinner." Heesok sneered at me. "Did you just see that in *The Brady Bunch*?" It stung because he was dead-on. I felt like a fraud.

The Asians we went to school with were predominantly Chinese. They embodied the model minority: hardworking, bespectacled, great at science and math, squeaky clean, and kept their heads down. There was also a group of Vietnamese kids who were in the English as a second language program at our high school. I used to look at them as other because we didn't speak the same language. I likened myself more to the white kids because of linguistic and cultural alignment.

By high school, I became aware that we differed not only in physical appearance, but also in class. Our high school sat at the bottom of a valley. We lived on the middle-class side, while many of the other students lived on the wealthy side. These kids alternated between their Whistler homes and

Hawaii for Christmas vacations. They would come back looking like raccoons because other than their eyes, protected by ski goggles or sunglasses, their faces were kissed by the sun.

The rich kids were also often the popular kids. They were white girls and boys with shiny, straight teeth and feathered hair, who cruised the streets of Vancouver in their parents' Beemers, Benzes, and Porsches. Though different, my brother and I were still very popular—my brother because he was so fucking smart and funny, but also because he was such a good athlete. I followed him in his other hobbies as well: I knew the name of every car, collected comic books, and could name most of the fighter planes from the Second World War.

Heesok and I attended the Mini School, a small annex of Prince of Wales Secondary School for self-motivated and bright kids. It was filled with brainiacs and misfits. One of the great things about our school, in addition to the rigorous academic program, was the diverse range of extracurricular activities. We did a lot of fundraising for our three annual field trips. We got to travel to places where we could ski, rock climb, hike, and kayak. The first and last time I saw a night of shooting stars was on our end-of-the-year trip on Salt Spring, one of the Southern Gulf Islands off the coast of Vancouver. It was warm and we lay in our thin down sleeping bags on the huge rocks that lined the beach. We were cracking jokes and yelling at each other over the sound of the crashing waves of the Pacific when someone said, "Look at the stars!" The stars shone brighter and seemed more plentiful, but I didn't see anything out of the ordinary as I stared into the clear endless sky on the stelliferous night. Then, out of the corner of my eye, I caught one flashing across the great black canvas. Then another and another and another until it seemed as if the stars were racing toward each other to reunite after a long separation. The first and only night I would bear witness to the wonder of a night of shooting stars.

Our school dances were filled with classic rock sprinkled with new wave. The perennial last song of every dance was Led Zeppelin's "Stairway to Heaven." For all the boys and girls who had been crushing on each other, this was their chance to grope and grind for eight unchaperoned minutes. Even though I was elected social coordinator two years in a row and painstakingly designed and printed the invitations on a mimeograph machine, I was never the girl who got asked to slow dance. I dreaded this part of the evening and always made sure I wasn't near the auditorium so I could avoid the humiliation of standing against the wall as the song started to play. I would go into the brightly lit administrative office and talk and laugh as if I didn't care, playing with the stapler or weighing myself on the scale in the nurse's office as if it would tell me anyting other than 107 pounds, which I was throughout high school and well into middle age. To this day, I bristle when I hear the opening acoustic guitar strains of the song. It takes me right back to those days of rejection.

In grade school, I grew up on Top 40 pop and classic rock, but it was disco that I loved the most because it was dance music. In high school, we started listening to new wave and punk: the Jam, Joe Jackson, and my favorite band of all time—the Clash. When *Sandinista!*, the group's homage to the Nicaraguan political party, came out, I rocked a red beret and went to the Vancouver Public Library to study the history of the movement. This album inspired my first interest in politics.

But there was something beyond the anti-establishmentarian and leftist leanings of the punk movement that drew me to the music. There was also the anger that swelled in those imperfect vocals and screeching guitars. Punk was my gateway to hip-hop.

In my final year of high school, Ray, a handsome Greek classmate known for being a music aficionado, brought a twelve-inch record to school, excited to share his latest discovery with a group of us assembled in the music room during lunch hour. He lovingly tilted his two-dimensional prize at a slight angle and slowly slid the paper-sleeved vinyl from its crisp cardboard cover.

I didn't recognize the label at the center of the disk. It was light blue and appeared to feature a colored snake. He set the turntable to 33 rpm and placed the needle onto the edge of the shiny black disc. As the familiar scratch crackled through the speakers, I studied the cover, which featured seven black men rocking studded leather belts, wristbands, and gloves, along with Kangol hats and tight designer jeans. I'd never seen anything like it.

I cocked my head as the first beats of "The Message" by Grandmaster Flash and the Furious Five sailed through the room. My whole body moved, almost involuntarily, when the synth notes came in. I had been a dancing fool since the age of three—from shimmying on the couch to making up routines in my bedroom to learning to do the hustle. The bottom of the song hit me in the solar plexus, and the lyrics set my imagination on fire. The urban jungle the MCs painted was so far from my quaint suburbia, but something in the music spoke to me.

Listening to that song was like taking the red pill in *The Matrix*. Once I'd heard it, I could never unhear it, and all music thereafter would be held to that standard of excellence and urgency and poetry and storytelling. In other words, I became a hip-hop devotee in precisely seven minutes and ten seconds.

My first boyfriend was a rakish Irish guitar player named Aaron. The moment I set eyes on him playing bass in a dive bar in Gastown, I knew he would be my boyfriend. We shared a love of music, mostly British punk and new wave, but diverged enormously when it came to hip-hop.

One night in 1985, we were sitting in the basement of my parents' house watching MuchMusic—Canada's version of MTV—when the video for Run-D.M.C.'s "King of Rock" came on. I was glued to the TV and could barely contain my enthusiasm. His face curled in disgust and disdain.

"You like this? How could you possibly like this? It's not music!"

That sentiment would be echoed by many all over the world for years to come. To me, hip-hop was a perfect potent parfait. It combined all the elements of the music that had informed my life: the compelling drama and narrative of opera, the infectious melodies and hooks of pop, the powerful vocal performances of crooners, the four-on-the-floor beats and danceability of disco, the rebellious messages and stripped-down arrangements of punk. And that's just what I could hear. Listening to "The Message" on repeat was ear-opening, but seeing Run-D.M.C.'s "King of Rock" video just that one time was eye-popping.

It occurs to me now that hip-hop was the first time I'd seen people of color telling their own stories as opposed to seeing them through the dominant white male lens of Hollywood. These artists were so physically assertive—stomping their feet, slapping their chests, and the ultimate B-boy stance: arms crossed high, hands tucked into the armpits, feet apart. This kind of unapologetic bearing was completely novel to me, an Asian woman who had been trained to shrink herself to accommodate others. It all spoke to an exhortation to be seen as they wanted to be seen. And unlike me, they were so proud of who and what they were.

Like most teenagers, I rebelled against my parents. Once I started driving at sixteen, it was hard to keep tabs on me. I didn't get drunk or high, mainly because I hated the thought of not being in control, but I started sneaking out to clubs in twelfth grade. I took Heesok's ID and used an X-Acto knife to cut out a photo of myself and covered his with a thin layer of plastic. I went to the Pit, the university pub in the basement of the Student Union Building, to dance every week. It was filled with frat boys in letterman jackets, drinking cheap beers by the pitcher. I would go to the center of the empty circular dance floor, which was in the middle of the room, like a stage in a roundabout theater, and let loose to whatever was playing, but my jam was Michael Jackson's "Wanna Be Startin' Somethin'." When Michael's voice proclaimed, "Yee-hah!" I would jump up on one foot and kick the other in the air.

Then there was the Luv-A-Fair, where the new wavers with gelled hair and asymmetrical shirts would dance to the likes of Depeche Mode, the Human League, and Culture Club. My signature song there was not a 1980s hit, it was Aretha Franklin's "Respect." I would get on top of the speakers and get down to the Queen of Soul. I also went to a number of venues downtown—the Commodore, the Town Pump, and the Savoy—to see countless live shows. I figured out how to get backstage and became a straight-up groupie, except I didn't want to sleep with the artists. Well, not all of them. I mostly just wanted to meet them. I loved talking to the people behind the music.

As I became friends with a few of the local bar bands, I also got to know their managers and talked to them a little about what they did. I learned about studios, sound checks, and touring. I was also constantly at the local record store looking at the new releases and asking for posters, many of which I have in my closet right now. The business side of music started to intrigue me as much as the bands themselves.

My going out was a source of tremendous tension between my father and me. Heesok told me that my father said to him, "We don't know what to do about Sophia, we never had these problems with you!" My father didn't know how to handle it when I asked if I could go shopping with a twenty-two-year-old guitar player. Why did I even ask? My father didn't really have a choice and was right to be concerned—I had sex for the first time with that musician on a dirty mattress on the floor.

In my life, I can only recall seeing my mother cry twice.

Neither was at my father's death or his funeral. The first was when I was taking a bath around eight years old and started scooping the water out of the tub with both hands, because she'd done something to annoy me. I watched as she got on her hands and knees with the omnipresent *gullae* (Korean rag for cleaning every surface) and mopped up the water. The second was when I came home at around eighteen and found her in the basement, by herself, crying. I asked her what was wrong, and she opened her hands to show me that she had discovered my birth control pills. "I just want you to have a good life," she sobbed. She couldn't stand having no idea who my partner was. She must have been concerned for my safety overall as well. Seeing her cry was devastating, but I didn't stop having sex and I only grew more enamored with the music scene and musicians. Naturally, my focus on school waned.

My parents didn't demand straight As. They didn't yell at us if we fell short of perfect grades; rather, they would kill us with silent looks of disappointment. I was a good student, but I was terrible at math, and when my father tried to teach me, it was dreadful for both of us: for me because *calculus* is Latin for "torture" and I was clearly disappointing my father, and for him because I was so terrible at the thing that was his lifelong passion, and he couldn't get through to me.

At some level, my brother and I understood the sacrifices our parents had made for us, particularly my mother, who took up sewing clothes for other people to make extra money. When I was nine, she went to work full-time at the UBC library, where she wrote out the catalogue cards in Korean, Japanese, Chinese, and English by hand, which involved romanizing the Asian languages. Because of the occupation, she was fluent in Japanese, and luckily, she had studied Chinese at night school because my father had wanted to visit China.

French was my favorite subject in high school. It came so easily and I had a perfect accent. I sucked at the sciences and think I failed geography. My English lit teacher told my parents that I wore my disdain for him openly on my face. Good thing he never found out that we used to call him Caliban, after the deformed beast in *The Tempest*. One of my science teachers definitely had a crush on me. I remember he once came up to the window of the door of the classroom I was in and licked it, knowing no one else could see him. When I met his Japanese wife, it was the first time I understood yellow fever.

When I got to the University of British Columbia, where my father taught and my mother worked, I followed again in Heesok's academic footsteps, still falling far short of filling them. There was an amazing interdisciplinary program called ArtsONE that provided three of the five required credits for the year. It was a combination of English, philosophy, and history. There was a weekly lecture on the given book, as well as a seminar and tutorials with your assigned professor. It was here that I truly learned to read, write, and analyze. We had to write a paper every two weeks. My favorite professor of all time was a tall bearded man, child of Russian immigrants, named Ed Hundert, a New Yorker, who told me that Barney's used to be a discount men's clothing store. He spoke slowly and deliberately with a booming voice and had a wonderful laugh and smile. When I think of my favorite lecture of all time, it was one that he gave about Dostoyevsky's *The Brothers Karamazov* and love.

In my second year, I started to focus on French and took literature classes as well as a pronunciation class. I remember watching my professor Jocelyne Baverel round her lips to show us how to make the "uuu" sound in French, which doesn't exist in English. And I had a professor named Ralph Sarkonak who taught us Proust and made fun of me all the time. There was one professor who reminded me of the actor Louis Jourdan. He was tall, dark, and handsome, from the south of France. I could tell he was attracted to me too. One day he drove me home and though nothing happened, I felt the chemistry. Total fantasy to fuck the hot French professor, but it never happened.

I got decent grades that would have been much better had I done the required reading, but I was too busy skipping classes to go to the newly opened Mexican restaurant with my friend Jen Fraser, whom I knew from high school. She, Stephanie Lysyk, also a high school classmate, and I used to go out all the time to the clubs. I would tell my mother I was going to Sedgewick Library because it closed at 1:00 a.m. She told me years later that she always knew that I wasn't going to study. I think it's pretty great that she never confronted me about it and let it rock. One of the best grades I got was on a paper I wrote about Dante's *Inferno*. Why *Inferno*? Because I hadn't read *Purgatorio* or *Paradiso*. There was a woman in the class who was really competitive with me and was furious that I got a 92 without doing all the reading.

As I made my way through college, skipping classes, neglecting reading assignments, and going out at every opportunity, it started to become clear to me that I had to get out of Vancouver. Neither the city nor my parents could contain me. I didn't have specific dreams, I just knew I wanted to leave. Like many of us raised in the suburbs or small towns, I longed to spread my wings in a major metropolis.

CHAPTER 2

NEW YORK STATE OF GRIND

During Christmas break in 1985, my junior year of university, I leapt at the opportunity to visit my brother's friend Steve Palmer in New York. He was doing his graduate studies at Columbia. I stayed with him and his roommates in a four-bedroom apartment close to campus. I loved the Upper West Side, with its brightly lit diners and cafés filled with students bristling with ideas, but it was the East Village, at the opposite end of the island, teeming with punks in leather and kohl-laced eyes, that spoke to me. Here was the epicenter of New York City nightlife, from clubs like the Palladium, the World, and Pyramid to live venues like the Cat Club and CBGB.

One night after poring through the show listings in *The Village Voice*, I dragged Steve down to one of the city's greatest live venues—the Ritz, now Webster Hall. I don't remember who was performing, and it didn't matter. I was determined to see a show in New York. By the time we got to the venue, we'd just missed the show. The crowd was filing out as the video for Stevie Van Zandt's star-studded anti-apartheid song "Sun City" filled a screen onstage.

Shit, that's it? This is my one evening at the Ritz? Maybe I'll see someone famous. Shortly before arriving in New York, I had seen a video of a blue-eyed English soul group called Curiosity Killed the Cat that featured the highly telegenic band with coiffed hair performing in a New York alley. I became obsessed with the fantasy of running into the pretty lead singer somewhere in the Village. I scanned the crowd from the balcony, hoping to spot him. Just as I was about to give up, Steve pointed toward the stage at a tall, gangly man with a mess of black hair covering his face and wearing a black motorcycle jacket, black jeans, and dirty sneakers.

"Sophia, isn't that Johnny Ramone?" Steve said.

Holy shit, standing alone by the stage was the guitar player for the Ramones.

"I'll be right back!"

I raced down the stairs and elbowed my way through the crowd that was moving in the opposite direction. I marched up to him and stuck out my hand.

"I'm Sophia Chang. You're Johnny Ramone, right?"

He took me in for a second and peered down at me over his rose-tinted, wire-framed glasses. "No, I'm Joey."

FUCK. A massive fumbling entrée into the inner sanctum of the New York punk scene.

"Well, you all look the same," I offered, playing off the fact that all the Ramones rocked matching bowl cuts and biker-esque uniforms and shared a last name. Joey spread his lips into a crooked smile and didn't say anything. *I'm in!*

I kept babbling and didn't inhale for three straight minutes. My verve and sense of humor must have worn him down and worked up an appetite because he invited me out for burgers. I asked Steve to come along. Joey and I walked slightly ahead of him, gabba-gabba-heying. At one point he slowed down to talk to Steve and asked, "I'm not causing a situation here, am I?" Steve told him no.

We went to a small dark spot near his apartment at Ninth Street and Third Avenue. We stood at the jukebox and played music for each other. He was smart and funny and so very New York. It was a magical night. I had been hoping to find the singer of an utterly forgettable one-hit-wonder band, and here I was, with the man who fronted the band that had defined the punk rock I grew up on back home. In retrospect, that single act of fearlessness had set into motion the events that would shape my entire career. It was my first big networking move, and I've been honing those techniques ever since. I spent the next several months drudging through classes, dreaming of breaking out of Vancouver. New York was so amazing, but Paris was the obvious choice for me as a French major.

In the summer of 1986, I went overseas for the first time on a tour of England, France, and Italy with Jen Fraser. We shopped, visited landmarks and museums, ate great food, and it was the only time in my life I drank coffee. The soundtrack for the many hours we spent using our unlimited student Eurail passes was the Fine Young Cannibals, Echo and the

Bunnymen, and Talking Heads, which we listened to on my Walkman by splitting a set of headphones. But seeing the Ramones in northern England was definitely the highlight of the trip. Their show was exactly as you'd expect: a nonstop jackhammer of three-chord rock and roll. And after the show we all hung out at the hotel. Joey slouched forward at one point and tugged gently at my big white plastic hoop earring (yes, it was just as ugly as it sounds). To his surprise, it slid right off my lobe. He pulled back suddenly and said, "Did that hurt?" It didn't because it was a clip-on.

Paris was exactly as I'd hoped—*les musées, les parcs, les cathédrales! Le pain, le fromage, les pâtisseries!* But everywhere I went, there were *les Parisiens.* I thought I would move there after school, but I didn't feel like I could fit in. I would speak French with a near-perfect accent in the stores, and they would respond in shit-ass English. The women were so impressive with their makeup and looking *tirées à quatres épingles*—dressed to the nines—that I felt even more invisible there than I did in Vancouver.

Having visited the City of Lights, I was more convinced than ever that the City That Never Sleeps was my destiny. Joey and I talked weekly over the phone, and I wrote him letters about my life in Vancouver. I loved making him laugh. His laugh sounded as if he were awkwardly reading a script, "Ha-ha-ha." Those conversations made me feel connected to New York in an almost palpable way.

On April 22, 1987, at twenty-one years old, I left home for New York. My friend Julianna Raeburn and I were up all night working on my French honors thesis on Racine's *Andromaque.*

I wrote my hurried thoughts onto a yellow legal pad, tore off the perforated sheets one by one, and handed them to Jules, who typed them up. We alternated between drinking Earl Grey tea, rolling around on the graying yellow wall-to-wall shag carpet (no respectable 1970s home was without), and working. I was writing until the moment I left for the airport. I was so anxious to get to New York that I didn't stay for my graduation. In fact, I didn't even confer with my parents, which seems remarkably selfish, in retrospect, particularly in light of the fact that I didn't have a real plan: no job, just a couch to stay on, and a couple of friends my folks didn't know.

My folks and I never had conversations about my future. For myself and any first-generation Asian immigrants, going to college was fait accompli. It never occurred to anyone in my family that I wouldn't follow the road to academia, that I would instead pursue the path of a hustler. My parents couldn't have been too surprised that their daughter ran off to New York—risk-taking was in my DNA. I sat them down in the living room and told them that I was going for six months, but I knew in my heart that it would be longer than that. I told them I had a place to stay and they didn't need to worry. They didn't have much of a response or any questions. They knew I had made up my mind.

When I arrived in New York, Joey had arranged for me to stay with his friend Legs McNeil, a renowned music journalist, and his girlfriend, Carol, on the Upper West Side. Carol worked for Paul Simon and got me a gig there as an assistant. It was a great first step into the music business, of which I so desperately wanted to be a part. Paul had just enjoyed a massive resurgence in popularity with *Graceland*, which won the Grammy for Album of the Year and sold more than fifteen million copies. My parents were relieved when I told them I was working for Paul Simon, because they had heard of him and it seemed solid.

It was a lush learning environment because Paul was a self-contained ecosystem: his whole team—manager, tour managers, business managers, travel agents, and publishing—was located on the fifth floor of the legendary Brill Building. Some of the greatest songwriters of the twentieth century—Burt Bacharach, Carole King, Leiber and Stoller, and Neil Diamond had walked through those same pristinely polished brass double doors. It wasn't until I learned more about the music industry and became a manager myself that I realized the genius of Paul's business vision.

I became particularly impressed that he owned all his publishing and had hired someone to administer it. For every song, the record companies typically own the recorded masters, and many artists do deals with publishing companies that give away half of their publishing income because they need the advance money. In return, the publishing company administers the songs and collects monies due the writer. They are also supposed to solicit work for the songwriter, which includes composing songs for other artists as well as placements in TV, film, and advertising. This means that every time you hear a Paul Simon or Simon and Garfunkel song, no matter who has recorded it, Paul is getting a check. That's extraordinary when you consider the depth and breadth of his catalogue.

Working with Paul, I was exposed to the most elite echelons of the music business. This was where I met the mighty Mo Ostin, who started his career in the 1950s at Verve Records, where he worked with jazz legends like Ella Fitzgerald, Billie Holiday, and Louis Armstrong. He was then hired by Frank Sinatra to run Reprise Records and went on to run Warner Bros. Records, where he signed Jimi Hendrix, the Sex Pistols, and the Red Hot Chili Peppers. I have to add that Mo would bristle at the adjective *mighty*. He is by far the humblest person I've ever met, despite his colossal accomplishments. I was also fortunate enough to meet Lenny Waronker, producer and president of Warner Bros., and Michael Ostin, Mo's son, who headed A&R at Warner Bros. Michael and I connected immediately. We shared the same dry sense of humor and a love of music and food. He would become my lifelong friend and mentor who taught me key lessons about parenting, family, and graciousness, all by example.

One of the greatest privileges of working with Paul was watching him create. It was one thing to see an artist perform or meet them backstage after a show; it was completely different to work in close quarters with one. Paul would sit in his office and play the acoustic guitar, but it was the studio that I found the most bewitching. Witnessing Paul interact with top producers and musicians opened a whole new world for me. This was the art of storytelling. Paul has one of my favorite voices of all time, but his songwriting gift, his ability to tell the story of someone's life in just a few minutes, is astonishing.

My direct bosses were Danny Harrison (rest in peace) and

Marc Silag, Paul's tour managers. Danny and I had a great rapport. He took me out to eat and taught me my first Yiddish terms, though he was an Irishman. Danny, in a stroke of genius, got me my first working visa by adding me to the application that Paul's agency was putting together for a tour. The list was long because of all the talent on the tour, and there was one standout name. It read something like this for about twenty-five names: Hugh Masekela, Miriam Makeba, Ray Phiri, Bakithi Kumalo, Joseph Shabalala, Headman Shabalala . . . and the very last name was Sophia Chang.

I quickly learned that to succeed, you have to be loyal to the right people—and have a backbone. One day Paul's manager, Ian Hoblyn, an intimidating, handsome, well-dressed Brit, came storming into the office waving a piece of paper. I was alone.

"Who left this on the copier?" he yelled.

I didn't know what it was, but clearly it was highly confidential.

"I did," I said, without hesitation.

"Well, you have to be more careful! Things like this can't be left lying around!"

When Danny got back, he went in to see Ian, who complained to him that I had left the paper on the copier. He could have let me take the fall, but Danny told him that he was the guilty party. My action and his response were both exercises in loyalty. And I believe I gained the respect of both those men that day.

Danny appreciated my efficiency, work ethic, and hunger to learn. He presented me with increasingly complex and difficult tasks, which I devoured. Less than six months after I'd started, Danny entrusted me with an assignment far beyond my pay grade.

On December 13, 1987, Paul put on a monumental benefit concert at Madison Square Garden that included Bruce Springsteen, Billy Joel, Lou Reed, James Taylor, Chaka Khan, and Nile Rodgers, among others. The proceeds would benefit a mobile medical unit that would provide health care to homeless children. Warner Communications, then headed by Stephen Ross, underwrote part of the show. Danny put me in charge of creating the financial reconciliation package that Paul would present to Stephen. I had to account for every penny spent—from lighting to sound to ground to laminates and catering—and provide all the backup receipts and invoices. It was a huge and daunting responsibility for a twenty-two-year-old with no business background, but Danny's belief in me was more important than my own. I knew that he would be judged as much as I would. I quadruple-checked every number and was thrilled to hear that everything went off without a hitch once it got to Stephen.

By the time I went home for Christmas that year, the six-month time limit I'd imposed on my stint in the Big Apple had passed, and it was clear that I hadn't gotten it out of my system. My parents must have been concerned. There was no such thing as a gap year back then, even between undergrad and graduate school. They must have suspected that I wasn't moving back any time soon; they knew their daughter better than I knew myself. My mother told me recently that their friends used to tell my folks that they were crazy for letting me run loose in New York. I think it's pretty fucking amazing that they never buckled to that peer pressure and insist that I come home. I'm really proud of them for that, especially considering how gossipy the Korean community can be.

When I tried to explain to my mother what I had been doing, the only thing she understood was that I was somehow in business, so her natural response was "come back to Vancouver and get an MBA." I lied and told her I'd think about it.

On that first visit home, Vancouver felt so small, so provincial—how people dressed, the shopping options, the restaurant opening hours. The fresh air and beauty of Vancouver never escaped me, but it wasn't enough to contain a twenty-three-year-old who had big dreams of being in the music business. I hadn't been away long enough to really miss Vancouver, and the excitement of living in the Big Apple overshadowed any kind of nostalgia I might have. Everything felt the same: the people, the restaurants, the streets, the theaters, the stores. Whereas New York felt like a city of endless adventures and possibilities. I remember on that first trip doing that annoying thing of talking about how everything was so much better in New York. Decades later, I would see my kids do the same and told them to reel it back because it might make their friends who lived there feel bad about their hometown.

Once back in New York, I told my roommate Kevin Bruyneel, a friend from Vancouver, that I was afraid to tell my parents that I wasn't going home. Other than suggesting the MBA, my parents didn't harp on me. It occurs to me now that they never asked *Why don't you get married? When are we going to get grandchildren?* or *Why don't you get a real job?* which was pretty damn extraordinary and gave me the freedom to chase my dreams.

My first five apartments were on the Upper West Side, with a brief stint in a studio above a Burger King near Grand Central. Then, after fully settling into New York life, I made the move to my sixth place in two years, this time downtown, where I spent all my nights. One of the women who worked for Paul sublet me her second-floor walk-up 360-square-foot studio on the corner of Fourteenth Street and Seventh Avenue, surely the noisiest corner in the Western Hemisphere. The floors rumbled as the trains passed below, and there was a steady sound of sirens from the ambulances racing to St. Vincent's Hospital, just two blocks away. My roommate at the time was Loren, whom I had met in the summer of 1984 at a French language program sponsored by the Canadian government at Laval University in Quebec.

We were two broke girls, but we didn't care because we were in New York! We slept on the floor and reused plastic plates. Every time we washed them we would laugh and say, "Too good to throw away!" which was the brand slogan printed on the bottom. My boss Danny took us to Macy's and bought us our first set of real plates, and Loren's boss, Michael, gave us two futons.

Going from our little hovel on Fourteenth Street to Paul's world was like stepping through the looking glass. Paul invited Loren and me to our first Yankees game. Our buzzer rang at precisely the prearranged time. Loren and I flew down the filthy stairwell and burst onto the sidewalk to find *the* Paul

Simon smiling in front of a pristine black stretch limo. His driver rushed out and opened the door for us. We had never been in a limo. It felt endless, as if we could swim in it. We bounced about the leather interior, fiddling with the knobs that controlled the air, stereo, and windows. Paul sat back, watched us, and smiled.

As we pulled off the Cross Bronx Expressway and approached Yankee Stadium, our eyes widened. We were about to enter the most famous stadium in the world with one of the most famous artists in the world. The driver took us to a special side entrance. Paul led us to our seats around the curved concrete corridors. When we reached the opening to the seats, I stopped midstep and gasped as I set my eyes on the enormous green, manicured field for the first time. During the seventh inning, a young boy approached Paul and asked for his autograph. The Yankees were losing badly, and Paul said yes, as long as the boy stayed until the end of the game. After the game, he gave the boy his autograph and asked Loren and me what we thought the clever headline would be in the *New York Post* the next day.

When Paul dropped us off, we invited him in to play Scrabble. I don't even remember feeling self-conscious as the three of us mounted the dingy stairs. We lay across our shitty New York futon, laughing and anagramming. I was really good at Scrabble and figured I'd win. At one point, Paul looked thoughtfully at the table and began laying his tiles across the board in a deliberate fashion: T-H-A-N. *Ha, he's going to play* than *and miss the double word score!* I thought. But he reached for a fifth tile. That could only be *thank*, which was impossible because I had the K and both the blanks were on the board. Paul laid down an E.

"What's a thane?" I asked.

"An aristocrat, like in Shakespeare."

I challenged him and looked it up. Note to self: Never challenge Rhymin' Simon, a man who made his living entrancing us with his lyrics, in Scrabble, or much else, for that matter.

During one of my parents' visits to New York, Paul gave us his season tickets to the Metropolitan Opera. Much like my first time at Yankee Stadium, I was stunned by the scale of the place. The stage was the size of a football field, the sets were extravagant, the costumes elaborate. And ah, the voices. Plácido Domingo was starring in Franco Zeffirelli's production of *Turandot*. That was an amazing experience for me, but even richer for my father. The child who listened to opera at the house of a friend who could afford a record player, he never could have dreamt he'd end up in seats in the orchestra section of the Met, front and center.

A few days after I'd started work, Danny asked me about a check I'd received. I hadn't been paid yet. When he showed it to me I saw that it was written to Sonya Chang, who was Paul's personal assistant. She was Korean American and would become a mentor. Twelve years my senior, she had a huge, authoritative personality such as I'd never seen in an Asian woman. She insisted that I, too, dominate space, rather than shrink in the corner, and move with unapologetic confidence and entitlement, like a white man. Sonya had impeccable style. She took me with her when she shopped for Paul, and those outings were my first glimpse into how the wealthy live—the top Armani salesman brought cashmere sweaters to his home, an army of Egyptians assembled and counted threads to make his bed more luxurious, and everything was perfectly tasteful and beautiful. She introduced me to my favorite designer, Azzedine Alaïa, and the Diptyque perfume that I've worn since I met her.

But more important than taking me for a walk on the fine side, Sonya imparted some of the most significant and enduring spiritual lessons of my life. She was the first person to talk to me about depression and addiction. She took me to my first Narcotics Anonymous meetings so that I would have a better understanding of what it meant to her to be sober. I sat in wonder as complete strangers got up and bravely shared their stories of addiction and loss. She was also the first person I met who spoke about spirituality in any meaningful way. She was a voracious reader and had studied many faiths and philosophies. I now believe she was a Buddhist by practice because she often told me to let things go, which is essentially the practice of nonattachment. She taught me to be more aware of my behavior and interactions with people.

Once she moved to LA in 1992 I continued to spend time with her friends. A few months later, she called from LA and said gently, "Soph, some of our friends told me that they love you but don't enjoy hanging out with you that much, because you're not present. You spend the whole time talking about work."

I had never been confronted like this. I was caught off guard, but Sonya's approach was disarming and so full of love that I didn't try to defend myself. I recalled telling her friends how busy I was, with pride and self-importance. I worked hard to alter my behavior after that. I came to have a deeper appreciation of the notion of being present, as it's a central tenet to Buddhism. Sonya taught me to have hard conversations, which remain an important component of all my relationships. She would always say, "Go to the love, Soph," because that's the foundation.

That philosophy served me well as I began to expand my circle of friends in New York. Now that Loren and I lived downtown, we spent most of our time in the East Village, shopping for clothes on Eighth Street, eating mustard chicken at Cafe Orlin (rest in peace) on Saint Mark's Place, where the wait for the bathroom could be endless because junkies would pass out in there. We saw countless shows by artists like the Godfathers, Squeeze, Fishbone, Big Audio Dynamite, and the Pogues, mainly at the Ritz. I went there so often that Anne, the woman working the door, started letting me in even if I wasn't on the guest list.

We were also deep in the hip-hop scene. We'd frequent Nell's, New York's premier hot spot, which we could practically see from our apartment. It was famous for being extremely choosy about its clientele and famously turned away Cher. Jessica Rosenblum and Mercedes, who ran the door, made sure I never waited more than a couple of seconds on the cold side of that red velvet rope. The crowd outside would be five to ten deep on all three sides, filled with Eurotrash, wannabees, and B&Ts (bridge and tunnels, our derogatory term for people from the outer boroughs and New Jersey; this was clearly long before Brooklyn became a thing). She'd grab me and hug me, then gently slide us through the doors into the world that was Nell's.

Upstairs, folks would lounge at tables or on velvet couches, eating fries and listening to a live jazz band, but downstairs was where we spent all our time, because that's where the dancing was. DJ Jules, a dapper handsome Brit, and DJ Belinda, a gorgeous Jamaican dancer, would move the crowd until 4:00 a.m., playing mostly hip-hop, R&B, and reggae. My girls and I were out at the clubs four nights a week. I would roll in at midnight with five or six badass bitches, many of them Asian—Korean, Chinese, Filipino, and Vietnamese. We gravitated toward each other by our shared race and love for hip-hop. We were beautiful and smart and independent. We rocked baseball hats, baggy jeans, and Timbs and danced our asses off for hours and hours. We were boy crazy and the boys were crazy for us. One of my friends told me, "Soph, we used to love it when you came through the door because we always knew you'd have a bunch of fly women with you." I had countless crushes and numerous one-night stands, but I was not interested in having a boyfriend. My job was my man.

Another regular spot was the Building, a decommissioned Con Ed power station. The gatekeeper there was Lysa Cooper, the queen of downtown New York nightlife. A beautiful black woman with big brown eyes and crooked, soft lips that either curled into a ferocious snarl or opened broadly into a staggering smile, Lysa had an eye like a hawk. She would see me approach from down the street and summon my girls and me in. The envious seas would part, and we would be pulled

THE BADDEST BITCH IN THE ROOM　　49

in by one of her big bouncers. The inside was raw and industrial but had been finely redesigned, incorporating the old elements with the new. The ceilings above the dance floor were at least fifty feet high. There was a mezzanine, an upstairs, and walkways with railings that allowed you to see the dance floor. The venue showcased artists like A Tribe Called Quest and the Beasties, and it was where I first saw Leaders of the New School perform. Even then, Busta Rhymes had boundless energy and walked on both sides of the high railings.

Our favorite spots were the underground hip-hop clubs that moved week to week. Social media didn't exist, so in order to know where to go, we had to get ahold of a flyer that the promoters distributed to the right people. We would call each other, and word spread. They named their clubs after chocolate bars, like $100,000 Bar and Payday. They rented out high school gyms, rooftops, abandoned Chinese restaurants, community centers. Back in the day, none of us ventured into the Lower East Side except for these clubs. We would get out in the early morning hours and wait for ages for a ride because the cabbies were never in that neighborhood. The writer Greg Tate once told me that if a white man was found on Avenue A, he was adventurous; on Avenue B, brave; on C, crazy; and if he was on Avenue D, his ass was dead.

It was a privilege to be in New York City in those days when the industry was taking shape. It wasn't just the music; it was the sense of community. People deliriously diverse across both race and industry sectors assembled around their shared love of hip-hop. MCs, DJs, B-boys, graffiti artists, managers, label execs, publicists, agents, attorneys, promoters, even artists like Keith Haring, Tony Shafrazi, and Francesco Clemente were regulars.

Outside of the clubs, the whole hip-hop industry convened at an annual convention called the New Music Seminar founded by Tom Silverman, owner of Tommy Boy Records, and his partner, Mark Josephson. Tommy Boy Records was home to artists like De La Soul, Queen Latifah, and Naughty by Nature. The NMS comprised showcases at night and panels during the day. Tom had invited me to be part of a group that determined what panels would be held and who would moderate.

The seminar was the first place I ever spoke publicly. I was invited to be on a panel about women in hip-hop in 1991. One of my co-panelists was Joan Morgan, self-described hip-hop feminist, and a friend for the ages. She was a surreal blend of South Bronx Jamaican who could talk shit and go hard like the boys, but attended Hunter High School and Wesleyan University. As we seated ourselves at the table, I was mesmerized by her beauty: closely cropped hair, big brown eyes, soft full lips, and high cheekbones. My infatuation rose to a whole other level once she opened her mouth and her brilliant words rang through the room. She talked about what it was like to be a black woman operating in hip-hop and the singular insight it gave her into how black men and women related to each other. She would eventually articulate this as the inherent conflict of being a hip-hop feminist. She was the first woman I met who called herself a feminist, and it would take me decades of learning and living to claim the moniker myself.

At one point during the panel, someone in the audience asked why there was a white British woman on a panel about hip-hop. I responded, "We are here today to talk about being women in hip-hop. What we are not going to do is question the validity of any of us talking about this." I was particularly sensitive to the topic because as an Asian woman my bona fides had also been questioned. It felt good to be on the panel, but even better to be outspoken. That was my first taste of holding a mic, and it was delectable. I wanted more, and it would come soon, but it would take decades for me to fully embrace center stage.

Over the next years, Tom had me graduate from being a panelist to moderator about a range of different topics. The hottest one was the LA uprisings after the Rodney King verdict came down in 1992. I wasn't nervous until I looked into the room and saw that it was huge and every seat was filled. Spike Lee was front and center, and somewhere in the back were the disheveled head and crooked glasses of Robert Christgau, one of the greatest rock critics of all time. *Now I'm nervous.* Once I started speaking, though, my fears dissipated. Christgau wrote about the panel in his weekly column in *The Village Voice* and alluded to me being smart. That was a huge boost of confidence for me.

One of the fixtures of the New Music Seminar was Dave Klein (rest in peace), a.k.a. Funkenklein, a big, blond midwestern boy who loved hip-hop to the core. We met in 1988 and he introduced me to a bunch of people in the industry, including the Jungle Brothers, De La Soul, and Queen Latifah. One night at Hotel Amazon, one of the moving clubs located in the Lower East Side, Dave introduced me to Q-Tip. We had all heard his verse on the Jungle Brothers' single "Black Is Black" and were curious to meet the body attached to this incredibly unique voice. We walked into a section of the club that was empty, and there was Tip alone in a hallway, sitting backward on a chair. Dave said, "Don't look into his eyes or you'll fall in love." As we neared, I understood the warning: Tip's baby browns reflected a soulful melancholy and could lead a responsible woman to make all sorts of irresponsible decisions, but what I remember most were his shoulders, which seemed to go on forever.

"Tip, this is Sophie," Dave said.

Tip looked up with a slight smile.

"Hey, Sophie, nice to meet you."

He shook my hand and his hands were big and strong.

"Nice to meet you too."

I looked straight into his eyes. And there, but for the grace of God, I didn't fall in love, but we became great friends.

Dave contributed to *The Bomb*, a monthly hip-hop magazine that everyone in the industry read. He wrote a quasi gossip column, "Gangsta Limpin'," so named because Dave wore a leg brace after he'd had an operation for spinal cancer. The column was funny, irreverent, and blunt. I laughed plenty at his thinly veiled takedowns. Good thing we were so close he'd never write about me!

Like Dave, Michael Ostin continued to bring me into his circle. In 1989, while I was working for Paul Simon, he introduced me to Russ Titelman, who, in addition to working with Paul, had made records with greats such as Nancy Sinatra,

George Harrison, Brian Wilson, and Chaka Khan. Russ recommended that I interview for an assistant job at the newly formed Alternative Music Department at Atlantic Records, which was being run by Peter Koepke. It would be a dream to work at a record company, because this was the central nervous system of the music industry; it was where the songs became hits and the artists became stars. I got the job and was one of two assistants covering a staff of five. I worked my ass off and liked the roster well enough, but hip-hop was my passion.

Fortuitously, right down the hall from us was the Urban Department, headed by the formidable Sylvia Rhone, who would become the first female CEO and chair of a record company. Sylvia was a marvel to behold: Wharton grad, beautiful, impeccably dressed. I wanted to be just like her when I grew up. I dreamt of running a department one day, maybe even a whole label. Only in retrospect, having navigated the business that is strangled by patriarchy and racism, do I realize the enormity of the fact that she was a woman of color, a black woman, to be specific.

I wanted to spend as much time as possible with Sylvia and her team. She knew I was a huge hip-hop fan, and I managed to convince her to let me promote her hip-hop records to the smallest college radio stations across the country. Peter let me do it because I got all the rest of my work as an assistant done. Because I was promoting some of her records, Sylvia was gracious enough to invite me to her weekly marketing meetings, which were attended by representatives from departments outside of hers, like sales, art, and video.

These meetings were no joke. Everyone was held accountable for their respective piece. An album release is like a machine: all the parts have to be working well and in sync for it to have the best shot at success. One small piece out of place could set the whole project out of whack, and Sylvia, as the head of the department, was the engine. I studied attentively as Sylvia ran shit, unflappable and confident in body-hugging Alaïa knit dresses. She knew the business inside and out and took no prisoners.

During one particular meeting, she sat at the head of the long conference room table and went around the room, asking each person where they were with their efforts. When she got to Rachel, a middle-aged white woman who was the head of the art department, she asked, "Rachel, is the album art done?"

"No, Sylvia, it ain't done," Rachel answered.

Sylvia turned her head sharply toward Rachel. The room, already quiet in deference to Sylvia, became deathly silent. "Pardon me?" Sylvia said pointedly, her eyes laser-focused on the woman. You could almost feel the collective cringe.

"It ain't done yet," Rachel repeated.

"You mean 'it *isn't* done yet,'" Sylvia corrected her.

I was astonished and inspired by Sylvia's commitment to calling out the bullshit, and I hoped that I would behave with such courage and candor should I ever sit at the head of a table. In one meeting we were discussing the latest Everything but the Girl single "Missing." I thought it could go on urban radio but kept my mouth shut. I didn't think I deserved to be heard and I was too scared to look like a fool. The very next week, Sylvia announced that they were taking the single to urban radio. I learned then that I had to trust my instincts and lose my fear around embarrassing myself.

Working at a major label was professionally rewarding, but I wasn't making a lot of money as an assistant. I was never one for the paper chase, but I did want to be comfortable. I had two roommates in a tiny studio apartment and was still feeling the squeeze. I called Sonya in a panic because I was feeling broke. I told her I was considering looking for another job. She said, "Soph, don't ever do something for fear of not making money. Money will always come to you. Is anyone going to die?"

"What? No!"

"Then don't worry, it'll all be fine."

Distilling everything down to life or death, though it may sound dramatic, helped me put things in perspective. Heesok responded differently when I called him in a state of alarm: "Sophia, we are all the authors of our own stories, and I just don't understand why you choose to write yours as a C-grade melodrama." Fortunately, soon enough, my money concerns would abate.

In 1991, Peter left to head London Records, and Mark Fotiadis, my direct boss, was promoted to head of the department. He made me head of marketing, which was controversial, because I was promoted over more senior people in the department. It was a big leap, one that I understand now I wasn't qualified to make. However, I was determined to do right by Mark and dove into the deep end of the pool.

Thankfully, I felt really good about the work that I was

doing with Sylvia. At one point I created a flyer to send to radio stations to accompany the new single by the artist Kwamé, who was only sixteen at the time. I bought a book about composers and compared him to the prodigies of classical music like Mozart and Chopin. God, that sounds so fucking pretentious now. I sent them to someone in her department for approval. A day or two later I got back to my desk, where she'd left the flyer and a handwritten note that said, *Great job, Sophia!* I'm sure she doesn't remember, but her approval meant the world to me.

Just two years out of college, I was the head of marketing in the Alternative Department at Atlantic and working part-time on Sylvia's rap records. The only thing better would have been focusing solely on hip-hop. No bother, though, because my nights were filled with it. One night at a club, Funkenklein introduced me to Sean Carasov (rest in peace), a.k.a. the Captain, a short Brit with a surly attitude who posed as a misanthrope but had a heart of fucking gold. He did A&R at Jive. (*A&R* stands for "Artists and Repertoire." A&R people are the scouts who find the talent, develop them, help them make their albums, and guide them through the label system.) *Wow*, I thought, *dream job*. The most coveted position at a record company and the closest parallel to a manager, the A&R person is involved in every aspect of an artist's career. Arguably, it's the role most critical to the success of a label because it all starts with the artists. No matter how good the rest of the team is, if you don't have a strong product, the records don't sell.

Not long after I met Sean, he told me that he was moving

to LA to be the Jive rep on the West Coast, which was a hotbed of talent, including N.W.A., Ice Cube, and Cypress Hill. He suggested that I interview to replace him in New York. He set up a time for me to meet with Barry Weiss, the president of Jive. Barry and I talked for a solid hour and a half about music. He knew more about the alternative world than I did. Later, he told me the moment I walked in the door he was certain I wasn't the right person for the job, and became convinced that I was when he understood how passionate and knowledgeable I was about hip-hop, as well as how completely immersed I was in the community.

Despite my enormous enthusiasm, I myself wasn't convinced that I was the right person for the job. How could I, a Korean Canadian French lit major, possibly be the right person to determine what rap artists were worth signing, when my experience was so far removed from theirs? A&R to this day is an insular boys' club. I'm not just saying that it's male dominated, I'm talking a *Little Rascals* "no girls allowed" joint. This meant I was entering a male-monopolized occupation in a genre that was testosterone driven and reigned over largely by men.

Having an opinion was one thing. "Opinions are like assholes, everyone has one," we used to say, because everyone thought they could do A&R. But A&R required a complex skill set: beyond having an ear for what was good and commercial, it was critical to be good at relationship building, instilling trust in your artists, and advocating for your artists within the label as well as without. There were also A&R people who were creative and actual producers, which I definitely was not. These were guys who could go into the studio with their artists and make records with them, which was incredibly efficient and created a bond that I could never share.

Despite my doubts, I accepted the job, hoping that my love of the culture and tentacles into the community would see me through. It wasn't easy to tell Mark, who had just fought for my promotion and raise, that I had been offered a job at Jive, but he said, "Sophia, as long as I've known you, what gets you excited is hip-hop. So you should go do that job. It's a fantastic opportunity."

I was really excited to tell Dave that I'd landed the job. He received the news lukewarmly. *Maybe he's having an off day*, I thought. Less than a week later, I was in the office reading *The Bomb*. As usual, I skipped forward to Dave's column. My heart sank as I started to read the first paragraph. The column was about unqualified people getting jobs in hip-hop A&R. The industry was tiny. Everyone knew he was referring to me. I was devastated. I never had the nerve to talk to him about it and it didn't end the friendship, but I was confused and hurt. This was the man who had introduced me to so much of the hip-hop world and wanted me to be a part of it, but he drew the line at me working in it? I was already insecure, never having done A&R, and this jab from a friend who had been so supportive until then knocked me down a notch or two. As if that wasn't enough, another close industry friend told Sonya, "Sophia better not start fucking rappers or she'll be done."

Yes, of course, all good for the men to fuck whomever they want and brag about it, but the second one of us women in the industry fucked someone, word got out and we were labeled. Unfair, but he was right, so I resisted sleeping with artists. Believe me, there were a number I would have slept with if I'd had one of those *Men in Black* wands that would have erased their memories the second we were done.

Once at Jive, I did the only thing I knew how to do: go hard. Barry Weiss was whip smart and funny as hell, and he ran a tight, nimble ship, which is so important in the music business, because the direction of an album can change at any moment, based on audience response. Barry's right hand was Ann Carli, a wonderful biracial Japanese American woman who headed Artist Development, unfortunately a relic of labels past. She was amazing with talent, including the staff. When I started at Jive I was making twenty-eight thousand a year. A year later, without me having to ask, Ann had gotten me a promotion and a raise to fifty-two thousand dollars a year.

We had weekly A&R meetings with Clive Calder, the owner of the company, in his cold, sterile, private conference room, going over the artists already signed who were actively recording and reviewing prospective signings. Clive had a killer sound system and he would listen to demo tapes ever so intently, head cocked, right hand pulling softly at his thin blond hair behind his ear. It was a nerve-wracking process. It was like auditioning every single time. I would try not to look at the reactions of everyone else. I kept my head down and waited for the song to end.

By the time an artist got heard in that room, I had already listened to the demo over and over and spoken to them or their reps. I had boxes of demos in padded mailers under my desk. At that time, we went through every single one, even the unsolicited submissions. Some labels don't do that anymore for fear of litigation—the concern being that an artist will come back and sue, saying the recording company stole their idea for artists signed to the label. When I started at Jive, I would listen to every song all the way through, but that was time-consuming and tedious, because the vast majority of the material was bad. I got to the point where I could listen to a verse and the chorus of the first couple of songs and have a keen sense of whether or not I wanted to sign the artist. It's certainly possible I overlooked some real talent, but I simply didn't have time to listen to everything.

At Jive we signed only self-contained artists, meaning they produced their own songs, which was better for Zomba Publishing, also owned by Clive. In hip-hop, the ownership of a song breaks right down the middle: half to the MC, who at that time was presumed to have written their lyrics, and half to the producer, who provided the music. It gets more complicated with sampling, because you have to give music publishing rights to the artist you sample. That portion would typically come out of the producer's portion.

The other way that we discovered artists was by reading the trades. Barry would put a red check next to the records that were moving units in different regions of the country. I would call the local record stores and ask about the artist and the fan base and if there seemed to be any promise, then get the manager's contact information. But the best way to find talent was through other talent, be it rappers or producers or

DJs, because they were in the streets and the studios. They didn't just have their fingers on the pulse, they were the pulse.

The first group I signed was the Fu-Schnickens, three West Indian MCs out of East Flatbush. Their whole aesthetic revolved around kung fu movies. I had originally met Chip Fu, the leader of the group, through a friend. Once I was at Jive, we met again at a Howard University homecoming, and we exchanged numbers. I listened to the demo and thought his style of rhyming was incredible, and the music was infused with their Caribbean roots. I invited my colleagues to a showcase they were doing at a local club and convinced the team to let me sign them.

We shot the video for their first single, "Ring the Alarm," on the steps of the Brooklyn Public Library. The group rocked orange-dyed karate uniforms and jumped out of a giant Chinese takeout box labeled with their name. It didn't occur to me that the iconography was clichéd.

Chip and I used to call Janine, a psychic in Woodland Hills whom Sonya had introduced me to. I once asked her if I would be accepted as an Asian woman doing A&R, and she told me I would become extremely powerful. While the Fu-Schnickens were in the studio recording the album, I met the group Das EFX through Parrish Smith, a.k.a. P of the Long Island rap duo EPMD. We all became very close and I wanted desperately to sign them. When I called Janine, I simply spelled out *Das EFX* and she said, "You won't get them, but you will go on to even better things."

She was right: the deal got too rich and they ended up signing with Sylvia Rhone at her newly formed Atlantic imprint

East West. Another group I wanted to sign was House of Pain, which I heard via DJ Muggs, DJ and producer for Cypress Hill, whom I had befriended years before. They ended up signing to Tommy Boy, another great small hip-hop label. Both groups went on to sell more than a million albums, but more important was that they had crossover success, having strong showings in the Billboard Hot 100 chart, the Holy Grail for pop records.

Once Das EFX went gold, Clive announced at a meeting, "We should just let Sophia sign whatever she wants." I didn't exactly have carte blanche, but I did go on to sign Mz. Kilo out of LA and Souls of Mischief and a couple of other members of the Hieroglyphics crew from Oakland. I also worked with KRS-One, A Tribe Called Quest, UGK, E-40, and Too Short.

Now that I was doing A&R as an active member of the industry, our apartment became what Jarobi from A Tribe Called Quest called "Soph's Home for Wayward Rappers." Q-Tip would come over to my little studio on Fourteenth and Seventh, and we would watch *Mystery Science Theater 3000* and *Midnight Run* so many times that we both memorized much of the dialogue. "So here come two words for you," De Niro says to Charles Grodin. "Shut the fuck up." We died laughing every time. I also used to crack Tip up by tying my then-waist-length hair into a ponytail above my head and doing a crazy dance. I would two-step *way* off beat, whipping my ponytail around like a ceiling fan, and then break into any stupid dance just to make him laugh. Some of my favorite moves I bit from the unforgettable dance scene in *A Charlie Brown Christmas*.

Despite the Lilliputian proportions of the apartment, we entertained constantly. Music was always central to any visits. There was a beatbox under the loft and a rack of cassettes loaded with the latest hip-hop, like Cypress Hill, N.W.A., and Public Enemy. In addition to Tip, Ali Shaheed Muhammad from A Tribe Called Quest, Fu-Schnickens, and Hieroglyphics were always at my apartment. But my favorite house guest by far was Reggie Noble, a.k.a. Redman.

I met Regman, as I called him, at a Too Short album release party in 1990. He was rocking an oversize North Face down jacket and what he called his "drug dealer bracelet," and had a tissue hanging out of his nose. I fell in love with him immediately. Who goes out with a tissue hanging out of their nose? REDMAN! He clearly did not give a fuck. He had terrible allergies and was always congested.

He was living on Long Island with Erick Sermon of EPMD and was often in the city late at the studio or doing God knows what. If he didn't want to drive home, he would just come to Sophie's. He was more like a boarder than a guest. He would come by my place at all hours of the night and yell up to my window, "Sophie! Open the door, goddamnit!" He ended every sentence with *goddamnit*. It was hardly the romantic yearning of John Cusack in *Say Anything*, more like, *I need to take a shit!* I would open the window and throw the keys down, and he would come upstairs and crawl up into the smaller loft and knock out.

There was no small talk. No "How was your night?" "How's work?" Nada. But watching him climb the small ladder and jam into that tiny space was worth being woken up at 3:00 a.m. The opening to the loft was only about four feet by four feet. Reggie is six feet one and, when I met him, kinda chunky, nothing like the lean machine he is now, and he would inevitably be wearing his puffy black North Face. It was like seeing a super fluffy Chow Chow squeeze through a doggy door. At one point I just gave him a set of keys.

During one of his many sojourns at my little pad, Redman said, "Sophie, I want to rap in Korean for my first single, 'Blow Your Mind.' Can you write it for me?"

"No, but my dad can."

I was a little embarrassed that I couldn't do it myself. My dad took on the task with pleasure and spent a lot of time writing something he thought would be suitable. This is what he came up with: "Get out of my way / Who are you? I'm Redman / There's no one better than me / In this world I am the best Redman, my man."

One night, we sat on my futon and I taught him the rhymes, word by word. He was so dedicated to getting it right. We ate Ritz crackers and laughed and practiced. Because the futon was low, we sank into it and couldn't sit up straight. When we were done, he looked down sheepishly at his Champion sweatshirt. It was covered in crumbs. He looked like a little boy.

That moment will stay with me forever because, in addition to our friendship and the laughs we shared, Redman appreciated my culture to the point of wanting to incorporate it authentically into his music. When the single came out, I got a call from Hot 97, the number one hip-hop radio station in the country. They had called Redman's label, who directed them to me. They didn't want to play the record because they thought that Redman was faking the Korean, and they found it offensive. I assured them that my father had written the lines and told them the meaning.

When I look back at all the guests who crossed my threshold and spent time in that tiny storied apartment, perhaps the most out of place was Chris Lighty, a South Bronx native who had come up carrying legendary Kool DJ Red Alert's record crates, then went on to work with hip-hop's biggest stars. He wasn't just physically big, he also had very imposing energy that barely seemed to be contained in that one room. He rubbed me all sorts of wrong ways when I first encountered him.

"Damn, Soph! What's that about?" asked Ali Shaheed Muhammad from A Tribe Called Quest as a patent look of disgust passed unwittingly over my face.

"I can't stand your manager. He's so arrogant."

We were in the Jive offices, sitting in a tiny cubicle, when Chris strode by. I found him insufferable. Shaheed is a beautiful, open soul. Born and raised a Muslim, he is far less judgmental than I am and has always wanted his world and those inhabiting it to be at peace.

"He might seem like that, Soph, but he's a really good guy. You should get to know him."

Chris had risen quickly because of his business acumen and naked ambition. I'm sure his looks didn't hurt, either. Chris was tall, broad, and impossibly handsome. He was nicknamed Baby Chris for his freckles and had a smile that could melt a thousand cones. That winning smile, however, didn't make its appearance very often. The expressions that more commonly graced his grill were indifference, inscrutability, and intimidation. I heeded Shaheed's advice and braved rough terrain in an effort to get to know Chris and eventually win him over, not a meager challenge. He was more Oscar the Grouch than Mr. Rogers.

Chris was working at Rush Management, whose roster boasted the biggest names in the business—LL Cool J, Run-D.M.C., the Beastie Boys, Public Enemy, as well as A Tribe Called Quest. I knew that we would continue to cross paths and that it was better to be on his good side than on no side. One day, I coaxed Chris into having lunch with me. I let him choose the restaurant. We ended up at the Shark Bar on the Upper West Side, the legendary soul food spot where the hip-hop elite broke bread. Cornbread and biscuits, to be exact. It was a long, narrow place with a bar downstairs and tables upstairs. When we walked in, the staff recognized Chris immediately. He simply nodded grimly and led me straight upstairs. The waiter had barely set the warm bread basket down on the table before I dove in like a barbarian. I'm sure Chris's eyebrows were raised in surprise. *Look at this little-ass Asian woman jumping on those biscuits like she just got out of Rikers!* Once my low blood sugar had been sufficiently raised, we got to talking. Or rather, I got to talking.

Our conversations were incredibly one-sided because I am garrulous and he was, as I told him on numerous occasions, the most laconic person I'd ever met. He did speak at length when I asked him questions about his past, however. And I had a bunch. Why is the crew called the Violators? Because they liked to steal other guys' women. What did you do before music? Hustled. Where did you grow up? South Bronx. As I pummeled him with questions while shoveling fried chicken into my mouth, he answered calmly, never with his mouth full.

Chris spoke in a measured tone, never raising his voice or getting excited. And yet he talked about his life in such vivid terms, it was pure cinema, and by the end of lunch, I had determined that we were going to write a movie together based on his past in the drug game. *The Violators* we would call it, after his crew from the South Bronx. He taught me about collections in Jeeps, beatdowns on corners, and re-ups in shadows. He told me about going to clubs where the Violators would set off the metal detectors with a smile but sail through because of who they were. He narrated harrowing stories about jumping fences and running across cemeteries with loaded backpacks. It's crazy that he entrusted this deeply personal story to me. I'd like to think that his intuition, finely honed by the streets, told him that this excruciatingly energetic Korean Canadian woman was a worthy vessel.

The world Chris painted for me reminded me of "The Message," and I felt a need to get his story out there. It was amazing the danger and adversity he had overcome to arrive at the table with music executives, megastars, and other power players. I was deeply impressed by Chris's entrepreneurial spirit, and I think he helped awaken that beast in me. The walls of my office at Jive started to feel as if they were closing in on me. Listening to him talk about the ways he was going to hustle to make money was so intriguing, and the idea of making a movie with him opened my eyes to the world of possibility outside.

I bought Syd Field's *The Screenwriter's Workbook* and Final Draft, the screenwriting software, and we started working on the script right away. We spent a lot of time together writing it, mostly at my place. It was funny to see his big body sitting hunched over at my little desk, crammed under the loft bed. Other times, I went to his new house in the almost exclusively white suburbs of New Jersey. He was proud of his new place and wanted to share it with me. The first time I visited, we went to the local theater. We were the only people of color there. When some white teens sitting close to us saw Chris, they started rapping. It was like when people see me and suddenly start talking about ordering Chinese for lunch. We looked at each other knowingly and laughed out loud.

When we got out of the theater, it was dark and we looked up at the clear, starlit sky.

"Damn, Soph, rich people even get the stars more than we do," he said. The bright lights of the big city dimmed the stars. I doubt he had spent much time looking up at the sky from the Bronx River housing projects; he always had to keep his eye to the street. All the lessons he learned from the streets combined with his ingenuity and ambition birthed the mogul he became. To me, the story of Chris Lighty is the story of hip-hop. From block parties in the South Bronx to rapid globalization to shiny corporate boardrooms to eight-figure deals. He was there through all of it and pioneered many of its metamorphoses.

Chris and I would continue to cultivate our friendship over

the years. We had so much ground in common: the music, the artists, the community. We were often out at the same places, but it was the times we spent alone that I cherished the most. The beauty of our friendship was that it existed outside all the grandiosity that came with his lifestyle and notoriety. I want to believe that Chris felt he was free to be himself with me. No chest puffing, no table banging, no cage rattling. When we were together, he let his guard down and let me love him fully and fearlessly. Chris was my first hip-hop ride-or-die, but he wouldn't be my last. Soon, I would meet my army of Shaolin bodyguards who watched over me, loyalists who defended me, friends who stood by me through thick and thin.

CHAPTER 3
ENTER THE WU-TANG

In early 1993, I received a demo tape that didn't get thrown into the boxes under my desk because there was already a buzz building around it. The slightly worn black Maxell sixty-minute cassette had three titles scrawled on the narrowly lined cardboard insert: "Protect Ya Neck," "Method Man," and "Tearz." At the bottom was the contact information for a Prince Rakeem, the producer and the founder of the collective, as I would later learn. I inserted the tape into my cassette player as I had done hundreds of times before, but the result was like nothing I'd ever experienced.

First, there were nine guys. *Nine.* And each killed his verses with unique vocal, lyrical, and delivery styles. Then there were the beats, which were like the underbelly of the city itself. Not the beautiful, romantic skylines that I'd seen in movies, but sidewalks piled high with trash bags, subway tracks filled with rats, and the massive crime-ridden projects of the 1980s and '90s at the height of the crack era. There are countless songs that marry the powers of incredible beats and killer rhymes, but there was an element here that went beyond technical mastery: a combustible energy. Prince Rakeem—now known as RZA—somehow harnessed this tsunami and mixed it in a forty-ounce bottle for our consumption.

It takes a master alchemist to flawlessly highlight and integrate so many disparate skills and personalities on what we called a "posse track" back in the day. Even the intro to "Protect Ya Neck" was ominous and compelling: the song opens with kung fu flick samples and launches right into "Wu-Tang Clan comin' at ya! Watch your step, kid, watch your step, kid . . ." ODB started his verse by singing his "come on, baby baby, come on baby baby, come on, baby baby, come ooooonnn," which could be the lyrics to an R&B love song, but then goes straight into "first things first, man, you're fucking with the fucking worst / I'll be sticking pins in your head like a fucking nurse." The song was an embarrassment of riches and I wanted more.

I played that demo for anybody who would listen. I was a true Wu-vangelist. I couldn't sign the Clan because RZA famously asked for a nonexclusive deal—meaning each of the members of the group could pursue solo deals at other labels—but I was determined to meet the man regardless, because he was clearly a singular talent who would have an exceptional future, and I was intrigued by the mind behind the music. The opportunity came a few months later when I received a demo for the Gravediggaz, the group that

RZA had founded with producer Prince Paul, the creative impetus behind De La Soul. I set up a meeting with him immediately.

It was a hot summer day. I wore a Club Monaco sleeveless long dress in a small navy gingham print. RZA was late, which was to be expected, because few rappers are punctual. An artist's tardiness was inconvenient, but today it was unnerving because I was so excited to meet him. I kept looking at the clock, worried that enough time would pass to signal that he wasn't coming. Finally, the receptionist called to tell me he'd arrived. I ran to the lobby to meet him. He was gangly and taller than I'd expected, as I would learn almost all of the Clan were. He greeted me with "Peace, Soph" and shook my hand warmly.

We went down the street from Jive to Lox Around the Clock for lunch. We talked about the Gravediggaz, their horror movie aesthetic, how he had come to collaborate with Prince Paul, and what they were looking for in a label deal. I then grilled him with questions about the Clan. He told me that most of them had met in Staten Island, which they called Shaolin. Some of them grew up in the Stapleton Projects, others in Park Hill, a.k.a. Killer Hill. Most of them had run in the streets, and they bonded around music and kung fu flicks. When it came time to record the demo, RZA said each member had to show up with fifty dollars cash to pay for studio time. RZA had a unique world view and clear vision for the group. When we parted, I thought, *That's one of the smartest motherfuckers I've ever met.* As I walked north on Sixth Avenue, wondering when we'd next meet, he called out, "Soph!"

I turned quickly.

"Next time lunch is on me!" He hasn't let me pay for a meal since.

Talking to RZA was like entering a house that has endless rooms, each more fascinating and complex than the last. He spoke with such intelligence, insight, and energy about everything. Beyond his business acumen and musical genius, I felt a strong spiritual connection to him. Though he had dropped out of high school and I had graduated from university, it was manifestly clear that he was far more erudite than I was, the ultimate autodidact. Guys like RZA and Chris Lighty helped me see that formal education is not necessarily the key to success in business, which is partly why I paid no mind to my mother's entreaty that I go back to Vancouver to earn an MBA. I hoped to learn from RZA via his words and actions. I made sure to stay in touch. To this day, I remember his home phone number and address on Staten Island, down to the zip.

Soon thereafter, RZA invited me to the studio, where I met the other Clan members. It's always a privilege to be in the room when people are creating, but this meeting was particularly fascinating because there were so many of them, and I was curious to see what the seemingly unwieldy process would be like. GZA, the Clan elder and the head of Voltron, was laid-back and almost a little shy; Inspectah Deck was low-key with kind eyes that took everything in; U-God was full of energy and verve and immediately started calling me Miss Chang, as he does to this day; Masta Killa clasped my extended right hand in both of his while looking me dead in the eye as he said "peace" with a quiet intensity; Raekwon the Chef had an easy smile and cocked his head when he listened to me talk, as if he was hearing something others weren't; Ghostface Killah leaned in to greet me because he's six feet three inches and looked at me with warmth and curiosity; then there was Method Man, who hugged me and enveloped me completely in his tall frame in a way that said, "I got you, Soph," from the gate. He not only said it, he walked it.

One Saturday afternoon I went to see the guys in the studio. I jumped down the stairs of my second-story walk-up, two at a time, in a white T-shirt and gray terry shorts that I'd nabbed at a DKNY sample sale. I raced up Seventh Avenue to Battery Studios, which was located in the same building as Jive. There was a heat wave throttling New York City, already choking with tension and humidity. When I got to the studio, I was sweaty and relieved to feel the blast of air conditioning. As I entered the control room, Method Man jumped up and dragged me by the hand into the back lounge, barely letting me greet the rest of the guys.

"Sophie! I just got my video and you've gotta see it!"

At this point, the world had seen only one music video from Wu-Tang, for "Protect Ya Neck." That song had catapulted the Staten Island collective into the hearts and minds of the hip-hop cognoscenti, and everyone knew their rise would be meteoric. Everyone also knew, after hearing just fourteen bars, that Method Man would be the group's biggest star. I was about to get a personal sneak preview of the video for his solo song, one of only two on the album, "Method Man."

He led me to a black leather love seat and gently patted the worn cushion with his big strong hand. The scars on his knuckles marked the countless times he must have used his fists to defend himself, his turf, his loved ones. I sat back as he slid the VHS tape into the machine and waited for it to click into the spools before pushing play. I slid over, expecting him to sit next to me, but he shook his head. "Nah, Sophie, you sit. I'm good." He receded into the wall like a long, lean phantom at an angle that allowed him to study my reaction. Sitting directly across from me, next to the TV, was Jamal, one of the Clan's crew, also intent on watching me. Chilled by his cold energy, I saw clearly that he was trying to figure out how this little Asian woman, clearly not a groupie, had made her way into the inner sanctum. But I was there for Meth and ignored Jamal's glare.

As the video played, my face broke into a huge smile, hands clasped in sheer elation. Like its predecessor, it was low-budget, grainy, and poorly edited, but the intensity and personality of the Clan were undeniable—in the video they brandished hoodies, Timbs, kung fu swords, and, of course, weed. And the song's star shone like Sirius A: Meth's raging charisma, spring-loaded agility, and scruffy good looks surged through the screen.

As the video finished, I started to gush but then Jamal interrupted me.

"Where are you from?" he asked, with thinly veiled hostility.

"Excuse me?"

"Where are you from?"

"I don't understand what you're asking me."

That was a lie. I had been asked this countless times before. I chose to play naïve because I was caught off guard and didn't want to be adversarial in someone else's house. *Where are you from?* is a loaded question for people of color. Like its evil stepsister *Who are you?*, it's a question that's not asking, but saying something like, "Who do you think you are to be in my world, because you clearly don't belong."

"Where-are-you-from?" This time emphasizing each syllable to drive his point home.

"Well, if you're asking my heritage, I'm Korean Canadian. If you're asking where I live, I live in Manhattan. If you want to know where I work . . ."

Before I could finish, Meth flew between us, yelling at the top of his lungs, "That's Sophie Chang and she's from Shaolin! She's down with Wu-Tang! And that's all you need to know! Who the fuck is you to ask her where she's from?! Don't you ever disrespect her again!"

I sat bolt upright, eyes wide, mouth agape. This total sweetheart, who had a kind word for everyone, transformed before my eyes into a fury-breathing dragon. As his words shot through the air like poison darts, I saw he was rocking a cape emblazoned with a giant *M*, rippling in the wind of his fury. He sucked all the oxygen out of the room and took up every cubic inch of space. In that moment, I swore my undying allegiance to Method Man. Not only did he defend me, an Asian woman whom he barely knew, against one of his own, but he also instantly understood the racial subtext of the query. His defense of me was at once potent and poetic. From that day on, each time I saw Meth, I knew he was watching over me. This was the first time, but far from the last, he would bring da ruckus on my behalf.

Despite their distinct and varying personalities, there were common elements among the members of the Clan: First, a sense that the Wu-Tang truly could be dangerous. Without a single raised voice or sudden gesture, it was clear that these boys had walked many times on the razor's edge of danger and would throw the fuck down in a New York heartbeat. Second, that they loved each other unconditionally. Third, that they were going to be huge. "Protect Ya Neck" was already getting a lot of attention, but being there while they were working convinced me that the dam was about to break, and we would all soon be engulfed by their music. Victor Hugo said, *"On résiste à l'invasion des armées; on ne résiste pas à l'invasion des idées,"* which has been loosely translated to "there is nothing as powerful as an idea whose time has come." Wu-Tang were, in fact, an invasion of both armies and ideas.

Being in the studio with the Clan was like being inside a particle accelerator, watching their subatomic creativity bounce off each other to produce killer gamma rays. But what was most profound for me was that I was welcomed without question. I had established wonderful friendships in hip-hop that would last for decades, but the Clan took it to another level. Wu-Tang didn't just love me, they claimed me. They made me important and created space for me wherever I went. They made it clear to their crew and the world that Sophia Chang, this petite Asian woman, was theirs.

Of all the guys, Ol' Dirty Bastard would be the most territorial. Ironically, he was the last one I met. People told me he rocked crazy braids, so I looked for him in every club. One night I was at a spot in Chelsea and I could feel tension in the air. It was hot and crowded, and there was a lot of testosterone in the room. Just as I was about to cut out because of the energy, something drew my gaze across the club. I turned to see braids sticking out awry like the random branches of an old oak tree. I didn't have to see his face to know it was ODB. His energy was vibrating clear across the room, through the throbbing crowd, sloshing drinks, and pounding drums. I made a beeline for him. I was not going to let him elude me again. I pushed my way through the hoodies and Timbs and introduced myself. He grabbed me and hugged me as if he already knew me.

He peeled me off to the side of the dark and crowded club; we leaned in to yell and laugh in each other's ears. I scrawled my digits in a dark brown MAC lip pencil on a napkin that he stuffed into his pocket.

"You're gonna lose that," I said, sure it would find its way onto the floor of the club or get left behind in a cab.

"No, I won't, Sophie," he said, patting his pocket.

Suddenly, we heard a *pop, pop, pop* like firecrackers. I looked at Dirty and saw something other than mirth in his eyes. They narrowed ever so slightly as he did a split-second 360 survey of the room. Before I had a chance to follow his gaze, he yelled, "Get down, Sophie!" and put his hand on my head to push me to the ground. Shots were fired. I was scared but felt much safer in Dirty's care, especially because he was laughing out loud by the time we hit the floor. When the gunfire stopped, everyone got up and rushed to the door. Dirty and I lost each other, but I stayed outside on the sidewalk, looking for him. Eventually, he found me and put me in a cab. Dirty looked me dead in the eye and said, "Get home safe, Sophie." Shortly after I arrived home, I got a phone call.

"Hello?"

"Peace, Sophie, it's Dirty. You okay? I just wanted to make sure you got home all right." Guess he didn't lose my number.

The notion of safety took on a new meaning for me in those early days. Before I moved to New York, I had seen harmless schoolyard skirmishes and clumsy drunken bar fights, but never full-on brawls, and I had certainly never heard gunfire. I started to develop a Spidey sense for when shit was going to jump off by trying to read and anticipate violent energy. Being at those clubs could actually be fatal if you were in the wrong spot at the wrong time, but it didn't stop any of us from going, because it was the only way to see the artists live, hear the music before it was released, and observe how people responded to records in real time. Having protectors like Dirty who were familiar with the fracas and weren't afraid was extremely comforting.

One of my girlfriends said, "Soph, aren't you scared when you're with them?" as we examined a picture of Wu-Tang looking threatening in *Vibe* magazine.

"Actually, I'm scared when I'm *not* with them."

What started as straight fandom would evolve into lifelong friendships, as well as several opportunities to spread the culture and make some C.R.E.A.M. along the way. A number of these opportunities would originate with RZA, whose inexhaustible entrepreneurship inspired the budding hustler in me.

While at Jive, I became very close with Denise, a colleague who had done marketing for some years. The major labels had started poaching talent from the hip-hop independents as it became clear that the genre was a revenue stream that was too big to ignore. I saw an opportunity. Denise was talented and we worked well together, so I began talking to her about starting an independent hip-hop marketing company that would consult to the major labels. I loved doing A&R, but the notion of running my own business was extremely inviting.

In the spring of 1991, SoundScan, a method of tracking sales by the bar codes of actual units sold, was implemented. The data was collected on Sundays and reported to *Billboard*, which used the numbers to compile its charts on Monday mornings. Before SoundScan, *Billboard* depended on the label to call the retailers, which was prone to mistakes and payola. N.W.A.'s second album debuted at number two on the Billboard 200 that year, moving up to the top spot the next week. Despite the power of racism, no one could deny the growth of hip-hop as a major cultural force. The album sold three million units, which told the world that it wasn't just young black people listening to hip-hop, it was white kids too, God forbid.

Around the time I proposed the idea to Denise, she had her first child and was trying to figure out how to spend more time with him. She asked her boss if she could work from home on Fridays and he said no. That was the final straw. We planned to quit on the same day at the exact same time. At 11:30 a.m. on a Wednesday morning, not long after I met the Clan in 1993 and less than two years after I had started at Jive, I left the company with Denise. She went into her boss's office on the ninth floor, I went into my boss's office one floor below, and we simultaneously tendered our resignations. I knew that my mind was made up, but I was concerned that Denise's boss would convince her to stay by offering her the Friday off, a promotion, more money. My boss simply wished me good luck, and I went back to my office, where I waited impatiently for Denise to call. Finally, she called and said that she had been offered more money but she held her ground. I heaved a sigh of relief and we giggled. We had just staged a minor mutiny. This wasn't a *take this job and shove it* moment. We liked our jobs; it was more that we were excited for the adventure ahead. This was the first time in my life that I would be working for myself, and it would become my road most traveled.

Chris Lighty, the serial hustler, supported this move, despite the fact that it meant we would be leaving his artists, A Tribe Called Quest, behind. Michael Ostin was the first person to hire our agency. We got a great deal consulting for Warner Bros., helping them shape their newly formed hip-hop department. Serendipitously, there we ended up working with another of Chris's groups, the Jungle Brothers.

RZA came to us with another proposal. He was going to do a label deal in partnership with a major record company and wanted us to run it. We sat strategizing in the Mondrian Hotel on Sunset Strip in West Hollywood. Label deals, particularly joint ventures, are very complex, as there are myriad factors to consider in the negotiations. RZA, as the owner of the label, would command a point override, meaning a guaranteed percentage of each release, as well as his points for producing. A point represents 1 percent of the overall income. At the time he was earning four points per song, which was high. Most producers were earning only three. There were also the recoupable and non-recoupable advances, meaning the cash the label paid up front that would have to be earned back in sales, and the portion would be straight C.R.E.A.M. in RZA's pocket that never had to be repaid. He also demanded guaranteed marketing budgets and releases; the latter are referred to as "puts." There were many other components of the equation, many of which I was familiar with, having negotiated some of them in our deal with Warner Bros. In light of the standard deals that we had done at Jive, I was deeply impressed by how clearly RZA valued himself. The deal didn't end up going with that label, but it was flattering to be considered to run it with my partner.

Having left Jive, I now had the freedom to move like I wanted to, and much of that movement was around the Clan. I tried to be wherever they were—studio, interviews, shows. I even went with them on their first promo trip to Cali. While we were there, I met the first wife: Tamika, Method Man's shorty, who sat on his lap in the video for "Method Man." There were a couple of things that struck me about meeting her: First, that she was on the road with the guys. It was uncommon to see the wives at shows, never mind on the road. Also, how happy Meth was to introduce me to her. And finally, how beautiful and sweet she was. *Yes*, I thought, *she's the perfect match for him.* She was the inspiration of his biggest hit, "All I Need," that was named "The No. 1 Summer Song of Love" in 1995 by *The New York Times.*

I also spent a lot of time with the other members, picking their brains about their lyrics. Ghost showed me where the bullet went in and exited his neck, Rae told me that a "lo sweater" in the song "C.R.E.A.M." was "what we called polo, Soph," and when I asked Deck, twenty-five years ago, about "handcuffed on a bus, forty of us, life as a shorty shouldn't be so rough," he looked down at me and asked, "What, are you writing a book, Soph?"

How did he know before I did?

Not long after that trip I got a call from Schott Free, who did A&R at Loud Records, Wu-Tang's label. Schott was having trouble getting the guys to focus on the "C.R.E.A.M." video treatment and asked for my help. I had already earned my reputation as the Wu whisperer and someone so devoted to the Clan that I would do anything for them. I jumped on a train and walked straight into the RCA offices, where the guys were doing a day of press. I pulled Raekwon out and we sat down at one of the desks.

We went through the song, line by line, and Rae extrapolated his vision while I typed away. I asked him questions, we fed off each other's thoughts and ideas, and we created a visual story that would translate the song into a film. "I want this shit to look like a movie, Soph! I don't just want us to be in the streets, we've also gotta be in boardrooms!" It was important to him to reflect the dramatic transition they'd made. There would be bags of cash, blunts, and fly gear. GZA told me later that he had wanted to flick a blunt across the conference room table like a ninja star in slow motion. I told Rae that there shouldn't be any women in the video and that one of the things that I loved about the song and the album in general was the conspicuous lack of women. He said, "Yea, yea, you get it, Soph!" Looking back, I understand that the twenty-eight-year-old me made the point because women were completely objectified at the time. The fifty-three-year-old me wishes I'd said that he should put a woman at the table as one of their peers. When we were done, I said goodbye to the rest of the guys, who were still conducting interviews. I poked my head into a conference room and silently waved goodbye to Meth and Ghost.

"How are you getting home, Sophie?" they both asked, with the tone of concerned parents.

"Train."

"We're walking you to the station!"

"Guys, it's Times Square in broad daylight and I only have a few stops. I'll be fine."

"Nah, fuck that, Sophie, we're coming with you!" They jumped up and walked out on their interview.

I couldn't have been more delighted to have my body-guards escort me. I walked through Times Square flanked by six-foot-three and six-foot-four like nothing could touch me. When we got to the train station, I looked up at their wonderful scruffy faces, stood on my tippy toes, and hugged my tall, strong bodyguards goodbye. As they enveloped me, I peeped: "I love you!"

"Love you too, Sophie!" they replied.

I could feel their watchful eyes on me as I descended the crowded stairway. They saw the hordes of people surrounding me in the rush hour crush and clearly didn't like watching their little charge disappear into the sea of bodies. To my surprise, and that of my poor unsuspecting fellow mass transit riders, Meth and Ghost leaned way over the railing and roared, "If anyone fucks with you, Sophie, you tell them you're with Wu-Tang 'cause we'll fuck them up if they come near you!"

Of all the guys, I became closest to ODB. We would spend hours at my place talking shit and listening to old R&B classics. Like Chris Lighty, he appreciated that he could leave his persona at the door and enter a chamber where he could be his own goofy, brilliant, sometimes vulnerable self. Dirty could be highly unpredictable, but there was one day that he genuinely caught me off guard. It was early 1995 and I had moved to the Archive, a luxury white-glove building in the West Village. One day after we'd hung out, I walked him downstairs. As we were crossing the cavernous, red-brick lobby lined with terra-cotta tiles, he stopped and sat me down on one of the polished wooden benches.

"Sophie," he said, turning to me with a seriousness he rarely exhibited, "I want you to manage me."

"What?"

"Yeah, Sophie, you know me, you understand me, and I love the shit out of you. When I'm around you I don't have to be Ol' Dirty Bastard, I can just be A Son."

Wu-Tang are members of the Five Percent Nation, a religious movement that was founded in New York by a former member of the Nation of Islam. GZA was the first of the Clan to enter the Nation and lead the others into it. I have no doubt that path of righteousness and discipline of the Nation saved some of their lives. The simple fact that they greet everyone by saying "Peace" sets the tone. ODB's Five Percent Nation name was A Son Unique because he was a unique child of God. He could be more impetuous than anyone I knew, but he had clearly thought long and hard about this name. RZA gave him his rap name, ODB, because "there's no father to his style." The Clan were the first artists to take on aliases, now a common practice in hip-hop.

I told Dirty I'd have to think about it. I went back upstairs and called Joan immediately. She had her reservations, but knowing how passionate I was about him and that we would do good work together, she gave me her blessing. I called him back.

"I love you too, A, and I'd be honored to manage you."

And just like that, I stepped into the shoes of artist manager, which I would wear on and off for the next twenty years.

I'd never managed before, but I would learn along the way. I fucked up plenty, but I put in good, hard work too. What I knew, unequivocally, was that I had to be passionate, thorough, loyal, and above all trustworthy. In return, he was wise, kind, generous, ferociously loyal, and protective. My golden ticket with Dirty was the trust that he had for and in me. Like all relationships, trust is key, especially with artists because they are sensitive by nature and so careful about whom they allow to help them get their creations into the world. It's an additional challenge to earn the trust of many rappers because of their backgrounds. I came to understand that the artists I worked with, all black men largely raised in challenging circumstances and having dabbled in criminality, had grown up with an inherent and justifiable distrust of a society and criminal justice system that had mistreated them for centuries.

As a middle-class, college-educated Korean Canadian woman, I didn't pretend to understand how that felt, but I checked my privilege and kept their histories in mind as I represented them. When people asked why Wu-Tang took to me so immediately and so deeply, I didn't have a clear answer. I know better now because I asked Rae and Ghost. They both said it was part of a bigger plan. Rae said I was a gift and the little sister that Wu-Tang never had; Meth said I was the group's muse. RZA said I was the yin to their yang and Ghost said I was like a ray of sunshine. When I was with the Clan, I felt truly seen, and I hope they would say the same.

My friend filmmaker Julius Onah said, in reference to his film *Luce*, that he believes all people should be granted access to the full spectrum of humanity. I think that the Clan and I did that for each other. When I was around them, I didn't feel like a little Asian woman on the periphery, I felt like a queen who was protected, respected, and adored. And I believe they know that I didn't see them simply as one-dimensional artists who could breathe fire with their lyrics; rather, I understood and loved every part of them.

Managing ODB might sound oxymoronic and it certainly came with its challenges, but we had a great working dynamic and accomplished a lot together. We did a promo tour through Northern and Southern California where people got to see him perform solo for the first time. Dirty was both a formidable MC and an outstanding performer. He gave a thousand percent every time he was on stage, running back and forth, stomping his feet, and swirling his head on his neck like a cobra.

The only time I fought with Chris Lighty was in 1994. We were at my apartment in the Archive and I told him about Dirty getting shot. How shaken I had been when just a day before, Dirty had stood where Chris was standing and lifted his shirt to show me the massive Frankenstein scar that ran up the length of his stomach. I wanted Chris to comfort me, but instead he laughed callously and said something sarcastic about him asking for it. My eyes instantly filled with tears.

"How could you say that? I love him and care about him like I love you, and you talk about him like he's nothing!"

Chris had never seen me cry. His big brown eyes softened, and his voice warmed with love. "C'mon, Soph, I didn't mean it like that." I fell into his chest, weeping, like I would do many more times. And as always, he just stood there and let me cry it out. He never hugged me back in an effort to console me, but he didn't need to, because through all his laconic silence and inscrutability, his stillness communicated his love and concern. He knew I loved him and needed him to soften up in that moment. To be human.

Chris and the Clan knew that I loved them as people above all. I had never experienced this level of devotion and protection. Hip-hop taught me my greatest lessons about loyalty. Being adopted by Wu-Tang Clan meant that I walked with a shield of protection at all times, as I did with Chris. It's as if the unseen *W* tattooed across my heart was a sign that I belonged to a crew that would come to my defense and rescue in a heartbeat. It meant that I never waited in line and would be ushered by one or two bodyguards directly to them and chaperoned when I went to and from the restroom. It meant that I always had a seat in the most crowded of studios or buses. It meant that if you were a man and wanted to date me, you were probably shook because of my nine giant older brothers who would hold you accountable to unimaginable standards. Who, indeed, could ever possibly pass this bar?

When I look back, it's remarkable that these nine warriors who "grew up on the crime side, the *New York Times* side," didn't hesitate to adopt me, a Korean Canadian woman who grew up in the green grass and fresh air of Vancouver, who didn't provide them with pussy, money, power, or access, but simply arrived at their doorstep armed with nothing more than a burning love that knew no bounds. Our experiences were diametrically opposed, but they gave voice to the outrage and frustration that I had felt being other. They taught me to honor my anger, to channel it and use it as a verbal weapon. Finally, I felt I was fully seen. It would take decades for me to see everything that they saw in me.

CHAPTER 4
WHEN THE STUDENT IS READY

The Fu-Schnickens used to talk to me about their favorite kung fu flicks. The steady stream of martial arts movies on Channel 5 every Saturday was a formative component of the Fu-Schnickens' childhood and adolescence, as it was for so many black men who grew up in New York in the 1980s. But I never watched kung fu movies as a kid, probably part of my cultural denial, so I had nothing to contribute on the topic because I wasn't a fan. "Sophia, how can you be Asian and not into kung fu flicks?" That question seemed silly and even offensive to me at the time, but now I get it. As Asians, we should be proud of that very important part of our heritage.

Then I met the Clan and everything changed. When they introduced me to John Woo's magnum opus *The Killer*, I went down the rabbit hole and watched every one of his movies countless times over, swooning over Chow Yun Fat, the effortlessly graceful and sexy leading man who could hold a baby, shoot a gun, and chew on a toothpick all at once. I'd later gasp at Jason Scott Lee's shirtless performance in *Dragon: The Bruce Lee Story* and delight in Jackie Chan, Jet Li, and Donnie Yen. People rarely talk about how women are empowered in Chinese martial arts movies, yet extraordinary actresses like Michelle Yeoh, Maggie Cheung, Anita Mui, Brigitte Lin, and Zhang Ziyi played integral, if not lead, ass-kicking roles. It didn't matter to me that these films were Chinese and I was Korean; it was about seeing someone who looked like me and my people on screen. Wu-Tang's love of Asian culture was greater than the love I'd seen in anyone, even other Asians.

Once I started watching kung fu movies, I recognized that Wu-Tang weren't just into the high kicks and explosive punches, they were also deeply invested in the Buddhist and Taoist philosophies, as well as the themes of brotherhood, loyalty, and resisting oppression that resonated with them. The first time they were on *Yo! MTV Raps* with Ed Lover and Doctor Dré, I saw clearly how seriously they took martial arts. After a break, one of the hosts, Ed Lover, came back to set in a wig and glasses, dressed in faux karate *gi*, and held a broomstick like a weapon. They were just being playful, but I could tell by the look on my boys' faces that they did not think it was funny. At all. When Meth was introducing himself, Ed got into his face, acting goofy, and Meth said, "Yo, what's wrong with you, man?" with a smile, but I knew he was annoyed. Then Raekwon, never one to mince words, said something like, "We take this shit very seriously.

This is not a game to us. You're here making it seem like a joke. If you ever do something like that again, we'll fold you up like a wallet."

My kung fu flick–watching partner was Maria Ma, one of my lifetime ride-or-dies, whom I'd met when we worked together at Jive. Like so many others, we decided, "Let's learn kung fu!" We visited a bunch of schools and saw the overweight so-called masters stand around, looking wholly uninterested in training the wide-eyed, gullible *gweilo*, which means "white ghost" in Cantonese and is a derogatory term for white people. Somewhere along the way, we heard there was a Shaolin monk teaching on Mott Street. Stop the fucking presses. That's like Pavarotti opening an opera school down the block.

The Shaolin Temple in Henan Province in northeastern China is a mecca for martial artists. It is the founding place of Chan Buddhism, which migrated to Japan and became what we know more commonly as Zen, and where martial arts first became codified. The temple had become run-down during the Cultural Revolution but underwent a massive restoration after kung fu superstar Jet Li's debut film *The Shaolin Temple* was released in 1982. It became a huge tourist destination, replete with kung fu schools, martial arts supply stores, souvenir shops, and noodle stands.

The winter of 1994 was brutal, but Maria and I braved the brick-ass cold to hunt down this elusive monk. We trudged up and down Mott Street through snow and slush and the throngs of Chinatown's residents on our wild-goose chase. When we didn't see any signs for kung fu, we just started

going into random doors asking about a Shaolin monk. We
went into some pretty seedy buildings and got some pretty
weird looks. We were disheartened but not defeated. We were
on a mission, like seeking the Holy Grail or the mythical
Prada sample sale.

We picked up the Yellow Pages and kept looking. We
called a bunch of kung fu schools, and finally someone
named Joe at the Tai Chi Association told us the monk had
just moved to Bowery. Readying for our quest, I put on my
winter gear, which consisted of extra-large black Gore-Tex
snowboarding overalls that I'd gotten off of Q-Tip, a black,
oversize North Face down puffer jacket inspired by Redman,
and black hiking boots with bright red laces. We found our
way to 96 Bowery and took the dubious-looking elevator to
the second floor.

When we emerged, we stepped into a long, narrow loft
space. The floors were covered in faded green carpet, and the
faux wood–paneled walls were marked with battery-operated
wall lights, spaced perfectly apart across the length of the
room. The thirty-fourth-generation Shaolin master was sitting at a table, reading the daily Chinese newspaper. He was
wearing a long brown wool monk's robe with bell-shaped
sleeves and looked to be in his early thirties. He stood up
quickly and strode over to us, then smiled and motioned for us
to remove our shoes. We were two well-raised Asian women,
so he could have saved that request for the savages who track
dog shit and piss into every house they enter.

His name was Shi Yan Ming. The first thing I noticed

was his posture. He walked and sat as if he had a steel rod in his back. He wasn't tall, but his shoulders were impossibly broad. His head was clean-shaven, and he had the eyebrows of a dragon. His lips were full and his smile inviting. In short, as Joan said as soon as she'd met him, "Soph, he's fine and I think he could beat Mike Tyson." Until this point, the guitar player in Vancouver had been my only serious boyfriend. After that, it was a series of unfortunate fucks, trysts, and crushes gone awry. And only one with an Asian man. I had bought into the notion that Asian men weren't sexy.

When Yan Ming opened his mouth, I was taken aback by how high and soft his voice was. Maria did all the talking, as she speaks Mandarin, and I just sat there, observing. I examined all the items on the altar: the ceramic happy Buddha statue, the apples and oranges on elevated plastic trays, the wooden bell, the vase of freshly cut flowers, and so much more. I studied the posters on the wall of the shirtless, fearsome, ferocious warrior standing on a bed of nails with arms outstretched, holding a massive jug of water in each hand, and the man in the saffron robes jumping in the air from atop the long wooden handle of a weapon that ended in a large silver blade. Then I looked at the man sitting in front of me, politely answering questions in a robe that cloaked his whole body, and I couldn't believe it was the same person.

What I did know, beyond the shadow of a doubt, was that this was the man I would spend the rest of my life with. The thousand-mile journey to him had started at birth and woven its way through my years in hip-hop preceding him. The most significant stepping-stone had been placed before me by the Clan.

I noticed there was a little boy running around in the back of the studio.

"Ask him if that's his son," I urged Maria.

"I'm not going to ask him that, Soph, he's a monk!"

"Ask him!"

Very reluctantly, she asked. Yan Ming looked surprised at the question and answered, "No."

It's hard to describe how certain I was that he was the one. It wasn't like a bolt of lightning, I didn't feel as if I were floating in the air on a bed of lotus blossoms. It was as if it was an empirical truth. I just *knew*. I was so certain that I went home and called my parents and told them, "I met the man I'm going to marry today." That must have sounded fucking nuts. But God bless my parents, they were right there with their nutty daughter. I told them he was a Shaolin monk, and my father immediately got some reference book and looked it up. "Shaolin monks are allowed to marry!" he said.

A week later, on February 10, 1995, just three months shy of my thirtieth birthday, I started training at the temple. The first class was repetitive and boring. We did the same kick, *caijiao*, or front slap kick, and stance, *gong bu*, or bow stance, over and over again for two hours. Patience, grasshopper. Then we stretched like crazy. *When do we get to the animal styles and weapons like Jet Li?* I left the class feeling cocky. *That wasn't so hard.* Two days later, I could barely walk. My whole body was shattered, but the most painful were my quads, glutes, and hamstrings. I wept at the sight of stairs, had to lower myself like a nonagenarian onto the toilet, and walked as if I'd been shot in both kneecaps. My muscles were shredded. And I went back for more.

Watching Yan Ming train was revelatory. He never lost focus nor intensity, no matter how tired he was. He was both strong and powerful, the latter being the more important. When I think of incredible strength, I think of those competitions where men pull trains. When I think of power, I recall Bruce Lee's famous one-inch punch that could send a man flying several yards back. Watch that footage in slow motion: you can see that he is summoning all the qi, or life force, in his body and channeling it through his fist.

Yan Ming could do this as well. He was well versed in an art called *dim mak*, a.k.a. the death touch. Before I started training, there was a student named Corey who had heard about the Shaolin monk teaching and went up to the temple to challenge Yan Ming to a fight. Bad idea. Yan Ming shook his head but Corey kept insisting. Finally, Corey tried to hit him. Yan Ming simply put his fingers on a pressure point on Corey's calf, and Corey collapsed onto the floor. His leg had been rendered completely useless. When he was able to stand again, he signed up for classes.

It's amazing how hard the simplest things were back then. Kung fu is a language, and my body was woefully illiterate. One day, we were taught a basic jump called *tantiao*, which consists of launching off your right foot, lifting your left leg, and bringing your right foot up to meet your left.

Simple, so simple. A couple of students went before me and looked kind of clumsy. I snickered to myself. *Let me show you how it's done.*

Everyone's eyes were on me, including Yan Ming's, naturally. I ran and jumped, feeling as graceful as a springbok leaping through the grasslands of Namibia. Then, as I was soaring through midair, which was only two inches off the ground, something went terribly wrong, and I busted my ass in spectacular fashion, crashing to the floor. I landed so hard that my right butt cheek developed a bruise the size of a Frisbee that turned brilliant colors reminiscent of a lava lamp. Training in kung fu was at once the most exhilarating and humbling experience I'd ever had.

Before the temple, I had made some anemic attempts at physical fitness, including going to the gym for twenty minutes or attending yoga classes, where all I did was watch the clock. I never needed to work out to stay thin, thanks to my metabolism, but I wanted to be in shape. What I didn't anticipate was being drawn so strongly to the spiritual aspect of the temple. Until this moment, I hadn't paid much attention to philosophy or faith outside of my university studies and was an agnostic. I was a literature major and my father an atheist math professor. We were beings of reason and rationale and logic, but as I started to open myself up to the transformation my body would undergo, I was also opening my mind. The mind-body-spirit connection was a catchphrase and marketing tool for many new age fitness centers, but none of them could have synthesized the three the way that Shaolin did because, I think, in some ways, Shaolin did it first. At Shaolin, kung fu is Chan and Chan is kung fu. You can't have one without the other.

Learning Buddhism from Yan Ming wasn't about rules, dogma, and doctrine, it was about exploring a philosophy and way of life. I can't quote the eight noble truths, recite sutras, or name the first five patriarchs of Chan, but I know that you can achieve enlightenment in a moment and that the transmission of the faith was only supposed to be heart-to-heart and mind-to-mind. And that's how I absorbed it from Yan Ming.

Less than three months after I'd started training, as my body began to undergo this transformation and I was drawn into the world of Chan Buddhism, I started falling for Yan Ming. Hard. I was amazed by his body, soul, and spirit.

I was having impure thoughts about Yan Ming and actually hoped that he didn't take this monk thing seriously. My dad did say Shaolin monks could marry, after all. But how to broach the topic without being a heathen? I swore he liked me too and that there was a growing sexual tension between us. I felt he paid special attention to me and watched even when he didn't need to. Just as I was coming to terms with my confusing feelings, I was forced to exercise patience, not one of my virtues, by leaving town.

When I was asked as a kid if I'd been to Korea, I would say, "No, I won't go to Korea until my thirtieth birthday." I was aware that I wasn't connected to my culture yet but figured I would be at some point. Sure enough, the first time I visited my homeland was on May 17, 1995, my thirtieth birthday. The trip was the most profound of my life. Korea was filled with historical sites, shopping, and delicious food: we spent hours in Itaewon shopping for fake designer bags and saw the legendary Emile Bell at Bongdeoksa Temple, where I ate the best *mandoo* and *samgyetang* to ever pass my lips. Seoul was industrial and dirty and crowded and exhilarating, all at the same time. And it was edifying to be surrounded by people who looked like me, everywhere, not just in enclaves dedicated to discrete immigrant communities like Chinatowns and K-Towns.

The excitement of discovery was palpable, but the overwhelming emotion I experienced in my homeland was shame. I had crossed the world to reconnect with my people, only to be stymied by the loss of my mother tongue—I had rejected this beautiful, vibrant culture that my family so eagerly welcomed me into. We spent time with my mother's older brothers and older sister, with whom she had escaped North Korea, as well as their children. I had already met them because they'd visited us in Vancouver, but in Korea I got to meet their children and grandchildren. I couldn't communicate with them except through sheepish smiles and my parents. My mother's sister lived in one of several huge, homogenous towers that housed thousands of residents in tiny apartments. I don't mean huge towers like the monstrosities in Columbus Circle, rather like the projects that lined my neighborhood on Avenue D in Alphabet City. When we walked into her home, I was shocked by its modesty. It was tiny, sparsely furnished, but oh so very clean. She hand-washed and hung dry all her clothes. Despite how modestly my relatives lived, they showered us with gifts and trips and meals.

My mother's brother took us to a fancy banquet at the Lotte Hotel in Seoul. I ate almost everything but positively blanched when they put the ultimate delicacy before us: a plate full of squirming tentacles of a just-killed octopus. I didn't even have the courage to try it, which was just so damn rude and ungrateful. I felt like the princess and the pea.

As we did our sightseeing, I noticed that my people were not particularly polite. I remarked as much to my father. One night we were on the train at about 9:00 p.m., and it was chock-full of wearied workers and students still in their school uniforms, holding their backpacks full of heavy textbooks close to their chests. When we got off the train, my father said, "You see, Sophia, these people have been working hard all day; they don't have the time and energy to be polite in the way you want them to be."

As we walked down the streets and through the shops of Seoul, people would stare. I don't mean casually glance my way, pretending to be looking at something just beyond me. Women behind the makeup counters at department stores would step out to stare at my short haircut. I hadn't noticed, but as I started looking, I realized that none of the women in Korea rocked short hair. My father was indignant on my behalf. He, too, then complained about how rude the people were. I didn't care that they stared at me, but it did bother me that it was having this effect on my parents. Little did any of us know that in a couple of months, I would do something that would make the nation clutch their pearls.

I thought about Yan Ming every day of the trip. At that

time, I dared not call him by his name, rather by Shifu, which means "master" in Mandarin. I met Maria in Hong Kong, where we browsed antique furniture stores, ate dim sum, and shopped for John Woo paraphernalia. While we sat on the Star Ferry, crossing from the mainland to Kowloon in the blazing heat of the summer sun, I professed my love for Yan Ming to her. Her eyes opened wide and she clapped her hands over her ears.

"No, Soph! Stop, that's our *shifu*!"

"I can't help it! And I think he likes me too!" I yelled over the splashing of the waves, shielding my eyes from the reflection of the sun bouncing off the water.

"Stop it, Soph!" she urged.

"Maria, I'm serious. I really think he likes me, and I don't know what to do! I can't ask him, it would be insulting to him and the temple."

"Okay, this is what you do," she said, more calmly. "When you go back, spend as much time with him as possible and it will become clear. If nothing else, you'll have a great friend."

Fortuitously, the hip-hop consulting gig wasn't too taxing, so I had the freedom to spend an inordinate amount of time at the temple. I started training seven days a week, spending all day and night there. Between classes, Yan Ming and I got to know each other, despite the language barrier. His story was the stuff of movies.

Yan Ming was one of nine siblings and got very ill and died when he was a baby. His parents, too poor for a proper burial, wrapped him in a blanket and took him into the woods to bury him. As they were walking, they encountered a man who asked why they were crying so bitterly. They told him that their son had died. He asked to see their child. They unwrapped the blankets and he inspected the blue baby. He took out needles and performed acupuncture. Miraculously, Yan Ming came back to life.

By the time he was five, it was the middle of the Cultural Revolution, when religious activities were banned. Yan Ming's parents took him to the Shaolin Temple, where every week, throngs of people would crowd at the doors, hoping to be chosen to enter the temple to train. When the abbot came out in his regal red and yellow robes, he scanned the crowds. When his eyes landed on Yan Ming, he studied his face and chose the boy, though small and sickly. Yan Ming would spend the next twenty-three years waking up at 4:00 a.m. to eat, pray, and train in cycles for sixteen straight hours a day.

Yan Ming got to the shores of America on the Shaolin monks' first-ever appearance in the country. On the last night of the tour, he snuck out, never to look back. The defection of the national treasure caused an uproar back home. As the temple became more commercialized, he saw that change was coming to his beloved home and wanted to spread Shaolin kung fu and Chan Buddhism in America. Yan Ming dreamed of replicating the Shaolin Temple in upstate New York, opening the teachings to the West. His vision was exalting, and I wanted to do what I could to help him realize it. This felt so much bigger and more important than the work I was doing in music.

During this period when I was trying to get closer to

Yan Ming, I pulled something in my back during class. Yan Ming ordered the class to keep training, sat me down, and gave me a massage. *OH MY GOD*. His hands were so strong and sure and hit all the right pressure points. When he was done, he told me that if it still bothered me the next day, I should come back. Later, one of his most devoted students, James, a total fucking stan whom I had become close with, said, "He gave me a massage too." Thanks for raining on my parade.

There was a clique of students who started looking askance at how Yan Ming was changing as a result of our liaison. When I met him, he looked like every tourist from Mainland China back in the day: he wore oversize, shapeless T-shirts tucked into ill-fitting khakis that were pulled *wayyy* over his waist and cinched tight with a cheap leather belt from Canal Street. *No, no, no,* I thought, *not my man.* I took him shopping and we bought him a pair of Prada sport shoes, which were beautiful and incredibly comfortable.

"I didn't think Buddhist monks were supposed to wear Prada," one of these guys scoffed, condescension and judgment in full effect.

"Buddhist monks aren't ascetics. Shakyamuni tried that and rejected it. Buddhists can appreciate nice things without being attached to them," I replied.

Yan Ming's spirit and soul weren't changing at all. As much as he liked comforts like heat, air conditioning, and Italian designer shoes, he would have been perfectly happy without them. What was really happening was that the men who had trained with him before I got there resented me.

Like with the hip-hop world, I had entered another super testosterone-filled environment. Unlike with hip-hop, however, I was not warmly accepted. They couldn't stand that there was someone who got to spend unfettered time with their beloved teacher, someone whom he would love more deeply than he could ever love them. In short, they were hating on the woman who took their boy away. My attitude? *I don't give a fuck.* I wasn't going to modify my behavior to make them feel better. Kind of my approach to most things in life.

Having immersed myself fully into the Shaolin way of life, I decided to take my dedication to another level and shave my head. Five years earlier, at twenty-five, just as I was getting my footing in the music business, I had decided to cut off my beautiful waist-length hair. I wanted to be taken more seriously, not be seen as a kind of doll. Sonya arranged for me to get my hair cut by hairdresser to the stars Angelo Di Biase. I struggled with the decision because my hair was such a big part of my identity. I spent so much time thinking about it that I finally told myself I had to do it, based on the fact that I had expended so much energy on something so superficial.

At thirty, my primary impetus behind deciding to go bald was the Buddhist practice of nonattachment. I told Yan Ming I was going to shave my head, and he said he wanted to be the one to do it. Now I was both excited and nervous about the process. I didn't much care about how I would look. I was thinking only about how this would play out. I figured it would be cold and mechanical. Yan Ming had been shaving his head for twenty-eight years, and he had it down to a science.

The setting was far from romantic. It was in the back of the temple over the large industrial-gray plastic sink, the kind you'd see in a basement laundry room. He waited until everyone was gone and got the clippers. He told me to lean my head over the sink. As I studied the drain, hot with anticipation, I heard the buzz of the clippers as Yan Ming turned them on and proceeded to slowly and carefully shave my head. I had felt his hands when he had massaged my back injury, but not on my skin and not on my neck. So many times I had watched his hands as they deftly handled chopsticks, powerfully punched bags, and superhumanly propelled his body into the air as he did push-ups across the length of the temple. That made him look like a fish on dry land, jumping up and down. But now his hands were gentle and warm, and, I dared think, full of emotion and desire. The strokes were methodical and measured, and it felt as if he took more time than he needed to. He handled the clippers with his right hand while his left held my neck in position or turned my head this way and that. When he was done, he guided my cold, bald, prickly head toward the faucet and rinsed it. It was indubitably one of the most erotic experiences I've ever had and a stunning mix of spiritual cleansing and tantalizing foreplay. If this had been any other man, I would have been absolutely sure that he wanted to be with me, but still, there was that monk thing.

With my hair gone, I discovered a whole new freedom. It was one thing to go from long, straight hair to a pixie cut.

It was completely different to go from a pixie to a fucking cue ball, especially because Asian women are known for their hair. I delight in obliterating stereotypes. With the training, I was ever clearer that I wasn't a China doll but a Shaolin warrior. The act was at once spiritual and political, the first in a myriad of middle fingers I'd throw up to white patriarchy for decades to come. You could almost say it was a process of de-beautifying myself. Don't get me wrong, I think I look dope as fuck with no hair, but I was keenly aware of how I would be perceived. The one response I didn't fully anticipate was my mother's.

The next time I went to Vancouver, my parents were waiting right outside the airport doors, craning their necks to see me. When I emerged and my mother caught sight of my head, her knees buckled. To this day, my hair is a source of embarrassment for her, and her embarrassment a source of frustration for me. I don't think my father liked it either, but he never said anything about it.

After Yan Ming shaved my head, I was more convinced than ever that something was going on between us. I came right out and asked James if he thought Yan Ming was celibate.

"Definitely."

Damn.

One night, James and I were both at the temple with Yan Ming. I stuck around, waiting for James to leave. *Ever heard of a third wheel, motherfucker? Read the room!* It was like playing a game of chicken to see who would leave first. Finally, at 10:00 p.m., I gave up and we both left. I walked into my apartment and started cooking myself some chicken. No sooner had the pan started to sizzle than the phone rang. My heart jumped. It was Yan Ming and he invited me back to the temple. I would say I took a cab, but I'm pretty sure I flew, powered by sheer delight.

We lay on the carpet in front of the altar, pillows under our heads, talking for hours. At one point, Yan Ming said, "Sophia, do you want to ask me something?"

I'm pretty sure that was an invitation to ask him if he liked me, but I was still too scared. I asked him what he thought about capital punishment. You can imagine how far that conversation went, considering the language barrier. Then I asked about his family, training, and China. Finally, at 3:00 a.m., I worked up the nerve to go a little deeper.

"Shifu," I said, a slight hesitation in my voice.

"Yes?"

"Do you ever want to get married?" I can't believe I said it. Call it late-night courage.

"Yes, I think about it sometimes."

Halle-fucking-lujah. And fuck you, James.

"Don't you want to have kids?"

"Yes, and kids love me."

"I think you should get married," I said.

"Why?"

"Because I think you'd be a great father."

"It's *yuan fen,*" which means something like destiny.

"Okay."

"Sophia, it's three in the morning, do you want to stay here or go home?"

"I want to go home," I said, hoping he'd come with me.

"Okay, I'll take you because I don't want you to go home alone."

"Do you want to come upstairs with me?" I held my breath.

"If you want."

Bingo.

We went up to my place and kept talking. We watched a Pierre Berton interview with Bruce Lee. Then I asked him to give me a massage. I tried to give him one back, but it's fucking impossible to give Yan Ming a massage. It's basically like kneading concrete. His skin was soft and smooth, but I couldn't get much deeper than the first two layers of his epidermis. I think I got far more pleasure out of that than he did. He fell asleep under the spell of my feeble fingers around 7:00 a.m., and I went into my room and slept for half an hour, hands frazzled. We got in a cab to go back to the temple. The second we got into the back seat, I laid my head on his lap. Only a few moments later, he leaned over and kissed me. The matter-of-factness with which I had called my parents the day I met him, which had transformed into taxing trepidation, now yielded into a perfect kiss that blissfully melted all doubts away.

When we got to the temple we went straight into his tiny, cramped room and made love for the first time on a quilt on the hard floor. And it was beautiful. There are many names for intercourse—sleeping with someone, having sex, or my current favorite, fucking—but with Yan Ming, it was making love, because that was the overwhelming sensation that I experienced. Don't get me wrong, the sex was wonderful, but it was because the connection was so deeply rooted in our emotional bond.

Yan Ming moved in right away—no discussion, no debate, no questions asked. It didn't make sense for him to stay in the tiny room at the temple if we were going to spend all our time together anyway. As surely as I knew on first sight this was the man I was going to marry, I was certain that we would be together forever. But he told me very early on, "Sophia, if you want to get married, I'm not the man for you."

"Why not?" I asked.

"Because, I'm already married and have two children in China."

"Oh, okay. Well, it doesn't matter to me. I don't care about marriage."

This may sound surprising, but I was so in love with Yan Ming and Shaolin and his dream of re-creating the temple that this revelation was truly of little import to me. This was my new man, my new path, my new destiny. In my heart and soul, he was my husband, even though we never legally wed. To this day, I don't give a shit about getting married. I was never the girl who fantasized about wearing the perfect white dress, with my hair and makeup done like in the magazines, who starved herself for weeks to be the same weight she was at her high school graduation. I never dreamed of that day when I would be the most beautiful girl in the world. As for his wife and kids, I would ask from time to time if he sent them money, and he said he did so through his brother. Other than that, it was clear that Yan Ming didn't want to discuss his family, so I left it alone. I figured I'd never have to deal with her, seeing as she was all the way on the other side of the world.

CHAPTER 5

THE SHAOLIN AND THE WU-TANG COULD BE DANGEROUS

Not long after Yan Ming moved in, Dirty called late at night and wailed into my answering machine, "Soooooooophieeeeee, where are you? It's me, pick up! Soooooooophieeeeeeeee!"

I ignored the call, mortified. Yan Ming turned to me in bed and said, "Sophia, why is there a man calling you after midnight?" It was a simple question, and completely appropriate. I was accustomed to people calling me in the wee hours, especially my West Coast artists. I had been single the whole time I'd lived in New York and now I was with someone. And that someone had grown up in a temple in China where they didn't even have running water until 1986. I called Dirty and told him to stop calling me so late. He was hurt, but making it work with Yan Ming was my priority.

The first time Yan Ming met Dirty, he was recording his verse for LL Cool J's remix of "I Shot Ya" at Chung King Studios. We went into the room and Dirty was in the booth. As soon as he saw me, he started saying gleefully, "Sophie's here!" into the mic. Then he saw Yan Ming. Dirty was protective, even territorial about me. He took off his headphones, hung them on the mic stand, and came barreling out to Yan Ming like the Roadrunner. He ran straight up on him, his energy frenzied, and Yan Ming stood like a statue. Dirty stopped just short of him, pointed at his chest, and said, "Oh, this motherfucker's for real."

After that, it was all good.

Yan Ming met RZA at GZA's *Liquid Swords* album release party in Tribeca in the fall of 1995. Because of my work, I was constantly surrounded by famous, testosterone-driven men. I made a point of introducing Yan Ming to them. I knew that the second he looked in their eyes and read their energy, he would know that there was nothing sexual there. In the several years that I had known these artists, they had never seen me with a man, so it was a novel process.

There was an immediate bond between RZA and Yan Ming. I believe they knew each other in past lifetimes. RZA started training right away. He would send a limo to pick up Yan Ming and bring him to the Wu Mansion in South Jersey. I didn't always accompany him. There were times when RZA made it clear that he wanted to spend time alone with Yan Ming. He would say something like, "This time it's just for the men, Soph." I appreciated his candor. On one occasion when I did go, I watched as RZA asked about every kung fu style he'd ever been curious about. Yan Ming would explain the style and the philosophy behind it, then demonstrate it. It was incredible to watch RZA's curiosity satisfied instantaneously by this living, breathing, practicing kung fu–pedia.

Naturally, I introduced Yan Ming to all my friends and family as well. My parents loved him. He was more culturally aligned with them than I was, because he was old-school Asian. He taught my parents stretches, and my mother loved cooking for him. Everyone loved Yan Ming, us as a couple, and who I was becoming with him. I was more patient and more present. Chris approved, probably relieved that I didn't end up with someone in the industry whom he'd have to violate if I got hurt. The Ostins welcomed him into their home and family immediately. We were fortunate enough to spend time with all three generations of Ostins. Michael's mother, Evelyn, God rest her soul, was uniquely wonderful. She was the matriarch of the family, and I see her influence in her three granddaughters, Anika, Leyla, and Annabelle, who are all smart and funny, but, most important, kind and generous and empathetic, as her first great-granddaughter, Phoebe, surely will be.

Mo took Yan Ming, Michael, Warner Bros. president Lenny Waronker, and me to lunch at Morton's, a high-end steakhouse in Beverly Hills. We were ushered in like royalty and seated at a central booth where everyone could see us. Yan Ming's eyes widened as a stream of people approached the table to say hello, lawyer Johnnie Cochran among them. When we left, Mo pulled me aside and said with a sly smile, "You know, Sophia, that place is full of movers and shakers."

What I remember distinctly about that lunch—and every other time I was fortunate enough to spend time with him—is that Mo never once looked at his watch. I never felt as though I was taking up his time. I can't say that for far-lesser executives. I took note and wanted to be sure that I would always try to make people feel valued, as he did. Yan Ming loved the Ostins, naturally. They were loving and super healthy and respectful of their bodies. California living.

Under Yan Ming's tutelage, my body was turning into a strong, lean, flexible machine, but it was my mind, soul, and spirit that were truly transformed. In Shaolin, we train every part of our being simultaneously. Yan Ming would say, "Stretch your body, stretch your mind." There's a brilliant movie called *Shaolin Soccer*, directed by and starring Stephen Chow, about a man who pulls together former kung fu masters to form a team. The movie ends with a montage of people incorporating kung fu into their quotidian routines like walking down the street, parking a car, waiting for a bus. It's a fun visual, but the meaning is much deeper: the idea is that we can incorporate kung fu into everything we do. I use my kung fu every day in everything I do, both physical and mental. RZA and GZA would say the same about how they incorporate chess into every aspect of their lives.

I learned my greatest spiritual lessons from Yan Ming. One of the most extraordinary things about him was that he never complained. Ever. He was always glass half full. I was the kind of person who would insist on taking the train because we couldn't find a cab and then when the train was taking too long, I would kvetch that we should have waited for a cab. I would complain about the rain, and he would say, "Sophia, the trees and the plants and the flowers need the rain." If someone at a restaurant or an airport counter was being a dick, he would kill them with kindness and positivity. He was extraordinary this way. I hardly have his spiritual constitution, but I strive to be mindful of my behavior and energy and how they impact those around me.

There was one person, however, who didn't embrace our relationship. My partner, Denise. For some inexplicable reason, she hated that I called him "my boyfriend."

"Why can't you just call him by his name?" she said, exasperated.

"Because I like calling him my boyfriend, Denise. I'm really happy to have a boyfriend."

I was taken aback by her anger. I understand now that she was not in a good place herself and was projecting onto me. She became furious when she found out that I'd confided in our attorney that Yan Ming was married, which I had done only to get a referral for a divorce lawyer. Clearly, there was something about my relationship with Yan Ming that bothered her. It couldn't be Yan Ming himself; she'd barely spent any time with him, and he was completely likeable.

Denise disbanded the company soon thereafter, which came as a total shock. She told me that she had spent her whole life standing in the shadows of brilliant men and felt as if she was doing the same with me. Whoa, what? I told her I wouldn't have had the confidence to start the company without her; that I needed her marketing expertise. I saw us as completely equal partners. Little did I know that decades later, I would have the same revelation about being unseen. I am grateful that she was forthcoming enough to tell me how it felt to work closely with me.

The company folding was a disappointment, but I was still managing Dirty, which was a wild ride and great learning experience. I stayed with him through the release of his debut album, *Return to the 36 Chambers*, but not long thereafter. The combination of the difficulty of managing him and my increasing involvement in the temple drew that phase of my career to its inevitable close. Beyond training, it was clear that I could help Yan Ming by managing him and the temple. My first client was ODB and my second was Yan Ming—Wu-Tang and Shaolin.

In 1996, RZA closed the deal he'd been talking to Denise and me about, but with a different label. He hired me as the general manager of Razor Sharp Records. "Soph, I've chosen you to run my most lucrative business yet," he said. Having been a GM of two small labels since then, I can see now how I was again not qualified to run the business, but I appreciate that RZA put his trust in me. I worked my ass off and did a fine job, but I was limited by my inexperience—I hadn't managed a team and knew little of finance. While there, I oversaw the release of Ghostface Killah's phenomenal debut solo album, *Ironman*. The photo shoot for the album cover, with all the two-tone Clarks Wallabee shoes, was one of my favorite sets ever. Ultimately, RZA and I parted ways because we didn't see eye to eye on how to manage the staff, but we remained friends.

I believed so deeply in Yan Ming's vision that I left music behind and fell into managing him and the temple full-time. In retrospect, I see I was walking away from a very promising career—managing one of the hottest rappers on the scene who was part of a hip-hop supergroup—that surely would have led to more opportunities, money, and power, but that didn't even occur to me then. In fact, I never thought that long and hard about any of my major life moves because I never doubted myself. If I fell in love and it didn't work out, there would be someone else. If I took a job and failed, there was always another gig. I try very hard not to be motivated by fear and I have my titanium confidence to thank for that.

By immersing myself so wholly in Shaolin, I was also distancing myself from my music community, and that was okay. Training at the temple was wholly fulfilling and consuming in the best way, so there was nothing to miss about the music business. I never looked back. Naturally, RZA remained in our lives because of his bond with Yan Ming, but we saw the other members of Wu-Tang less often.

The same can be said of Chris. I didn't expect the guys in the Clan to call me to hang out—that's not how we engaged— but I was disappointed that I didn't hear from or see Chris much during that time. I didn't reach out to him enough, either, but I was very aware of his movements because he was becoming a major force in the industry. Regardless, when I did see the Clan or Chris, it was like visiting my hometown and seeing my high school friends—like no time had elapsed and our love picked up right where it had left off.

I knew that the temple and Yan Ming were my future. It was a big endeavor because I was building something from the ground up with a largely unknown figurehead. I knew that getting the word out about him was key to our success. A big part of the strategy was his association with RZA. It was such a great story, and Wu-Tang was at the height of its popularity at this time. RZA was incredibly gracious and never said no to anything to do with the temple.

In September 1999, I pulled off a remarkable, if somewhat underhanded, PR coup. I got Yan Ming on the covers of the four top kung fu magazines in the world: *Inside Kung-Fu*, *Kung Fu*, and two magazines in China. I managed to do it without any of them knowing about the others. It meant that as a martial arts fan, when you went to your local bookstore, martial arts supply store, or magazine shop to look for the latest issue, you saw Yan Ming on every cover. Once the covers ran, the Discovery Channel called and asked Yan Ming to participate in a martial arts documentary called *Secrets of the Warrior's Power.* Yan Ming was prominently featured in the program, and his picture was on the packaging. After the show aired, our phone rang off the hook, and our membership ballooned quickly. And as is the case with all press, more soon followed: National Geographic, CNBC, TNT, and more.

It felt glorious to be a part of this burgeoning movement. I love managing artists because I believe that their art has transformative power, but the impact of this work was much more direct and immediate. I watched people's bodies, minds, and spirits evolve before my eyes. And I was doing the same. I flung myself out of my comfort zone and rushed to meet every challenge. But I was about to be faced with the biggest hurdle of my life.

Not long after the Fourth of July weekend in 1999, I was lying on the couch while Yan Ming cooked his daily meal of a giant bowl of noodle soup. He loved Chinese brown vinegar, which has a very strong smell. I'd gotten used to it, but on this particular day, it turned my stomach. I knew immediately: "Holy shit, I'm pregnant." Less than a year before, Joan had told me she was pregnant and that her sense of smell went through the roof. I went to Duane Reade and bought a pregnancy test. I had never used one before.

I went into the bathroom, peed on the stick, and waited for the pink lines to appear. If it's one line, you're not pregnant. If two, you are. It takes about three minutes. The first line always appears. It's waiting for the second that pushes you to the edge of the toilet seat. We weren't trying to get pregnant, but we weren't trying to avoid it either. When that second line appeared ever so slowly but surely, a big-ass smile spread across my lips. I went into the living room and showed Yan Ming. Our love was going to climb to another level.

The very next day, I made an appointment to see Dr. Allen. I peed in a cup, they drew my blood, and it all came back positive. When I got home, I called Joan and asked her to meet me. We had lunch on DeKalb, close to her place, and I brought out a small, flimsy, blurred black-and-white image. She took the sonogram from me and started crying immediately. Our pregnancies would overlap by a month.

During pregnancy, I didn't glow, I glowered. Throughout my first trimester, I was exhausted; lifting the remote seemed like a Herculean task. For someone as energetic and active as me, I hated being slowed down. As much as I just wanted to lie on the couch and watch TV, I had already committed to the biggest undertaking of my life that demanded my full attention.

In less than six weeks, we were going to lead a group of fifty students, disciples, and friends on a tour of Shaolin Temple and other sites in China. I had found the travel agent, dealt with all the visas, created the itinerary, and hired a documentary crew. It was everyone's first time to Shaolin Temple, and for many, including myself, the first time to mainland China. We were a diverse crew that ranged in age from teenaged to middle aged and across the racial spectrum. The tie that bound us was a love for Shaolin kung fu and a reverence for Yan Ming.

On the day of the flight, everyone met at the temple. The room, piled high with luggage, was buzzing with anticipation. The excitement was barely contained by the time we boarded the plane. The one person who would meet us at the airport was RZA. While everyone else was taking pictures of themselves on the plane before takeoff, I was trying to reach RZA because he hadn't boarded yet. When I finally contacted him, he was at the airport but went to the wrong terminal. He missed the flight by minutes. Even after we landed in Hong Kong and the entourage was jumping for joy, I couldn't relax until I knew RZA was on the next plane. Finally, he made it to the gate back in New York and I exhaled. With the itinerary tightly organized, I anticipated no other bumps. But the best laid plans of mice and Soph oft go astray.

Shaolin was the first place I had ever visited that felt like a third world country. There were people sleeping outside on mattresses, toddlers shitting in the streets in broad daylight, and stand after stand of noodles, trinkets, and souvenirs, run by people who looked bone weary. It was the fifteen hundredth anniversary of the temple, and huge celebrations were planned. Every morning before dawn, we were awakened by the synchronized footsteps of boys as young as five up to their early twenties chanting, "*yi, er, yi, er, san,*" or "one, two, one, two, three."

After all the movies we had seen and the lessons learned, visiting the actual sites was profoundly moving. It was like the first time I had gone to Paris and laid eyes on the landmarks I'd read about in college, but with an added spiritual component. My soul was tied to this hallowed ground: the huge red doors, the pagoda garden of masters past, the elevated plum blossom stake on which the monks trained, the cave on Mount Song where Bodhidharma had sat and meditated for nine years.

Yan Ming's master, Shi Yong Qian, was quiet and reserved but clearly powerful. Meeting him was like meeting Yan Ming's father. Then there was his kung fu brother and closest friend, Shi De Yang, a thirty-second-generation Shaolin monk, one of the top-ranked at the temple. From the moment we arrived at the Dengfeng airport, we were greeted and escorted by De Yang and his disciples. On the second day of our visit, RZA performed for the monks, the first artist to ever do so at Shaolin Temple. De Yang's disciples formed a human chain around RZA. They stood guard and watched him bob and weave and sway as he rhymed in words they couldn't understand but with an energy that they absorbed. I was proud to create that piece of history, where martial arts and hip-hop intersected, Shaolin and Wu-Tang, old and new.

At the end of one particularly wonderful day full of training, sight-seeing, and the best Chinese food I'd ever had, Yan Ming, De Yang, and I were walking through the main training center near the temple when we came upon a woman holding two children, around five and seven, by the hand. She looked angry, resolved, and nervous all at once. Yan Ming and De Yang stopped in their tracks. They definitely recognized her, and she was definitely waiting for us. It took a moment, but I realized that she was Yan Ming's wife and those were his two children. De Yang gently took my hand and led me away.

I didn't hear any words and I didn't look back. Clearly, this was something he'd have to handle on his own. My mind was filled with questions: How had she found Yan Ming? Why did she feel compelled to stalk and ambush him? Something wasn't right about the picture. I knew very little about how much Yan Ming communicated with her while we were in New York, but clearly, not enough if she went to such measures to speak with him. As a mother now, I feel bad for the kids. What must they have been thinking?

It was a couple of days before we were scheduled to leave Shaolin Village, but Yan Ming decided that we all needed to leave immediately, because he understood that someone pretty high up at the temple and/or the government must have conspired with his wife to find us. Staying would only become more complicated and potentially dangerous, particularly because he was not yet a U.S. citizen. That night, we gathered everyone up in the dark. Suddenly mobilizing a group of fifty people is not easy. De Yang escorted us to the edge of Shaolin Village and I hugged him tightly.

Next stop: Wu Tang Mountains. We had all seen Jet Li's classic kung fu flick *Tai Chi Master* multiple times and were well versed in the legend of Zhang San Feng, a Taoist master who founded the martial art Taiji in the Wu Tang Mountains. The anticipation was palpable.

We took a two-hour bus ride from Shaolin Temple to the Zhengzhou train station. From there, it was an eight-hour ride to Wuhan in Hubei Province, where Wu Tang is located. The train was an anachronism, like something out of an old western. Yan Ming and I had a private cabin with a double bed. Once he'd put our bags up, I ate a protein bar, which my ob-gyn had scared me into thinking was the only thing I should eat on the trip. Then the rocking train put me to sleep. I slept for hours. When I awoke, I was very groggy and made my way to the bathroom car. When I opened the door to the stall, I was shocked to see not a toilet, but an opening in the floor. *Well, when in China...* As I squatted over the gap and watched the tracks roll past below me, I wondered whose literally shitty job it was to clean up after me. I got up and stopped by the food car, where RZA was drinking with a bunch of students. I returned to my car and went back to sleep.

When we finally arrived at the station, we loaded ourselves into two small buses and made our way to the hotel. I was relieved to be off the train and put my feet on terra firma. I felt as if I were still rocking. The trip up the winding mountain road was terrifying. The drivers swerved into the oncoming traffic to switch lanes. Luckily, one of our Chinese American students introduced me to *bai hua you*, Chinese white flower oil. This miraculous combination of wintergreen, peppermint, menthol, eucalyptus, camphor, and lavender immediately abated my nausea. It has the added properties of being a decongestant and mosquito repellant.

When we finally arrived at the hotel, I sprang off the bus ahead of everyone else. I shook off the journey and took in the breathtaking scene. High on the mountaintop, we could see mountains for miles in every direction. More spellbinding still was observing RZA. One of ten children raised by a single mother in the projects of Staten Island, he was the boy who had memorized the miraculous moves, archetypal characters, and poorly dubbed dialogue of the kung fu flicks that had provided him with an escape into another world. That boy grew up to be the man who founded the greatest rap group of all time and named it after the famed mountain range, and here we were now, standing at its mile-high peak.

RZA slowly rotated a full 360 degrees to take it all in. When he was facing me again, he said, "Soph, take a picture. Look at the mountain behind us."

"What about it?"

"It's a *W*," he answered serenely.

And goddamn if he wasn't right. Behind him, the mountains were shaped like a *W*, like the Wu-Tang logo. Not only did RZA have an ear, he had an eye. He wore his white, raw-cotton Shaolin Temple vest with yellow trim. He looked regal and proud and as though he had arrived.

The next day, we visited the Temple of the Purple Cloud, which had been constructed in the twelfth century. As we approached, I knew immediately that it was going to be different from Shaolin. Wu Tang was pristine—no souvenir shops, no roadside vendors, just a magnificent temple. Everything felt ancient, centuries old. Even the master of the temple, with his beautiful, long, thick black hair tied in a bun atop his head, and his traditional white silk suit that moved gently with him as he descended the stairs, looked as if he'd stepped out of a time machine. Yes, he was fine. The only thing that betrayed we were, in fact, in the twenty-first century was the cordless phone he held to his head.

As he reached us at the entrance, he clasped his right hand around his left fist, a greeting of respect, just like they do in kung fu flicks, and welcomed us with a huge smile. Watching him and Yan Ming approach each other was historic. As a fan of the genre, I knew that Shaolin and Wu Tang were always pitted against each other. And again, there was RZA.

The first order of the day was for the schools to perform for each other as a sign of respect. There's something important and honorable about being chosen to perform for another master. You are not representing yourself but your master and his tradition. Demonstrating in perfect synchronization as a team takes a lot of practice and chemistry that is established by the master. When done right, it's like a single beating heart. Like their leader, the Wu Tang crew wore off-white silk robes, with their long hair tied into a knot at the top of their heads. They performed with and without weapons, and yes, they exhibited a Wu Tang sword style. Our team kicked and stomped and yelled like warriors in our bright saffron robes. The students on both sides performed with dignity and pride.

But they were just the undercard. Here came the main event: the masters would now present their skills. Our host went first. He walked slowly and deliberately to the center of the stone square and proceeded to perform Taiji. His flow was slow and mesmerizing, like water. Most people think of elderly Chinese people in the parks doing Taiji, which is good and real, but it doesn't paint a full picture of the art form. It is a martial art. Done well, it's beautiful and awesome, and you have no doubt that the practitioner is a fighter. Our team all wondered what Yan Ming would perform. I had seen his whole repertoire and knew that his Taiji was superlative. But he wouldn't actually do Taiji in the house that built Taiji, would he?

Yan Ming clapped slowly and heartily, then strode into the center of the crowd, bald head high and back erect, a winning smile on his face. His smile quickly disappeared as he focused and summoned his qi. He had told me that you can tell a martial artist by their eyes. If they don't look like Mike Tyson stepping into a ring, they're not legit. We watched breathlessly as he raised his shoulders and hands as if he were pulling the energy out of the ground he stood on. *Oh, shit, he's gonna do Taiji. My man is a competitive motherfucker.* He transitioned into a fighting form that showed his awesome power. He is a fighter to the core, and it takes only one side kick to demonstrate beyond the shadow of a doubt that he is a stone-cold killer. He was the national fighting champion of China, not a small country, two years running.

Throughout the demonstration, RZA stood quiet and erect, taking it all in. Though he was Wu-Tang, he wanted to rep Shaolin today, for Yan Ming. He wore the saffron Shaolin robes with a black sash and carried a monk's bag over his shoulder. He wasn't the blunt-smoking, nut-grabbing, bottle-popping MC of the West. He was a humble disciple, full of wonder and reverence. After the demonstration, the abbot welcomed Yan Ming, RZA, and me into his chamber, where he served us tea. The abbot listened attentively to RZA's questions via the interpreter and answered that many of the stories he had heard were, in fact, myths. The abbot of Wu Tang then presented RZA, the abbot of the Wu-Tang Clan, with the gift of CDs of instrumental Daoist music. It was a surreal and sublime moment.

The next day, we rode gondolas to the top of the mountain. RZA and Yan Ming sat on a wall that looked as though it was the edge of heaven. In my bones, I felt that this trip had been predestined and that we had all met before, perhaps right here, which is why we were meant to return. This was a spectacular culmination of an odyssey that had started when I heard the first notes of "Protect Ya Neck." I had brought the Shaolin and the Wu-Tang together to Shaolin and Wu Tang.

Truthfully, the deepest discovery I made on this trip was a realization about myself. It took me a long time to arrive at this epiphany, because I was so hardwired to be in the service of brilliant men; I had been so focused on the task of ensuring their prosperity and fostering their internal growth. This trip was the culmination of a journey of self-discovery during which I truly embraced the formidable beauty and power of my Asian heritage. And like so many things in my life, all roads had led me to Wu-Tang. And though I had brought RZA to China, it was, in fact, he who had delivered me there.

CHAPTER 6

EVERYTHING YOU NEED TO

KNOW IS NEVER ENOUGH

On the way home from China, Yan Ming and I stopped through Vancouver and told my parents that we were expecting. They were out of their minds with happiness. Their daughter, who had skipped graduation at twenty-one to run to New York for nothing in particular, had shacked up with a good Chinese man, and they were going to be grandparents. In retrospect, I appreciate that my parents had never pressured me to get married or have children, though I'm sure they talked about it between them. They probably knew saying something wouldn't have had any effect whatsoever.

Motherhood, as I would soon find out, could be summed up in its entirety with these three words: *it's fucking hard*. On Christmas 1999, exactly three months before my due date of

March 25, 2000, Yan Ming and I made our way through knee-deep snow deep into Alphabet City to visit John Leguizamo and Justine Maurer, whom Rosie Perez, a devoted student, had brought to train at the temple. At the time, their neighborhood seemed so far away and remote. Funnily enough, I would end up moving just a block away several years later. When we entered, John approached me—Justine now six months pregnant—and handed me a paperback entitled *Healthy Sleep Habits, Happy Child*. He said, "Sophia, this book will change your life," with deadpan conviction.

Because I would be almost thirty-five when I gave birth, my OB recommended an amniocentesis, a procedure that involved inserting a needle into the uterus to draw out amniotic fluid from which to screen for genetic abnormalities. At the top of 2000, Yan Ming and I went to the hospital to meet with a genetic counselor before the amnio. She told us about genetic risks based on the profiles of the parents. The line on the graph for likelihood of complications like Down syndrome was pretty flat until the mother's age hit thirty-five, at which point the increase was dramatic.

I had the amnio at twenty weeks. The procedure sounded worse that it was, but it was still pretty awful and there were a number of things that could go wrong, like infection, miscarriage, or leaking fluid. That night, I noticed a drop of blood in my urine and called Dr. Allen. She put me on bed rest immediately. I could get up and go to the bathroom and wander around the apartment, but being too active was out of the question. This was a really difficult state for someone used to training in kung fu every day and being out and about. I went stir-fucking-crazy. I had a dry-erase calendar and would cross off the days until I could get out of bed.

During this time, a nurse from the hospital, where I was to give birth, came to show Yan Ming and me a video about childbirth that covered topics like Lamaze classes, cesareans, and epidurals. I asked how many first-time mothers got epidurals and was alarmed to hear the rate was about 90 percent at that particular hospital. It seemed inevitable that I would have an epidural, despite wanting to give birth naturally. Dr. Allen called first thing the next morning and summoned us to her office. The nurse, God bless her, had called Dr. Allen after the visit and said, "Dr. Allen, I don't think we can give Sophia and Yan Ming the experience they want in childbirth."

Dr. Allen said gravely, "When you give birth with me, it will be in a brightly lit and steely room. I see childbirth as a medical procedure." Then she turned her steady gaze to Yan Ming. "You see it as a natural one. So I've decided that you're going to see my friend Barbara Brennan, who runs a midwife service. You're at thirty-six weeks and she's not supposed to take anyone past twenty-eight, but she's an old friend and is doing me a personal favor. I will also refund all the money you've paid me."

We hear nightmares about the medical system, but I was the beneficiary of two incredible women—the nurse and Dr. Allen—who put my interest first. And then the midwives. I went to see Barbara immediately. There were five midwives in the practice. Seeing as it was my last month, I would see a different one each week. They were all wonderful and made me feel so comfortable and safe. Still, I was nervous and scared because both my brother and I were C-section babies. And then there's the pain. When I asked Joan what it felt like, she said, "It's like taking the biggest shit of your life, and it's all about your relationship with pain." Thankfully, having trained so intensely with Yan Ming, pain and I had become fast friends.

On March 16, 2000, shortly after Yan Ming had wrapped taping *The Dr. Joy Browne Show* at CBS studios, my water broke, nine days before my due date. I called my midwives. They said I had time to go home and pick up my bag. The midwife on call was the only one I hadn't met, but they were all so lovely that I was confident she'd be great. Yan Ming's student and friend of the family, Joe, drove us home.

We got our things, rushed back to the hospital, and checked into the birthing center around 5:30 p.m. The room looked like a very clean Holiday Inn. There was a queen-size bed with a colorful floral quilt, a rocking chair, and a Jacuzzi. Yes, a fucking Jacuzzi. It was the perfect atmosphere for me: I wasn't high risk and wanted as little medical intervention as possible. However, should anything go wrong, I was just one floor away from Labor and Delivery. We settled in and waited for the midwife to arrive.

Her name was Anna Porizkova and she was beautiful—fiftyish, blonde, slight wrinkles around her eyes. The second I laid eyes on her, I felt a huge sense of relief. As much relief as I could feel while my entire midsection was contorting like a beach during a tsunami. The contractions felt like unbelievably intense tightening and cramping, and I could barely breathe. I was mesmerized by Anna's beautiful full lips as I focused on her breathing and followed her lead. In, out, in, out. When it finally came time to push, they asked if I wanted a mirror to see what was going on. *What? Hell fucking no.* I understood it was a miracle and the circle of life, but I had no desire to see my vagina torn apart while I bled and shit uncontrollably.

My labor was mercifully short, only three and a half hours. And because I'd been under the care of the midwives, there was no pressure to get an epidural, an episiotomy, or oxytocin. I did it naturally. Despite the pain, I didn't scream "I hate you!" at Yan Ming, like we see in the stupid movies. I barely broke a sweat. While I was pushing, I looked up at Yan Ming over my right shoulder, and he was sweating beads the size of quarters. It was as if he was absorbing the stress and the pain and helping me push. That's kung fu.

I didn't hate him at all: I loved him even more in that moment.

When our son came out, the umbilical cord was wrapped around his neck and he was blue. Yan Ming panicked. I wasn't scared because I looked at Anna and the nurse and they were completely calm. Our baby was in the hands of seasoned professionals. They took him to a table and were working to get him to breathe. Yan Ming was yelling, "Come on, *erzi!*" which means "son" in Mandarin. He didn't stop until we heard that first wail. We named our firstborn Jin Long, which means "Golden Dragon" in Chinese. In the Chinese zodiac, the dragon is the most powerful animal, and gold the most powerful element. The year 2000 was not only the year of both, but also a new millennium.

I can't describe the feeling when Anna laid my Golden Dragon gently on my chest. Looking down at this tiny life that I had carried inside me was almost otherworldly. He was so small and gentle and vulnerable. There were two things that I understood the moment I gave birth: first, that I would die for my son; second, that I would kill for him without hesitation or compunction. If someone threatened him, I would summon all my strength and power and use whatever was within reach to hurt that motherfucker. I could grab a bagel and asphyxiate someone, if necessary.

Before Jin Long was even born, Yan Ming and I had discussed asking RZA to be his godfather. We had spent a lot of time with his wife and children and were certain that they would take good care of him, should anything befall us. When we asked him, he answered immediately and humbly, "Wow, I've never been asked that before. Of course I would be honored to be the godfather to the Golden Dragon."

When Jin Long was an infant, I would stare in disbelief at him sleeping in the bassinet. Is that my child? This sense of amazement never dissipates. Even as they get older, doing whatever mundane thing, I can be struck by this sense of awe. Just looking at my kids doing nothing in particular, I could start crying because the love is that profound.

Having children was a natural extension and manifestation of the love between Yan Ming and me. Witnessing this fierce warrior, who had been training and hardening his body his entire life, metamorphose into a gentle and doting father was beautiful, but his soft approach to the children left me in the unenviable position of being the disciplinarian. I used to wonder what kind of father Yan Ming would be, having been raised in such a harsh disciplinary environment. I think after enduring a childhood that included training twelve hours a day, getting the shit kicked out of him, and doing handstands until his eyes bled, Yan Ming chose to take the opposite route.

When we fell in love and decided to have children, we never discussed the practical issues: nursing versus bottle, private school versus public school, family bed versus crib. And why would we? Any concerns had always managed to get worked out, but once Jin Long was born, the stakes were exponentially higher and everything changed. And when I say everything, I mean everything. Especially for me.

I read the book that John Leguizamo had told me would change my life, and it did, in more ways than one. The author supports the idea of letting your child cry herself to sleep, also referred to as the Ferber method, after the doctor who founded it. That notion was untenable to Yan Ming. He could not stand the sound of Jin Long crying; it was as if someone was stabbing him in the eyes with hot needles. It didn't bother me as much. I knew that crying is the only way babies know how to communicate. And, as a mother, you know intuitively when your child is crying from discomfort—"I'm hungry/tired/wet"—as opposed to being in pain. The first big fight we ever had was over sleep patterns for Jin Long.

Because Yan Ming taught at night, I was able to start training Jin Long to fall asleep by himself, but Yan Ming would be home on weekends, so the program was interrupted, and I was never able to complete it. I nursed Jin Long to sleep, often falling asleep with him . . . in the crib! I would wake up, neck sore, completely discombobulated. When I called my parents to complain, my father said, "Sophia, just do what Yan Ming wants. It's not worth the fight. It will only be a couple years." A couple of years at the time seemed like an eternity.

Looking back, it wasn't so bad and I'm grateful that I got to spend as much time as I did with Jin Long. I nursed him for fifteen months. Never mind the health benefits of a baby having mother's milk, it really is a beautiful bonding experience. That said, after being pregnant for nine months and then nursing for another fifteen, I was ready for a break. Thing is, I didn't grant myself one. I had a temple to build.

In the spring of 2001, when Jin Long was only a year old, I started to plan our second tour of China, which would follow in late August. The two-week journey included visits to the Forbidden City, the Shaolin Temple, and the Terra Cotta Warriors. On September 9, a temperate day in Beijing, our trip was drawing to a close, and I wrangled our forty disciples into the airport. The trip had been amazing, but we were tired, hungry, and ready to go home. Yan Ming and I were anxious to get back to Jin Long, who had never been separated from us for so long and was being cared for by my parents. I made sure everyone had their passports with their visas and sent them to the line for "foreigners," a.k.a. non-Chinese citizens. Yan Ming was in a separate line because he didn't have a passport. The government had confiscated it when he defected, and he was not yet a U.S. citizen. He was, in essence, a stateless individual.

Like any good tour manager, I made sure the entourage

was on the plane and waited for Yan Ming to clear customs before going through myself. Derrick Waller, Yan Ming's faithful friend, a New York City cop, also stayed behind. We knew that it would take a minute because of Yan Ming's status. I heard Yan Ming yell from across the room, "Sophia! They're not going to let me go!" I turned suddenly toward his voice. Two police officers were holding my husband's arms tightly behind his back.

You really don't know what you're going to do in a situation like that until you're actually in it. I did the only thing I could think of: stand by my man. I rushed over, grabbed Yan Ming around the chest and held on for dear life. Derrick was sitting on the floor, both of his arms locked around Yan Ming's right leg, saying, "If you take him, you're gonna have to take me too."

The Chinese police pulled me off of Yan Ming and yelled in my face in Mandarin, "We know who you are! You're Sophia Chang! You're Canadian! This has nothing to do with you!"

Then—and I have no recollection of this; Yan Ming and Derrick told me—the police kicked me and punched me in the face. Before I knew it, Yan Ming, Derrick, and the Chinese police disappeared behind an ominous steel door. Emmerich, one of our most senior disciples, ran back from the gate, wondering what the delay was.

"Get everyone off the plane!" I yelled. "They've taken Shifu and D!"

I watched him sprint down the long hallway back to the departing gate. Just as the plane was about to take off, he yelled for everyone to deplane. Imagine forty Americans dashing off an aircraft with all of their luggage. If it hadn't been for their rigorous training, discipline, and ability to follow orders, there's no way they would have been able to mobilize that quickly. They were bewildered and shaken. I ordered them to sit down and calmly told them what had transpired. As the tour leader, I knew that I had to maintain my cool, that I would set the tone, and though I was panicking inside, I could not betray that emotion.

I feared for Yan Ming's life. This was China—I feared they could throw Yan Ming in prison, or even kill him, without any recourse, and we might never see him again. Even with that, my overwhelming instinct was to get back to our eighteen-month-old son. I called the U.S. embassy and arranged for someone to come and get Yan Ming and Derrick out. I assured everyone that everything was going to be okay, though I had no way of knowing that. Despite my level demeanor, a number of the forty students were terrified and weeping.

Yan Ming and Derrick finally emerged. Derrick was silent. He looked as if he was in shock. A single tear trickled out of one eye. He told me the cops had beaten both of them, but that's not what had scared him. As they were trying to explain who they were, Derick had taken his badge and passport out to show them he was a U.S. citizen and an officer of the law. They grabbed his passport and threw it with utter disregard into a garbage can. In this single gesture, they had expunged his existence.

I looked at Yan Ming and said with little emotion, "I have to get home to Jin Long." He agreed wholeheartedly. I had already worked out who would stay with Yan Ming and how everyone else would get home. A small group of his most senior and loyal disciples would stay behind at a hotel in Beijing to continue to communicate with the embassy and ensure his safe passage back to the United States.

I walked away from the crowd of students and changed my ticket. I stopped through Narita, Japan, where I played *Crash Bandicoot* like an automaton on a public PlayStation. On the flight home, I wondered how the police knew who I was, how they knew we were going to be at the airport at that exact time. Clearly, we had been flagged and they were waiting for us. It had to be an inside job. But who? I had no answers. I ate a little, slept fitfully, but still, no tears. When I landed at JFK, I stood in an interminable line at customs and, thankfully, got through with ease. I walked out to the curb and got into a yellow cab.

As my taxi drove over the Brooklyn-Queens Expressway, I looked across the East River at the iconic Manhattan skyline. On that day, the comfort was mixed with unease. I called RZA as we neared the city, traversing the Williamsburg Bridge, and watched Brooklyn receding into the distance, the projects lining the FDR before me, the East River below. *I'm home. I'll be holding Jin Long soon. I'm okay.* But the second I heard RZA answer, "Peace, Soph," I started to cry uncontrollably. I could barely breathe.

"Soph, what's wrong?"

After sobbing for a solid minute, I managed to get the story out. When I'd finished, RZA asked calmly, "Is he safe? I mean physically safe? Are they going to hurt him?"

"No," I answered, as by that point I knew the U.S. embassy had gotten involved, "but I don't know when he'll be back."

"Okay. We'll work it out." Those simple words made me feel so much better, and I heaved a sigh of relief. RZA had defended himself successfully against a murder charge and dodged bullets. If he told me it was going to be okay, I believed him. Waiting to exhale indeed.

As I pulled up to the building, my parents were out front, sitting on the concrete stairs with Jin Long in their arms. I barely recognized the boy before me. Even in those two weeks he'd grown so much. I rushed out of the cab, and his round little face lit up as he saw Mommy. I grabbed him and I couldn't hold him tightly enough. I wanted to squeeze him so hard that somehow the pressure of our combined love would make his father suddenly appear.

Two days later, I was watching Pat Kiernan on the local news station NY1, as I do every morning, and there was a story of a plane flying into one of the Twin Towers. I called Heesok, who was at home in Poughkeepsie, immediately.

"Sophia, that's not an accident. There's no way someone flies into a building by accident."

While we were on the phone, the second plane hit. I hung up and rushed up to the rooftop of our thirty-six-story building. We lived less than three miles north of the World Trade Center, and it was a clear day, so *we* could see everything. I had Jin Long on my hip and watched in disbelief as the towers fell. I ran back downstairs and watched as the news reported that four planes had been hijacked, two United and two American Airlines flights. My parents had just boarded an 8:30 a.m. flight out of JFK back to Vancouver. I called American Airlines and asked them if my parents' plane had been hijacked. They couldn't tell me it hadn't. Finally, my mother called from JFK. They had been turned around and brought back to the gate. Luckily, our student Joe, who had taken us to the hospital for Jin Long's birth, lived on Long Island and was able to pick them up and take them to his house. They wouldn't have been able to come back to the city, because all the bridges and tunnels into Manhattan were closed. I called Yan Ming immediately, who at this point was at a hotel with our students. They had seen the towers fall on TV.

The next day, I walked six blocks down Broadway to the temple to check in with Jason and Etienne, the disciples who had taken care of it in our absence. The streets were filled with people, but the energy was off; it was as if the city was at once traumatized and fortified. My own energy was off-kilter too. There was the shock of watching the towers go down on top of not knowing if I'd ever see Yan Ming again. As I stepped into the temple, I was comforted by the familiar surroundings of the room. I sat at the desk and attended to the business: checking attendance, payment of dues, and new enrollments. Meanwhile, Jason and Etienne dusted each tiny item on the altar and changed out the roses and lilies, apples and oranges.

Jason, Etienne, and I talked about the horror of the fallen towers. I told them briefly about the trip and what was going on with Yan Ming. When we were done, I backed up, stood before the altar, took a deep breath, and prostrated myself before Buddha. On my knees, palms humbly outstretched,

I rested my head on the carpeted floor for a beat longer than usual. *Please bring him back safely*, I prayed. When we got onto the tiny elevator, I suddenly noticed Jason's body odor, which had never struck me in the hundreds of times we'd trained together.

Holy shit, I'm pregnant.

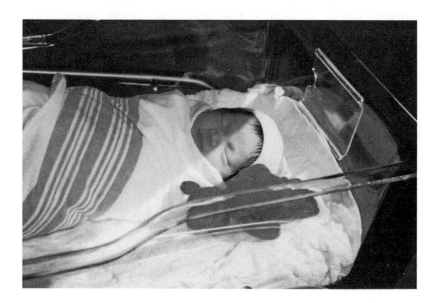

CHAPTER 7
I WANT ME BACK

On the way home from the temple, I bought a pregnancy test, but I already knew. Sure enough, two pink lines appeared. I saw Dr. Allen the next day to confirm that I was pregnant. She said, "Sophia, you are very lucky. Many women have trouble conceiving, and you got pregnant the first time you had your period after childbirth." I had never considered myself fortunate for being able to conceive, but knowing what I do now, I am extremely grateful. That was the first time anyone had ever talked to me about fertility, other than scaring the shit out of me about getting pregnant in high school. I wish I had known then what I know now: that our fertility peaks in our early twenties and declines steadily thereafter, with a precipitous heightened risk of birth abnormalities after age thirty-five. I would give birth to my second child at thirty-seven. I also wish I'd thought about my parents' advanced age and how long they would have to enjoy their grandchildren.

My parents got back to our place from Long Island the next day, but I wouldn't tell them about the pregnancy until the end of the first trimester, when it's considered safe to do so, especially under my uniquely stressful circumstances. I even waited a couple of days to tell Yan Ming. Things were still too tense in Beijing. When I did, he was predictably thrilled and more determined than ever to settle everything and get back to our little growing family. He, too, had a revelation for me: he and his brother had figured out that it was his wife who had arranged the airport ambush. Fuck. After nine days (which felt more like ninety) of the U.S. embassy facilitating negotiations with the local Chinese government, and Yan Ming's loyal younger brother making the nine-hour drive from Dengfeng to Beijing several times, Yan Ming was finally able to come home.

I told Yan Ming that if this baby made it through being beaten by the Chinese police, the worry that I might never see Yan Ming again, and the largest terrorist attack on American soil, we would have to give our baby a name that signified that he or she was a warrior. I reminded him that on our first trip to China, De Yang, his kung fu brother, had arranged for a master calligrapher to make a beautiful piece for both him and RZA. RZA wanted his to say something like, "If you can survive the fire, you'll emerge stronger." I said to Yan Ming, "I want the name to reflect that she's been through the fire." He came up with Jian Hong, which means Straight Sword That Cuts Through Fire. I didn't know the gender, but I hoped for a girl. A big brother and little sister, just like Heesok and me. On the last day of my first trimester, I called my parents and they were ecstatic.

My wish was granted, and we were going to have a little baby girl. I was put on bed rest again in my second trimester because I had premature contractions. We told Jin Long that he was going to have a little sister. He was only two, but seemed to have some grasp of what that meant. On May 2, nine days before our daughter was due to make her entrance onto the world stage, I started having contractions late in the evening. I called the midwife and she sounded unconvinced that I was in labor. I feared being one of those women who gives birth in the back of a cab, because the second birth is often faster than the first, so I went back to the birthing center to be sure. The midwife on call examined me and told me I was contracting but barely dilated. I walked around a little, was examined again, and was sent home. At 5:30 the next morning, the contractions woke me up. They were so intense that I had to lean against the wall to take a shower. When I called the midwife and could barely get out my words between breaths, I could hear her smiling as she said, "Now you're in labor." We rushed back to the hospital and I was immediately put into a bed.

While I was waiting to be examined, there was an emergency that required the midwife to take her patient up to Labor and Delivery. She was gone a long time and I started getting nervous. When she finally came back, I saw it was Anna, who had attended Jin Long's birth. She examined me and told me my cervix was already six centimeters dilated, only four away from pushing. For some reason, the moment she said that, my legs started wobbling involuntarily. We moved into the birthing room, and I had a very easy labor. Jian Hong's umbilical cord was wrapped around her wrist, a minor complication. What was worse was that the midwife and nurse weren't sure that the whole placenta had come out. How could they even tell? They dug inside me for several minutes. It felt awful, but again, nothing could mitigate the joy. The very moment Jian Hong was born, I knew she would be different from her brother. Her energy was more intense. I had no doubt that this sword would cut through many fires.

Just as it was beautiful to see Yan Ming as a father, it was overwhelmingly touching to see Jin Long as a big brother. My parents brought this gorgeous two-year-old soul to the hospital, and he laid a little red IKEA teddy bear next to his baby sister. From the day she was born, he has loved her so unconditionally and protected her so ardently, it's breathtaking to witness and yet another blessing of motherhood.

And thank God for the gifts, because the sacrifices are great.

Anyone who says being a mother is easy is either full of shit or not doing it right. How can it not be hard? You are creating a human being. You are responsible for their physical, spiritual, mental, psychological, and emotional development and well-being. You have to impart the right values and instill a sense of confidence, all while juggling the logistics of budgeting, education, health insurance, playdates, and so much more. It's overwhelming and you're constantly filled with doubt and guilt. You ask yourself if you've done enough and the answer is almost always no. This pure little vessel looks to you for everything, and whatever you do is never ever enough.

Having two children, naturally, was more exhausting in every way. Even when they were infants, barely weighing as much as a large roasting chicken, lifting, carrying, changing, feeding, and bathing them added up. None of these single activities was particularly tiring, but the aggregate of them, in addition to sleep deprivation, was depleting. I also chose to nurse both my children for more than a year.

By the time I was done breastfeeding Jian Hong, I had been either pregnant or nursing for four straight years. All I could think at that point was *I want my body back!* I was desperate to move freely without having someone sucking on my breast, sleeping on my lap, or clinging to my leg. When I became pregnant the first time, a friend of the family who had four children said to me, "When the baby comes, Soph, you need to take an hour a day all to yourself. I don't care if it's reading a magazine, taking a nap, or going for a walk. Believe me, you'll need it." How right she was. I remember thinking that Kmart was Shangri-fucking-la. I practically tripped the light fandango down the aisles. I needed independence; even just a soupçon would do.

Managing the temple was a beautiful and rewarding experience. It challenged my marketing, business, and leadership skills, and I grew so much as a leader in those years. But overseeing the temple, Yan Ming's career, the household, and the children began to feel insular and suffocating. I wanted to break out and try my hand at other creative endeavors.

Before Jin Long was born, I had started developing an

idea for a movie called *Wu-Tang and Shaolin*, based on the unique bond between Yan Ming and RZA. It was a tale of reincarnation and unlikely friendships. I love bridging cultures, and this was the perfect vehicle for that fascination. I was thrilled by the idea of reimagining the story that was unfolding in front of me between two of the most important men in my life, outside my immediate family. Looking back, it's still a brilliant idea, and yet there was no Sophia character in the movie. How could I write their story without including myself?

I thought I could see the concept as clear as day, but I learned pretty quickly that it wasn't fully formed. I met with some development people at Miramax about the project, and though they didn't bite at the idea, one of the development executives, Michelle Sy, would become my closest friend. I kept working on the idea part-time, but I still craved something outside of the temple, Yan Ming, and the kids altogether.

In 2003, the opportunity arose. On one of those thrilling field trips away from the kids, I went to a Vivienne Tam sample sale in the heart of New York City's Fashion District. As I browsed through the racks and tables full of clothes, I noticed that the designer herself was there. I introduced myself and told her that I was the person who had been responsible for Julia Roberts showing up at her store years before.

Back in January 1998, Michael Ostin had invited me to the opening night of Paul Simon's musical *The Capeman* at the Marquis Theatre in Times Square along with his father and Lenny Waronker. It was my first Broadway opening night, and I was brimming with excitement. I chose to wear a Vivienne

Tam floor-length, netted, close-fitting Buddha dress. It was my first of her pieces, gifted to me by Julianna, who had typed out my final essay more than a decade earlier. The after-party was filled with the cast, crew, press, and celebrities in silks, satins, sequins, and tuxes. As I surveyed the space, I noticed a tall, dark, and handsome man at the bar across the room, eyeing me. If I had had eyelashes to speak of, I would have batted them. Curiously, he seemed to be focused on my chest. If I had had a bosom to speak of, this might have seemed normal, but I was an A cup on my best days. As I gazed back at this tall drink of water, he leaned in to talk to a woman who was clearly his partner. *Damn.* She had shoulder-length, reddish-brown hair, and as she turned toward me, I recognized Julia Roberts, making *him* Benjamin Bratt. When I realized that they were admiring my dress, I marched across the room.

"Hi, I'm Sophia Chang," I said, sticking my hand out to Julia first.

"I'm Julia, and we were just talking about your dress. It's beautiful! Who made it?"

"Vivienne Tam. She's from Hong Kong and my favorite designer! You should go to her store on Greene Street in Soho, it's beautiful!"

"I will, thanks!" she said earnestly.

Five years later, I relayed the story to Vivienne. She was surprised. She asked if I would interview to be her part-time assistant. Here was a job that I was massively overqualified for, but Jian Hong was still a baby, and this was my chance to get out of the house. It was also an opportunity to explore the world of fashion, one of my childhood dreams. I went back the next day and got the job. On my first day, Vivienne told me half-jokingly that she wished I could be her CEO; we would have this same discussion more seriously years later, only to have the plan disrupted by the 2008 recession. Some months later, I got bored of taking calls and ordering lunch. I wanted a challenge that would allow me to pursue my passion, which, at this point, was film, but I had to figure out a way for it to bring in money.

That same year, Jim Jarmusch had asked RZA to score his incredible samurai movie *Ghost Dog*, starring Forest Whitaker. In 2001, I had arranged for RZA to host a screening of Donnie Yen's kung fu classic *Iron Monkey*, which Quentin Tarantino was presenting in the United States for Miramax. Being around Donnie and Quentin lit a fire under my ass about our movie and I put more focus into it.

In 2003, I partnered with Esther, a Chinese American film producer. Yan Ming and I had met her years before, when we did our first rounds of Hollywood meetings. Esther and I continued to work with Yan Ming and RZA to develop the idea. When the time came, we set up pitch meetings in LA and New York. While we were in LA, we met with an agent friend of Esther's who told us we weren't ready and that we'd never sell the idea. When we left his office, Esther suggested that we cancel all our pitches. *Fuck that and fuck him. I didn't come all this way to give up the second one person tells me I won't make it.*

We went on to do eleven meetings and sold the screenplay to HBO, the brass ring. The film never got made, but I learned a lot about the industry and further developed my love for pitching, which is like a very condensed form of storytelling.

One of the greatest gifts of that experience was meeting Sam Martin, the executive who acquired the rights. After we'd gotten a few underwhelming drafts from a screenwriter, Sam told me I should write the script myself, seeing as I had created the story and knew it best. It had never occurred to me to take a stab at it. I didn't think of myself as a writer until that moment. Once again, it took someone else seeing potential in me for me to pursue the endeavor. A decade after I'd started writing Chris Lighty's story as a screenplay, I was doing the same for Yan Ming and RZA, two more singular men in my life. It was yet another example of facilitating the telling of others' stories.

The next spring, I proposed to RZA that I manage what I called his extracurricular activities, meaning anything Hollywood related, like scoring, acting, and directing. It was an organic and perfect bridge between my two worlds of Shaolin and Wu-Tang, of kung fu and cinema. He said yes, well aware of the doors I had opened for him in the past, and he knew I would give it my all.

Managing RZA was a pleasure and an honor. There was no door that his name, and GZA's, couldn't open. This was my math: the people running the companies that I was reaching out to, not massive corporations, were usually men in their late thirties through early fifties. There was a 90 percent chance that they had been hip-hop fans at one point, and if so, a 95 percent chance that they were Wu-Tang fans. They grew up on Wu-Tang or their college years were marked by memorizing every word of GZA's *Liquid Swords* and Raekwon's *Only Built 4 Cuban Linx*, and you can't be a Wu fan without worshipping the Abbot. I got callbacks 90 percent of the time.

The greatest door that RZA's name opened was that of John Woo, though he wasn't necessarily a hip-hop fan. On RZA's behalf, I wrote a letter to John that explained how deeply his films had impacted and influenced the music of the Clan. We heard back immediately. John's response was so touching and appreciative and humble. This exchange culminated in meetings in New York and LA. The first face-to-face was at Shun Lee Palace on the Upper West Side on John's next trip to New York. John and his partner Terence Chang arrived on time, as did Yan Ming and I. Ghostface was a little later, and RZA was hours late. He was driving in from Ohio. I was mortified, even though John and Terence were incredibly gracious. I was so hungry and we ordered food but I remember that John wouldn't touch his chopsticks until RZA arrived. When he finally burst into the restaurant, it was like talent overload having him, Ghost, John, and Yan Ming all in the same room. On another visit to John's office in Century City, RZA talked to him about his aspirations to be a filmmaker himself and John took him very seriously. He told RZA, "Rakeem, the most important person on your team will be your editor." RZA had never forgotten those words.

As I watched the two interact, I saw a parallel between this rapport and that of RZA and Yan Ming. They came from disparate worlds and experiences, but what they shared was a mastery, which meant there was a mutual respect and allowed for a sort of shorthand. It wasn't verbal, it was more heart-to-heart, mind-to-mind, as in Chan. When I think about it, I believe that part of my gift of speaking with these extraordinary talents is that I, too, have a level of mastery that involves listening, empathy, translation, and communication.

RZA and I learned a ton and met a bunch of people together. I realized that I hadn't been feeding the social beast in me. I wanted to get out and broaden my networks and experiences. One of the key lessons I learned while managing RZA was the art of negotiating, of which I'd done little before then. I didn't care much about money, but that didn't mean shit because he was my client and I was serving him. While I was working on a big deal for him, he said, "Soph, you've gotta get me more money." The studio had made an offer and he said he wanted double. His agent and I had a conference call with the studio executives. When it came to his fee, RZA's agent dummied up. After a couple of moments of awkward silence, I gathered myself and said assertively, "We need to double his fee." Though he kind of threw me under the bus, I'm grateful to his agent for pushing me out of my comfort zone. And we got the money.

During this same project, the company drew up some artwork that included an illustration of RZA that they shared with us. I knew immediately that he wouldn't like it and, rather than have him articulate it on the next conference call, I said it myself so that he could avoid it. Part of being a manager, in addition to the babysitting aspect of it—"wake up, the car is outside and the flight leaves in an hour!"—is that you have to be comfortable playing the bad cop. Everyone has to love your artist; everyone has to respect you.

Managing RZA gave me a taste of the autonomy that I

yearned for and it made me want more. Unfortunately, Yan Ming saw it as a display of disloyalty. He was disappointed that I did work outside the temple. He thought that if I gave as much energy to him and the temple as I did to RZA, things would be even more prosperous. Thing is, I'd already given so much. I understood his perspective, but I needed something that was completely mine. It wasn't only the work around the temple and his career that consumed me, it was also that we had two small children, to whom I was tethered. He had fallen in love with my spirit of independence and hustle. I don't think he had imagined it would seek other outlets. But he couldn't be that unhappy that I was working with RZA, because he was one of our best friends and godfather to our children. Ultimately, Yan Ming would never deny my attachment to the Clan. One that was about to be punctured by tragedy.

One day that summer, I heard that Dirty was at RZA's 36 Chambers studios on Thirty-Fourth Street. I rushed over because I hadn't seen him in a very long time and wanted to reconnect with him. I knew about his stints in rehab, and apparently, he was back, *so fresh and so clean clean*. I said peace to all the guys in the lounge, the kitchen area, and the control room, but no sign of Dirty. Someone told me he was in the bathroom, so I waited for him in a chair across the hallway.

I sat patiently outside the bathroom for what seemed like several minutes. When the door finally opened, I jumped up from my chair and called out, "A!" My heart started to drop as I watched Dirty emerge ever so slowly, completely disheveled and in a haze. When he heard my voice, he turned toward me, but he didn't seem to recognize me. It felt as if he were looking right through me. It was as if all the precious memories we'd forged together vanished. I stood there, silently, as he went into another room. I didn't even bother going after him, he was too far gone. I went to the elevator and left.

I got in a cab and called the studio. When one of the guys answered, I said, "Is Dirty high?"

"No, Soph."

"He's fucking high!" I insisted angrily.

"No, that's just Dirty."

No, that's just Dirty. Those dismissive words would soon take on a much more serious meaning. But I knew he was high. Now I wish I'd chased him down and hugged him instead of leaving so soon, even if he didn't know who I was, because I wouldn't get another chance.

A few months later, on November 12, 2004, the Clan had a big reunion show at the Continental Airlines Arena in New Jersey. There was a lot of anticipation because they had promised that every single member would be there, which was rare for Wu-Tang. RZA had our temple demonstration team perform too. It was a great night. But Dirty wasn't there. No one was alarmed because he could be unpredictable.

The very next night, I was at Da Umberto, my favorite Italian spot in Chelsea, waiting on RZA for dinner with his agents. He was later than usual and I was getting hungry. I called him, and his sister Sophia answered the phone, which was odd.

"We were supposed to have dinner with RZA but he's not here. Do you know where he is?" I said, a little impatiently.

"You don't know?"

"Know what?"

I heard her hand the phone to RZA.

"Peace, Rakeem, what's wrong?" I said.

"He's gone, Soph. Dirty's gone."

I hadn't heard him like this since his mother had passed in 2000. My whole body went numb, save for the faint sensation of hot tears streaming down my cheeks. The last place I had seen Dirty was the last place he would lie. RZA had found him on the floor of the studio. He'd OD'd on tramadol, a prescription opioid, and cocaine. Five days later, we laid him to rest at the Christian Cultural Center in Brooklyn, the borough where he was born. Yan Ming was serious and calm. I was sad but still in a state of disbelief. I'd never been to a funeral and for this to be the first, for the man lying in the casket in a pristine white suit to be just a few days shy of his thirty-sixth birthday was hard to process. I surveyed the huge church, which was packed with friends and family. I remember looking at Shaquita, his lovely wife, and three children, whom I adored. There was Mariah Carey; there were photographers. And then RZA delivered a stunning eulogy and my wandering eyes were brought sharply into focus until they were blurred by tears.

"When we can't be satisfied with ourselves and can't find happiness . . . you find other things to make you happy . . . alcohol, drugs, and sex. And the abuse of alcohol, drugs, and sex will take any one of us outta here . . . I don't think that God kills any of us. He wants us to have life. But I do believe that we kill ourselves, or we allow each other to kill ourselves . . . When I think about A Son, I said to myself, I'm going to take 5 percent of the blame because . . . when I saw him doing things that were wrong, I refrained myself from intervening . . . Never neglect each other. If you see somebody . . . hurting, reach out . . . Dirty told me, 'Yo, I'm dying' . . . I took it as he's just high or he's just talking out of his mouth, but it was real . . . Don't ever take what somebody is telling you from their mouth or their heart as a joke, as a jest, or a pass-by, because everything is real. And if you don't believe that it's real, then the Most High will show you how real it can be."

After Dirty's funeral I called Chris. "I just went to my first funeral and it made me think about you."

"Why?"

"Because, so young, you've been to so many funerals of the young."

"Yeah, Soph."

While all these things were going on, I had begun to feel extremely detached from Yan Ming. The kids were two and four. Though he was a loving father, he wasn't as engaged as I'd hoped, probably because he hadn't grown up in a traditional way. There were no playdates, birthday parties, afterschool activities, or homework at Shaolin Temple. It was all on me. I took the kids to the playground or Central Park on the train by myself. That meant carrying the toddler in the stroller up and down the subway stairs while holding the other child's hand. I had to time it perfectly, like a bank heist, because I had to leave after the morning routine, but get Jian Hong back by 1:00 p.m. for her nap. I was like Cinderella—if she doesn't go down by 1:00 p.m., I'll turn into a pumpkin!

Sticking rigorously to the schedule, the kids were asleep by 7:00 p.m. Then I'd be by myself, sitting on the daybed, watching TV. I would eventually fall asleep, alone. Yan Ming taught until 9:00 p.m., then there was the cleaning and eating and drinking ritual that happened every night with the students. He often got home after 11:00 p.m. and sometimes not at all. Let me tell you, there is no loneliness like the loneliness you feel in a relationship. Yan Ming was as unhappy as I was. The difference was he had the freedom to do whatever he wanted.

I was a slave to the schedule: bedtime, wake time, mealtime, nap time, rinse and repeat. I would wake up early every morning and feed the kids breakfast, make their lunches, get them dressed, and have them brush their teeth. The biggest part of the morning was doing Jian Hong's hair. Because I had had long hair, I already knew how to French braid and got really creative with multicolored barettes and matching hair bands. My kids were also always dressed in perfectly coordinated outfits and scrubbed clean. Then I would walk them to school and come home. I spent several years being the drill sergeant every morning, yelling at them every step of the way. God, it was tedious. At one point, I said to my kids: "Here's the deal: when I ask you to do something, I'll ask nicely twice, but the third time I'll yell." And yell I did. Way more than their father. At one point I printed out a grid of the chores that alternated between Yan Ming and me, and it helped a little, but not much.

When Jian Hong turned three, God bless her, she stopped taking naps and wanted out of the stroller to walk with her big brother. I'm sure *Healthy Sleep Habits, Happy Child* said the kids should still be napping at three, but fuck that. When I had just one child, nap time was mommy time. With two, it was a pain in the ass, especially because I was so determined to stick to the schedule. Then there was all the fucking paraphernalia, which adds to the baggage, literally and figuratively. Getting rid of the stroller, diapers, wipe warmers, and plastic everything was so liberating. I felt like Angela Bassett in *Waiting to Exhale* when she sets her cheating husband's shit on fire in his BMW.

The good thing about the second child was that we had experience and weren't as afraid of every fucking thing. We didn't have to watch literally every movement as we did with Jin Long. By the time Jian Hong came around, I was happy to let her play with a steak knife and lighter next to an outlet if it meant I could take a shit uninterrupted.

When I became pregnant with Jin Long, Joe, our student, said to me, "Sophia, once you have a baby, all this"—he formed a *V* with his index and middle fingers and directed them from his eyes to mine—"turns into this." He rotated his fingers downward, indicating that all the attention that we put on each other would now be diverted, as it should be, to our baby. At the time I didn't understand it, but, man, did those words come back to me.

CHAPTER 8
THINGS FALL APART

When I hear someone's getting married, I think, *That's not gonna last. At least not if they have kids.* I am aware of exactly how fucked up that sounds, but I can't help it, based on what I myself have experienced and seen. Believe me, there was nothing I wanted more than to stay together as a happy family. *Happy* being the operative word.

I started seeing a shrink in 2004 to work through my feelings about my relationship with Yan Ming and doubts around motherhood. The disintegration of the relationship naturally affected how I parented.

When I told my shrink that I thought I was being too draconian about the schedule and boundaries, she said, "Sophia, I can't tell you how many people have sat across from me, exactly where you sit, and told me that their parents never established boundaries, and now as adults, they're completely lost." That was very reassuring because I wasn't sure if I was overdoing it.

On another occasion, I told her about yelling at Jin Long for no good reason, and she said, "You know, Sophia, in the pyramid of well-being, the foundation is food, water, and shelter, and right above that is emotional well-being. Some people think that emotional abuse is worse than physical abuse." That grabbed me by the collar and shook the shit out of me.

I am the most confident person I know, except when it comes to motherhood. As a philosophy, I choose to live with no regrets. I am grateful for my mistakes because they're opportunities to learn. When I've hurt people, I analyze my behavior and take responsibility, but with adult interactions, there's usually agency on both sides. When I've been a shitty mother, however, the only lesson I've learned is *You're a shitty mother.* There is no power as awesome as that of a parent, and no victim as helpless as a child. To this day, there are occasions when I'm a horrible mother that I wish I could take back, that I would do anything to erase. There is no greater guilt and shame than in those moments. My bad-mommy highlight reel would be extensive and appalling.

Yelling at the kids was a huge source of tension between Yan Ming and me. Though I could never justify the times when my behavior was egregious, my children, thankfully, came to appreciate how strict I was. When they went on playdates, their friends' parents marveled at how well-behaved they were. Yan Ming said I would kill their spirits, especially Jin Long's, as he was so sensitive. And he was right. I had to find the right balance between caring and discipline.

When I yelled at Jin Long for leaving his toys out, not brushing his teeth, or poor grades, he would look at the floor and shut down completely. On one such occasion in Vancouver, Heesok said to me, "Sophia, far be it from me to tell you how to parent, but you have to be aware of how much Jin Long cares about what you say. Your approval means everything to him." The flip side of that, naturally, was that my disapproval would have long-lasting deleterious effects.

Jin Long used to love little toy cars—sports cars, sedans, muscle cars, trucks, everything. When one of Yan Ming's disciples returned from Italy, she brought Jin Long a small toy Vespa. It was a thoughtful and unique addition to his collection. He loved that little silver Vespa. One night, when I was trying unsuccessfully to put him to sleep, I yelled and hurled the Vespa across the room. It hit a wall and broke into two irreparable pieces. Even as it was hurtling through the air, I felt an instant pang of regret and thought, *Well, there's one for the couch when he's older.*

In 2015, Pixar put out a brilliant movie called *Inside Out*, which personifies the emotions in a young girl's brain. In one scene, one of the characters falls into the valley of memories, depicted by glowing balls, and she is told that the balls eventually fade and disintegrate. I cried so hard during that scene because I knew it to be true. My kids could never hang on to every wonderful memory and experience I tried to create for them; there's no space. I just hope the good ones outweigh the bad ones.

My kids were remarkably well behaved because I was so strict. They had only one tantrum between the two of them, and it was my daughter at three. (Buyer beware: the terrible twos extend right through three as well.) Yan Ming and I had taken them to Kmart, and she didn't get what she wanted, so she had a meltdown on the street. It was so odd and funny at the same time. This tiny little girl was crying and emanating so much energy.

Over the next couple of years, the yearning I had for some detachment from Yan Ming, the temple, and the kids continued to build as it became more and more clear that Yan Ming and I were growing apart. We were less affectionate and more argumentative. And each fight created more distance, which only fueled the estrangement. It got to the point that any little thing would set us off. It was as if a surface scratch could cause a hemorrhage. We started to hear each other through our selective and respective filters. Everything he said sounded like resistance to me, and everything I said felt like control to him. There was truth to both of those perceptions.

Maintaining control made me so good at my job, but my shrink told me the trait wasn't necessarily a benefit when it came to human relationships. It was so easy for me to take care of all the business because it was my wiring. Having grown up inside the temple, Yan Ming had no experience in any of it. I paid all the bills, I called the realtors and scoped out spaces for the temple, I had the patterns made for the uniforms and found where to have them made, I imported the famous Feiyue training sneaker from China. When I look back, I should've taught Yan Ming to be more independent, rather than letting him rely on me for everything, which created a cycle of dependence and resentment. I saw what was wrong but didn't know how to undo the damage that had already been done, how to take back the harsh words we had hurled at each other.

Worse than feeling alienated from Yan Ming, I started to suspect him of cheating, but I had no evidence. I would walk into the temple and look suspiciously at all the women. Even on the streets, I would look at a woman and wonder, *Are you fucking my husband?* The level of paranoia was deranged. The temple was full of adoring disciples who angled to spend more time with their dear leader. And of course, a number of them were women who found him attractive, as I had. I had helped create this cult of personality, and once I started to have some distance from it, it repulsed me. Having worked with count-less celebrities, I was very familiar with sycophantism, but it didn't make it any easier to swallow.

One day, I went to the temple, as I had done thousands of times before. I went up the elevator, walked into the space, and dutifully removed my shoes. I crossed the forest-green carpet that was worn in the lanes where we had kicked and jumped across the floor. I knew every dip and irregularity. But this day something was different. Rather than hanging around in the main space, I walked directly into Yan Ming's private room, the abbot's chamber, where we changed and had all our personal effects.

For some reason, my hand reached straight onto a shelf under a stack of sweaters. It was almost involuntary. Between the wool and the wood, my fingers touched several square plastic pouches. As I withdrew my hand, I was dumbfounded to see condoms filling my palm. *These are not for use in my vagina*. I know God directed me to that stash of contraband contraception. I looked around the tiny space—the space where I had folded his clothes, where I had nursed our son, where we had made love. And now I was so utterly alone. I marched out and threw them down in front of him.

"What is this?"

He glared at me. "It's none of your business!"

I became so suspicious that I studied our most recent cell phone bill, which I paid monthly. I knew every number except one with a 410 area code. Baltimore. Several calls had been exchanged with that number, some late at night. I picked up the fax phone, punched *67 to block the number, and dialed. A woman's voice answered and I hung up, my stomach in my throat.

Around this time, I had met a film director named Andy Tennant who was married with three kids. We hit it off right away. One night he invited me out for dinner with some friends. When I arrived, I sat there, despondent, not my usual cheery self.

"What's wrong, Sophia?" he asked.

"I just went through my husband's cell phone bill and called one of the numbers I didn't recognize. I can't believe I've become this woman."

"How old are the kids?"

"Two and four."

He looked at his watch. "Right on time!"

In February 2005, Andy invited me to the premiere of his movie *Hitch* starring Will Smith. I was really excited to go and naturally invited Yan Ming to accompany me. I was imagining it would bring us closer together, still holding out hope to reconcile what seemed to be irreconcilable. The afternoon of the premiere, he said blithely that he wasn't going. I was so angry and hurt. As bad as it was losing my husband, losing my best friend was just as heartbreaking. By dint of habit, I still thought about him all the time and wanted to experience everything with him. If I walked past a store, I would think that something would look good on him. If I ate at a restaurant, I would think that he might enjoy the food. As I watched the movie, I thought about all the places he would have laughed.

A few months later, *The New Yorker* published a piece entitled "Drunk Monk" about Yan Ming's recent birthday party, which was attended by RZA, Masta Killa, Wesley Snipes, and Jim Jarmusch, among others. One of Jin Long's classmates' mothers, Laurie Liss, a beast of a literary agent, started talking to us about doing a training manual. Even though the seams between Yan Ming and me were coming apart, I was enthusiastic about the thought of memorializing Yan Ming's take on Shaolin training and Chan Buddhism. It was part of not only his legacy and a culmination of his work, but mine also.

I still needed to find something to help me through what seemed like an inevitable transition out of the temple. I yearned for something else, something bigger, much like my desire to break out of my hometown. A step toward that independence had come earlier that year, when Vivienne had asked me to produce her runway show. It was exciting to help translate a designer's vision and to work with a team on the technical aspects of lighting, music, and staging. It was here that my skills as a producer began to gel. I loved creating and overseeing the budgets and timelines. It wasn't hard for me to stand out in an industry that seemed to thrive on chaos, which was the antithesis of my MO—I'm the one who holds things together. During a meeting with Jim Jarmusch and RZA, we discussed *Ghost Dog 2*, which everyone wanted to see happen. We all acknowledged that coordinating logistics and communications would be a challenge, considering both of their hectic schedules. With little hesitation, Jim nodded his frosty-white coif toward me and said in his baritone, "No need to worry, we've got Sophia. She's the glue." I doubt he remembers even saying that, but I was deeply flattered, and the moniker stuck with me. Pun wholly intended.

At the end of that year, Michael Ostin came to town and took me to lunch at Trattoria Dell'Arte, an upscale Midtown Italian spot. He started the conversation, as always, by asking about the family. I shared that things could be better between Yan Ming and me. I tried to put on a brave face, but I could see his concern. Family means everything to the Ostins. He didn't probe. He knew I hadn't fully processed my feelings. He told me that he and the legendary producer and artist Nile Rodgers were starting a management company.

"What a great idea! You'd be a fantastic manager and teaming up with an artist like Nile is so smart!" I said.

"Well, we want you to run it, Soph."

My jaw dropped.

"What? Why me? Michael, you know so many people out of work who are far more qualified!" The digital revolution had caused the business to implode and led to the mergers or closing of several labels, leaving a host of very talented executives out of work.

"Because, Soph, I've never known anyone better with talent than you," he said matter-of-factly, and with the love and kindness of someone who wanted to help his friend.

Tears welled. The former head of A&R at Warner Bros. Records and president of DreamWorks Records, who had worked with the likes of Madonna, Prince, Eric Clapton, Van Halen, the B-52s, Talking Heads, R.E.M., Red Hot Chili Peppers, and Green Day, was telling me that I had a singular gift with artists. I'd never thought of this quality, but I've come to believe that he's right. I don't know to what to attribute this propensity, I just know that it exists and is powerful. With just a few words, Michael boosted my confidence and put a much-needed battery in my back.

I started work with B-Hive, the management company, in January 2007. We worked with composers that Nile knew, and I brought in Organized Noize, the team from Atlanta who produced OutKast's and Goodie Mob's first albums, as well as "Waterfalls" for TLC and "Don't Let Go" for En Vogue. Managing composers meant spending a lot of time in LA, which represented escape for me, both personally and professionally. It was the perfect antidote to the cloistered ecosystem of the temple. I was able to spend quality time with some of my closest friends, like Michelle, who had moved out West to pursue their careers in film. I threw myself into the world of composing, learning everything I could about the process in TV, film, advertising, and trailers. I got to know the heads of music at all the major film studios and broadened my network in this world that I was so excited to occupy. I loved exerting those hustle muscles again.

I started traveling more frequently to LA for business for a few days at a time. It was my first time away from both the kids and Yan Ming. When I was traveling, I wouldn't call the kids very frequently because it would take me out of my business head and make me miss them too much. At least they were a little older, neither of them toddlers anymore. Jin Long was in kindergarten at a public school in the Lower East Side called NEST+m, the first dedicated K-12 gifted and talented school in New York. Until this point, he was a pretty shy kid, but he grew right out of that and became very outgoing. Jian Hong was going to the same private preschool her brother had just graduated from and she was always the smartest in her class.

While I was in LA that March, Universal Pictures arranged for Organized Noize to meet with Michael Mann, who was shooting *Miami Vice*. When we arrived at his office, we were escorted to the dark editing suite, where someone showed us a scene from the film. We huddled around the small monitor in black swivel office chairs. I was captivated even in those few minutes and studied everything intently. When we were done, the door opened and the bright light from the hallway flooded in, backlighting the person who had just entered. I squinted at the silhouette. *Holy shit, it's Michael Mann.* I was disarmed by how low-key and unassuming he was. He sat across from us and asked us what we thought of the scene. The guys didn't speak, so I leapt in. I told him how

I felt about Gong Li's presence, conflict, and motivations in the scene. Michael tilted his head down a little and looked at me for a few seconds over his wire-framed glasses. *Shit, I fucked up.* But then he said: "Yes, that's exactly it, Sophia."

He elaborated on the scene, the narrative arc, and how he saw Organized's bottom as critical to rounding out the traditional score. Like the times I got to see Paul Simon in the studio, listening to Michael Mann was like taking a master class in storytelling. I'm sure he has no idea how inspiring I found that single brief interaction.

On May 16, 2006, a day before my birthday, Yan Ming's story was immortalized in the form of his book, *The Shaolin Workout.* It was beautiful to see the book on the shelves of Barnes & Noble, particularly the stores where I had read to the kids countless times. I grabbed a bunch of copies and spread them all over the store in highly trafficked locations. We did book events in New York and LA. It was interesting to watch him with some emotional distance. He was still the charismatic, effortless, powerful warrior and teacher that I had fallen in love with, but no longer the perfect partner. That book would be the last project we worked on together.

That fall, Yan Ming and I were invited to a disciple's fiftieth birthday party. I declined, but Jeff, the disciple, said it would mean a lot to him for me to be there. The dinner was at a Chinatown restaurant. Yan Ming and I sat down toward one end of the long table across from Marcie, Jeff's girlfriend, who managed the temple. Next to her, directly across from me, was her sister, Janine. As soon as we settled in, Janine started talking to Yan Ming, without acknowledging me.

"You know who's in town?" she said excitedly.

He said nothing, almost as if he knew what she was going to say.

"Alex!" she said, almost triumphantly.

Who the FUCK is Alex? I wondered.

"Oh, you remember Alex, don't you?" she prodded.

Silence.

"Well, she definitely remembers you and she's really excited to see you!"

This bitch right here.

Still nothing.

"She said we're all going out dancing again later!"

Her insouciance was utterly galling and I would not soon forget it.

And yet, Yan Ming remained quiet.

There's no fucking way he made plans to go dancing. I know my husband; he doesn't dance.

I was blind with rage. I looked Janine straight in the eye with a glare that could pierce titanium.

"You do realize who I am, don't you? I am his wife and the mother of his children and you're talking like I'm not even here!" I said, punctuating the statement with a hard tap of my index finger on my chest.

"Oh, I didn't mean to . . ."

I turned to Yan Ming and hissed into his ear. "Imagine if a man sat across from us and started telling you that there was another man that you didn't know who was excited to see me and go dancing? It never would have gotten this far because one of my friends would have shut him up. And you just sit there saying nothing. I need you to go sit at the other end of the table."

I got up and walked outside, seething. I called Karina, a woman who had produced a National Geographic special about Yan Ming. We had become close during the shoot. I told her what had transpired, and she knew immediately who Alex was. Some months back, a group of them had gone out for drinks while I was at home watching the kids. She said Alex and Yan Ming were drunk and started flirting right away. They moved to sit next to each other and even danced together. *Hold up, they fucking danced?* In our ten years together, Yan Ming had never danced with me, not even at our closest friends' weddings.

Later, once I started going out again, I couldn't believe I had forgotten that dancing was a huge part of my self-care and self-expression. I had spent all those years on the couch night after night, waiting for Yan Ming to come home instead. Why hadn't I been more proactive? Part of it was sheer exhaustion, but part of it was social lassitude. I wish I had been more vigilant and ambitious about maintaining my independence when it became clear that he didn't want to spend time with me. I had lost myself more than I cared to admit.

At a weekly session with my shrink, I told her that separation felt inevitable, but that I hated the idea of walking away from my decade-old dream of helping Yan Ming build the temple upstate. We had looked at land and imagined the summer programs for children. When I was done, she rested her hands on her notepad, peered at me, and asked gently, "Sophia, are you sure that's still your lifelong dream?"

Yes, of course! I wanted to blurt out, but I had learned to let go of all presuppositions and try to be tabula rasa. Her question carried the weight of a ton of bricks, yet it made me feel light as a feather and freed me of that emotional anchor. I had become so imbued with Yan Ming's dream that I didn't consider the possibility that it was time to let it go. Ironically, I had not adhered to the key Buddhist tenet of nonattachment. I sighed and sank back into the couch.

"Oh my God, you're right: it's not my dream anymore."

Thanksgiving night, a couple of months after Jeff's dinner, I addressed the Janine situation with Yan Ming after we'd made love. Toward the end of our marriage, I had committed to having sex once a week to try to maintain some degree of intimacy. Romance and friendship were gone. When we made love, it was the only time that he was tender. And I missed that so terribly.

"That night at Jeff's birthday party, I was really hurt. I can't believe you didn't stand up for me. I was so humiliated. You just sat there as Janine talked to you about another woman and you did nothing. Imagine how that made me feel."

Then, for maybe the second time in eleven years, he apologized. I told him to tell Marcie that Janine couldn't come to his birthday party, which was a huge bash that I planned every year. He promised to take care of it. Even with his assurance, I doubted he would do anything, and that night didn't fix what had been wrong for years.

At Christmastime, I sat alone at a bar waiting for Joan, and my mind turned to Yan Ming, wondering where he could be. I started imagining whom he could be fucking at that very moment. As I had done many times before, I pictured the act and started filling in the details—what room they were in at the temple, what she looked like, what he was saying. Then I had the most astonishing revelation: I didn't care. Word. I didn't care. I rewound the tape and played it again, this time with another woman in a different room, and the outcome was the same. This thought that had tortured me in the past and turned me into a paranoid wife had completely dissipated. Holy shit. When Joan got there, I immediately shared this discovery with her.

She listened quietly, then looked at me and said calmly, "Soph, it's over."

And right then I was free. The emotional yoke was broken. I was free from the doubt, the suspicions, the humiliation. That might sound like an appalling epiphany, but for me it was an exquisite emancipation.

A week later, at my first shrink session of 2007, I launched into a diatribe about Yan Ming, then stopped myself.

"I'm saying exactly the same thing to you that I did this time last year. I am officially the hamster on the wheel. I'm done."

Shortly thereafter, I told Yan Ming I was leaving. I would stay in the house for a while to ease the transition on the children and my wallet. We both knew it was over, but I knew I had to be the one to make the break. Why would he walk away from the woman who ran everything in his life? I didn't deliver the message with any triumph or anger, and he didn't offer any opposition. All those hours of emotional excavation I had spent with my shrink led me sadly, but resolutely, to this final decision. Once I walked away, I never looked back. My eyes were firmly fixed on the future, whatever or whomever it might bring.

Just a couple of weeks later, I was heading to LA. Alone. My girlfriend Sam had invited me to the legendary HBO pre–Golden Globes party at the Chateau Marmont. I wasn't just in a new mind state, I was also on a manhunt. The summer before, I had met Brian, nothing more than a typical actor crush. He was talented and committed, but his height, broad shoulders, and mischievous smile had me infatuated. I was at the premiere for a friend's movie in New York and there he was, in the flesh, with a young model dangling off his arm. I introduced myself, but he couldn't have been less interested. What would I have done if he had been? Things between Yan Ming and me had eroded, but I was still in a committed relationship. But now, as I packed for LA, I told myself, *Fuck it, you're single.*

I knew Brian would be at the party, and I thought about him as I pulled my tight Plein Sud navy pinstriped leggings over my thighs and closed the zipper high on my waist. I turned and looked at my ass at a three-quarter angle from behind, smiled, and said, "You've got this, Soph." I topped the outfit with a Vivienne Tam white faux-fur jacket and a white beanie that had *Shaolin* embroidered on it. It was the first time I'd been out as a single woman in twelve years, and I'd call this the night I let the veil down.

Michelle and I drove to the Marmont, and my anticipation grew as we reached the legendary hotel in West Hollywood. I felt emboldened with every step I took across the

FAMILY

CHINA

CHRIS LIGHTY

HIP HOP

Andre 3000 and Rico
Wade of Organized
Noize Productions

Redman

Q-Tip

KIDS

WU-TANG CLAN

Ol' Dirty Bastard
(RIP)

Raekwon the Chef

Ghostface Killah

Method Man

Method Man, Raekwon, U-God, Redman

RZA

Ghostface Killah

RZA and GZA

YAN MING

RZA, Donnie Yen, Quentin Tarantino

faded Persian rugs. I dragged my fingertips lightly along the backs of the velvet couches, as if I were imagining a man's hands on the nape of my neck. Everywhere we turned, there was another celebrity—Chris Rock, Bill Maher, Helen Mirren—but I only had eyes for one. When I finally spotted him across the star-spangled room, my knees went weak. The only other man who had ever made me feel that way was my favorite actor, Chow Yun Fat, director John Woo's muse.

I clutched Michelle's arm. "There he is!" We worked our way over to Brian and I did some reconnaissance: he was with another woman, another tall, young model with long hair. Not the right time to engage. This hunt would require patience. I saw him a couple more times, but he was always surrounded by a bunch of people, the skirt right by his side. At one point, I managed to make eye contact. New York bitches are bold. If we want you to see us, we will stare at you until you look back. You might not even know what's drawing your gaze. That's Empire State magnetism. He looked back, and I thought there was a glimmer of recognition.

Michelle and I spent the rest of the evening making the rounds. One of Joss Stone's songs that Raphael Saadiq had produced, "Headturner," ran through my head and would become my anthem. I was like a kid in a man-dy store. I felt myself gathering power, like a video game character picking up coins. Flirting and fucking are like riding a bicycle: once you know how, you never forget, no matter how long it's been since you've been on two wheels. And coming back as a confident forty-two-year-old who'd been married and had kids, I was Lance Armstrong out this bitch, except I didn't need steroids.

By the end of the evening, I was exhilarated by all the male attention that I'd received but still nowhere with Brian. All good. We'd seen each other twice in six months; our paths would cross again. As Michelle and I made our way to the elevator, I looked up to the landing, and lo and behold, there was Brian. Standing tall on the red terra-cotta tiles, a-fucking-lone. I didn't hesitate. Carpe dickem. I marched straight up to him and stuck out my hand.

"I'm Sophia Chang. I met you before at the premiere for your last movie."

He looked down at me with a mischievous smile. "I remember you."

"No, you don't, but that's okay." Then I stood on my tiptoes and put my mouth close enough to his ear so that he could feel the heat of my breath. "You're lucky I have a husband and two kids at home, because if I didn't, I'd be so far up your ass you wouldn't know what to do."

He pulled back quickly and looked down at me, surprised and intrigued. "Call me tomorrow at eleven a.m. at the Four Seasons. I'll make you come over so I can do bad things to you."

"You're not listed under your real name."

"Yes, I am. Call me in the morning."

The next day, I called the Four Seasons at exactly 11:00 a.m. and he was, in fact, listed under his name, but he wasn't there. I rang back around 5:00. I was just about to hang up when the phone picked up and I heard his sexy, raspy voice. He didn't have time to see me because he had done interviews all day and was leaving town, but we had a great conversation.

"We know a lot of the same people," I said. "I bet we have about twenty people in common."

"I'm sure we do."

"Well, I can't have any of them knowing that we're talking."

We exchanged numbers and promised that we'd see each other soon in New York. I was elated. Here I was, planning a tryst with my fantasy man.

I called Chris to tell him I'd met Brian. I started off the conversation like an excited schoolgirl with a crush, but as I continued reporting what had happened, inexplicably, I started to cry. All my certainty melted away and I was suddenly shaken by the prospect of actually being with a man after all this time with my husband. As always, Chris just listened.

Back in New York, Brian and I continued to have thought-provoking conversations. On his next visit, he invited me to his hotel again. I was still too nervous. I had dipped my toe into the water, but I wasn't ready to get wet yet. I made up an excuse not to go see him.

My wise friend knew of my crush and was going to invite him to a dinner party through a mutual friend. I expressed my nervousness to her.

"Why are you nervous, Soph?"

"Because he's dating all these beautiful, young models and actresses, and I don't think I can compare to them sexually."

"What? You think those young girls are better in bed than you are?"

"I have no idea."

"They're not."

"I'm also concerned about just being another notch on his belt."

"Soph, why wouldn't he be a notch on yours?"

Thank you, friend. Notch on my motherfucking belt. That was exactly the boost that I needed. After having only one partner for twelve years, I had completely lost touch with my sexuality, my sense of adventure, and therefore my confidence. My body was a finely tuned, constantly advancing machine when it came to kicking and punching but pretty much on autopilot when it came to fucking and sucking.

The dinner with Brian never transpired, and when I told Chris, he said, "That's a good thing, Soph. I didn't want to say anything, but I know several women who were tangled up with him." Seems I dodged a bullet. A full year would pass before I engaged with a man again.

The night of Yan Ming's much-anticipated forty-third birthday party arrived. Despite our breakup, there was no fucking way I wasn't going. It was important for the kids, and I had made all the arrangements: planned the menu, invited the VIPs, coordinated the performances, arranged for his gift. There were toasts, cake, a DJ, and lots and lots of alcohol. It was always a great party, but it was different this time because I felt so removed from it all, as if I were a guest instead of the host.

Shortly after the fanfare had died down, and people were mingling, I spotted Janine walking off the elevator. The fucking nerve of this bitch. With her was a nondescript white woman with mouse-brown hair. I knew immediately that it was Alex. I approached Yan Ming and said, "She's here. You told me she wouldn't be."

"It's my birthday party! You can't tell me what to do!" he said angrily.

"If you don't tell her to leave, I will. And I promise you, you don't want me to do it," I responded, serious as a heart attack.

He just stood there, as mute as he had been at the restaurant.

Before I could get across the temple floor, Jian Hong, five at the time, approached me. I took her by the hand and walked up to our friend Beau Sia.

"Take Mei Mei," I ordered.

I strode resolutely across the floor, almost in slow motion, like an assassin in a kung fu movie. I was wearing my Gucci fedora and a custom black silk suit embossed with dragons from Shanghai. The floor-length jacket flowed open to reveal blood-red lining. I got right in Janine's grill, and as I did, Alex scurried away. She knew exactly who the fuck I was too. I was amped, and she was shook. Janine greeted me with a clueless smile.

"Hi!"

"I want you to know that the last time we saw each other you disrespected me like I've never been disrespected in my life."

"What?"

"You sat across from me and told my husband that there was another woman waiting to go dancing with him later that night."

"Uh . . ."

"So, here's what's going to happen: I'm going to walk away," I said, looking at my watch, "and I'll be back in five minutes. If you're still here, I'll kick the shit out of you and your friend."

I turned around and, with a whoosh of Shanghai silk, left her choking on my words. I got my daughter back from Beau and he whispered to me, "What just happened? Your energy when you handed me Mei Mei was crazy."

My adrenaline was surging. Yan Ming walked up to me, angry.

"This is my party! You have no right to tell people to leave!"

"I told you to handle it and that if you didn't, I would. So I did."

He was enraged but I didn't give a fuck. I had warned him three times and he still let Janine, and worse, Alex, that trifle of a woman, come to the evening that I had planned. I watched them scurry out of the temple like the vermin they were. Let me be clear: even though I don't think he fucked that entirely forgettable white girl, the infidelity began when he started acting single. I don't give a fuck if you don't touch her. Flirting, dancing, and exchanging numbers with another woman is a betrayal. If I do any of that shit, I've checked out and need to leave. I barely looked at other men when I was with Yan Ming. When I'm in, I'm all the way in. Ain't no half-stepping.

You know how people caution, "Don't say anything you might regret"? There are many things that have come out of my foul mouth that I wish I could take back, but the threat that I leveled that night felt exquisite and still does, even as I repeat it now. Once I let my rage loose, I felt empowered, like that day back in Balaclava Park. And I felt free, so fucking free, even though Yan Ming and the whole temple looked at me like a pariah. I didn't give a fuck. Guess what, I built this house, motherfuckers. You wouldn't even be here if it wasn't for me. I danced my ass off completely alone with utter abandon, silk swirling around my body as I swayed, swerved, and dropped it like it was hot. I felt untouchable when Michael Jackson's "Shake Your Body (Down to the Ground)" came on. Everyone was watching me. One of the students told me later his friend had said, "Who's that? She dances like a porn star." A porn star? That's a new one and I'll take it. In that moment when I felt so alienated from everyone and everything around me, it was music that was my deliverance. Music, which had receded so far into the background of my life as I immersed myself in Shaolin, came back like a faithful friend who had never left.

Walking away from the temple also meant relinquishing my place of training. Now I had to figure out where I could continue my kung fu practice, because I knew I would train for the rest of my life. Studying with another master was out of the question. First, I would never find someone as great as Yan Ming, and second, I wouldn't do that to him; it would be disrespectful. I joined a gym around the corner from our place. It was awkward at first. And lonely. I was accustomed to the hum and energy at the temple, and now I was training by myself.

But the community that I had helped assemble started to

turn on me. I had been the matriarchitect of that institution for more than a decade and had been treated with the commensurate respect. But once I left Yan Ming, I was persona non fucking grata. Without any formal announcement, everyone knew that Yan Ming and I were not getting along. I wasn't spending as much time there, and when I did, the former warmth between us had congealed into frosty exchanges.

Being separated from the students wasn't a big deal, because none of them were true friends. On the other hand, when the real friends disappeared, I felt hurt and betrayed. Someone had warned me, "Wait till you see who you lose in the divorce." Naturally, my ride-or-dies stuck by my side, but there were a number of folks whom Yan Ming and I had met together who surprised me. I expected the men to side with Yan Ming because they spent more time with him, drinking, playing video games, going to bars. But there were women who had been much closer to me who stuck with him, which was hurtful.

One day as I was walking out of our apartment building, Natalie, one of Yan Ming's disciples, who I suspected was sleeping with him, was entering with Julie, whom I'd considered a close friend. She had spent a lot of time with me, both with the kids and one-on-one. What the fuck was she doing with Natalie, and why were they visiting Yan Ming when I wasn't around? Even though we were no longer a couple, we were still living together, and I found it galling that they would waltz insouciantly into my house with utterly no regard for me. They seemed surprised to see me. *I do live here, bitches.* They forced smiles and said, "Hi, Sophia!"

I didn't feel like engaging in bullshit small talk with people who I felt had betrayed me. I walked right up to Natalie and asked her point-blank: "Are you in love with my husband?"

"No!" she answered, shocked.

Honestly, I don't think she was, but she couldn't have been confounded by the assumption. She was spending a lot of time with Yan Ming, much of it alone, which was totally fucking inappropriate. Slapping her in the grill with that question felt good and bad in equal measure. I'm glad I let that bitch know how I felt, no punches pulled, but by the same token, that moment was some reality-TV shit, which I could not abide. This was what I had been reduced to.

Aside from the trauma that the separation put the kids through, I have no regrets about my time with Yan Ming. I didn't leave a minute too early or a minute too late. Though I felt betrayed by his interactions, in the end, I don't think he actually slept with other women. He remains the single most remarkable human being I've ever met. We changed each other's lives for the better and that is a gift.

It was time to move the fuck on.

CHAPTER 9

THE JUGGLING ACT

Freedom didn't exactly feel like *Shawshank*. I was faced with the daunting task of pulling my life back together and excavating the identity that I'd allowed to be buried. In one fell swoop, I had lost my husband, my best friend, my coparent, my business partner, my career, and my professional dream. I never wavered on my decision to leave, but swore that I still loved Yan Ming. I recalled all the magical moments—the trips, the training, the children—they were real! And then I had a simple, stunning revelation: *This isn't love, Sophia, it's nostalgia.*

I abandoned the Hallmark notion that we were meant to be together forever. It's not impossible, but I don't think I have a single soulmate, I believe I have many. And, God willing, I'll be blessed enough to encounter some of them in this lifetime. I've never stayed long in a relationship—romantic, platonic, professional—that wasn't satisfying. Nor do I trust that love conquers all. I think timing trumps love. When Yan Ming and I met, it was synchronicity: he needed someone to help grow the temple, and I was ready to train and settle down and have kids. Our needs and desires were in lockstep with each other. However, as we grew, so did we grow apart. I mean, what was the likelihood that we would develop in the same direction . . . at the same rate . . . for the rest of our lives? I've met potentially amazing partners, but we were at such different places in our trajectories that it made a relationship impossible.

To my surprise, my family wasn't disappointed that I was leaving Yan Ming, they were relieved. They'd seen our dysfunction up close. One day, Yan Ming and I got into a fight. My mother shocked me by saying to him, "I used to think it was Sophia's fault that you were fighting all the time, but now I see that it's you, and I don't like the way you're treating my daughter." That was devastatingly out of character and must have taken so much for her to overcome her aversion to confrontation. I had never heard my mother challenge someone like this. Yan Ming stayed silent. He was ashamed. It didn't change anything, but she had spoken her piece, and I was moved by and proud of her for doing so. When I told Michael that Yan Ming and I had been reduced to fighting in front of the kids, he looked at me sadly, without a hint of judgment, and said, "Soph, is that the model of love you want to provide to your children?"

A bright light during this dark period appeared on March 17, 2007, when Heesok married Carrie Goldberg, his former student, a brainy, ballsy, beautiful blonde who had been a case worker for Holocaust survivors and had just sat for the bar. It was a sunny affair in Palm Springs. Carrie's big, wonderful family filled the sprawling green lawns along with our little clan—me, my folks, the kids, and even Michelle. But no Yan Ming. It was the first signal to my family that it was over. Nothing was said, it just was. And it was all good because the children and I were so loved.

I would have to be more explicit with the Clan about the separation, which I dreaded because they didn't see it coming and were very attached to our union. RZA, naturally, was at the top of my list. On a warm spring evening, we had dinner with Power, one of the Clan's executive producers. I kept waiting for an opening in the conversation, like a girl trying to get in on a double Dutch skip, but the opportunity didn't appear, or I was too nervous to seize one. Then came the check and we were out. *Damn, I blew it.* Luckily, as I was walking RZA to the parking lot, he stopped by a deli for a drink before the long drive home to South Jersey. I followed him to the back of the store. As the large refrigerator door opened and the frosted air escaped, I saw my opening.

"Rakeem, I have to tell you something."

"What is it, Soph?"

Here we go.

"It's over between me and Shifu. I'm leaving."

He had just reached for an iced tea and stopped cold, leaving the door half-open. He slowly let it close and turned to face me.

"That can't be true, Soph. I don't believe it."

"It's true, it's over. It's been bad for a long time."

"What happened?"

"Nothing, we just grew apart."

"I'm gonna talk to Shifu about it."

"There's nothing to talk about. I've been trying to make it right for years, but we're at the end of the line."

This was a blow to RZA. He was the godfather to our children, our families spent a lot of time together, and he was very close to each of us.

Next up was Ghost. I went to see him before his show at the Highline Ballroom in the Meatpacking District. I put on a pretty powder-blue halter dress, a white Kangol, drop pearl earrings, and Prada white leather pumps. When I pulled up, there was a massive line, but no worry, Ghost sent someone to get me immediately. I was escorted to his dressing room, where he was seated on the couch, surrounded by his boys. When he looked up and saw me, his eyes widened. He'd never seen me look so feminine. I suddenly felt ridiculous and self-conscious. I wasn't dressed for a late-night hip-hop show, I looked like I was going to an afternoon wedding! But I wanted him to see me differently tonight. I wanted him to see the woman, the girl, who needed him to protect my neck and heart again, not the drill sergeant who ordered everyone around.

"Come here, Soph," he said, standing up. Even with that slight Starks slouch, he towered over me at six feet three inches. He was wearing a red-and-white velour tracksuit, and I buried myself in his chest. Sinking into him was like being swallowed by a Downy-scented teddy bear. I looked up at him and said, "I need to talk to you. Alone."

"Oh, yeah?" Ghost managed to make something as simple and common as *yeah* sound like slang.

"Please."

"Guys, get out," he ordered.

His crew immediately got up and left the room.

Alone on the couch, I turned toward him and held his big, coarse hands in mine.

"What's up, Soph? You okay?" he asked, softly.

Ghost had never seen me like this. So serious. I was usually like a Jack Russell terrier, jumping up and down around him.

"Shifu and I aren't together anymore," I said quietly.

"Nah, Soph, that can't be true." Like RZA, he couldn't believe his ears. I think that to these guys, we were the ideal couple: we built a business together, had kids, walked the straight and narrow.

"It's true. It's really over."

"So, what happened, Soph? I know there was no wickedness going on." That was his euphemism for infidelity. I think in his mind, that was the only thing that could have caused the rift. No one suspected the gradual erosion of our friendship and passion.

"No, no wickedness. We just grew apart. So, I'm here to tell you that I need you to take care of me again. I need you to be there for me. I need all of you to surround me like a forest of tall trees."

"C'mon, Soph, you know we got you, always."

"This means that one day I'll have to bring someone else around you guys and get your approval."

"That's easy, Soph. You know how I'll judge?"

"How?"

"By looking at his shoes. I can see everything I need to know by looking at a man's shoes."

The Wally King had spoken.

The most suprising response I got was from Method Man. That July, the Clan were performing in London the night of RZA's birthday. My girlfriend Sam Martin, who had bought my screenplay at HBO, and I decided to go meet them. I called Ghost the afternoon of the show and asked what I should wear: black or green. He came to my room later and said, "Green, because I'm wearing green." So I wore my favorite dress: a spectacular first-season Alaïa shimmery forest green body-hugging cap-sleeved number with snaps down the back.

It was an awesome night. RZA had told me that his and his wife's favorite album at the time was Corinne Bailey Rae's debut project. I looked up her manager online and sent a cold email, and she came to the show to surprise RZA. Never fear the cold email! She arrived in a shimmery dress with her sister Susan. She was so sweet and gracious and the guys were completely taken by her. Idris Elba and Clive Owen were also in attendance. The show was great but the after-party was amazing.

It was a lavish affair. There was a huge cake, magnums of champagne, and beautiful women in bustiers, shorts, and heels walking around serving everyone drinks. I kept asking the DJ to play "Put Your Records On" and he finally did it after I went to him for the nth time and said, "Listen, it's RZA's birthday party and he wants to hear the song and Corinne

Bailey Rae is here." We all danced up a storm, including RZA. She told RZA that it was the first time she'd heard her song in a club! I was very proud of that moment.

Late into the evening, or, rather, early into the morning, Ghost, Meth, Killa, U God, Sam, and I went back and hung out in the hotel lobby. I sat next to Ghost, who was being super attentive and sweet. He said, "Soph, I'm gonna give you this hat. It's a really special hat: Halle Berry touched it." And he gave me a New Era kelly-green NYC skyline cap. I treasure it to this day. And he'll ask me about it from time to time. "You still have that hat?" I wonder if he regrets giving it to me. Too bad, he's not getting it back.

Meth went up to his room and got his portable iPod dock. He sat up on the back of a couch and started playing classic R&B songs. The rest of the guys were saying, "Oh, shit, that's my jam" or "Damn, you killed that one, Meth!" Then they got into a competition, trying to outdo each other with the hits, passing the little dock around. We sat there listening to Marvin, Al, Stevie, the Isleys, the Temps until the sun came up. It was magical.

The next day the guys had a bunch of press. Nobody likes press days. They are so fucking monotonous. The label and the artist's publicist set up a string of consecutive ten- or fifteen-minute interviews that last for hours. What makes the day so long is that everybody asks the same boring questions. Luckily for the Clan, there were nine of them, but writers almost always wanted to talk to Meth, and he was such a good sport about it. I parked myself in Meth's room and sat across from him quietly as he graciously answered every shallow question.

He was his usual goofy self. He was using a black Sharpie to draw faces on mandarin oranges and kept showing them to me across the room. I had to stifle my laughter because the interviews were being recorded. He loves an audience, especially one as captive as Sophia Chang, who thinks he can do no wrong.

At one point RZA came into the room to do an interview, so Meth decided to take a shower. He said, "Come on, Sophie, come in here with me!" He got into the shower and talked and made me laugh the whole time. If it was any other man, I would have taken it as a come-on, and if it were any other woman, it probably would have been, but not with Meth and me. It was totally normal. I remember thinking how many women would love to be in that bathroom and pull back that shower curtain, but there was no part of me that wanted to see him naked. The thought of it was and remains quite appalling, frankly.

Later July the same year, the Clan performed at Rock the Bells at Randall's Island. I was wearing a backless navy Indian cotton top that tied across the back, tight jean culottes, and navy espadrilles. This is around the time that Raekwon started saying "Miss Chang got them legs out!" in a warning tone that bordered on disapproval. I think they were all grappling with seeing me in a different light. Before that show one of the members of the Clan came up to me and confessed, "Pardon me, Sophia, but I've been thinking about you differently lately." It was so polite and honest. I answered the question at the show the next day. I walked up to him and said, "I should have told you yesterday. You're probably seeing me in a different light because I'm single now." Once again, shock.

As requested, all the guys in the Clan circled their tall imposing wagons around me, but no one quite as ardently as Meth. He had me ride on his bus from San Bernardino to San Francisco for the next show. I felt warm and comfortable and safe.

Just as the other Clan member told me he had started seeing me differently, I actually started thinking of my body-guard romantically, though I wasn't remotely attracted to him. That was the summer of Corinne Bailey Rae and the song that spoke to me in this moment was "Breathless." Then one day Meth predicted: "Sophie, he's gonna be someone you've known for years. He's right under your nose and you'll just start looking at him differently one day. He's been watching you, but he's too scared to say anything because it might ruin the friendship. And you'll look back and start analyzing everything."

A few months later a bunch of the guys in the Clan attended the *American Gangster* premiere at the Apollo Theater. RZA had a great role playing an undercover cop alongside Russell Crowe. That night I wore my Gucci fedora, a revealing Vivienne Tam tiger-print halter top, Prada black patent wedges, and some very short shorts. It is also entirely conceivable that I wore a layer of baby oil on my legs as well. It was fall, so I wore a Vivienne Tam embossed black satin padded trench. When we got to the after-party, which was a huge affair, I took off the coat and Meth was standing right in front of me. He looked down at my bare legs and his eyes widened in disbelief and, like Rae, semi-disapproval, as if he were looking at his little sister about to hit the town. Always the protector. When we said goodbye in the street, as he was getting into his car he said sternly, "You be careful out here, Sophie."

I hadn't seen much of Chris while I was with Yan Ming. He hadn't even invited me to his wedding, a huge affair in Miami attended by A-list artists and industry brass. I was neither, but still. If I wasn't important enough to be invited to his wedding, I had receded too far from his heart, and I was crushed. Now I needed his support and love. I wanted him back in my life. I started calling him more frequently and going to his office, which was the easiest place to see him. I wanted the big male energy of Chris and the Clan to surround me again now that Yan Ming was gone.

After a visit to Chris's office, he offered me a ride home. We walked to the parking lot across the street and got into his big, shiny black Bentley. As we made the drive from Chelsea to Alphabet City, we laughed about the time he had shown me where he hid his gun in his Range Rover and other moments we'd shared. As we turned right onto Avenue C from Fourteenth, I took a deep breath and said, "Why didn't you invite me to your wedding, Chris? That really hurt my feelings."

"Soph, you were invited! I couldn't believe you didn't show! Even your old partner Denise was there. How could you not have come?"

"I never got the invitation!"

We figured that it had gotten lost in the mail. I am so

thankful that we had the conversation, otherwise we would have both carried this disappointment and sadness with us. He told me he wanted me to meet his wife.

"Look, Soph, you and Joan are the only two women from my past who mean anything to me anymore, and it's really important that you meet her."

"I'd love to, of course!"

Eventually, I met her and didn't see the fit but vowed to love her because he so clearly did. I was grateful that he wanted me to be a part of his life, as I wanted him to be part of mine. I attended his fortieth, my kids and I went to his son's fifth birthday party and watched the fireworks with his family, and he and his wife came to my birthday dinner. I cherished every single minute with him. I felt reassured that, now that we'd reconnected, we'd never be apart again, we'd be friends until we were old and graying but happy, laughing about the ridiculousness of artists, still amazed by how far he'd come from his childhood in the BX, and beaming about our grandchildren.

As ludicrous as artists could be, Chris and I loved working with great talent and would go so hard for our artists. In spring 2007, I was in LA on B-Hive business and ran into Raphael Saadiq at a café. I introduced myself and asked if he'd ever thought about scoring, and he said he had. I arranged for Michael and me to visit his studio the next day. Being there reminded me of the Paul Simon days; it was a full-fledged recording facility. He led us to the A room, the big room. I settled into a black office chair and swiveled around slowly, surveying the décor: the wood-paneled walls, green velvet couches, countless instruments, and big-ass speakers.

"Do you wanna hear my new album?" Raphael asked.

"Of course!" Michael volunteered.

Raphael walked over to the Mac laptop next to the board and scrolled through his iTunes and hit the space bar. I was not prepared for what would come out of those big-ass speakers.

It was a song called "Sure Hope You Mean It," the opening track to his album *The Way I See It*. It was Raphael's homage to Motown and, in my opinion, his magnum opus. Everything sounded familiar yet fresh, analog, a little imperfect, and dirty in the best way. I hadn't been inspired by new music in so long. I'd heard that most people stop exploring music at thirty, which was definitely the case for me. Raphael single-handedly gave me back the gift of music. He reminded me how deeply it can touch me if I connect with it, and how hard I'll go to champion it, if given the opportunity.

After listening to the album, Michael and I proposed to Raphael that we manage his entire career, not just composing, and he agreed. Co-managing with Michael was the perfect arrangement. I happily took on the day-to-day, which was below his pay grade, though he would never have called it that, but I wasn't simply his mouthpiece. We had daily conversations about every aspect of Raphael's career and arrived at conclusions together. Michael valued my opinion and empowered me to lead many initiatives, discussions, and negotiations. But when certain big issues arose, Michael stepped in and spoke to the label president, who wouldn't necessarily respond to me.

I hadn't managed an artist at a major label since ODB. I had to win over the team, because everyone at the labels was overworked since the industry had collapsed with the advent of digital. The job that had once been done by two people at two different labels was now done by one. There were still constant rumors of staff cuts that had everyone dreading the call from HR. In this environment of extreme corporate paranoia, people resorted to backstabbing, credit stealing, and throwing colleagues under the bus in an effort to keep their jobs. *I am so glad I don't have to deal with this shit*, I thought. I would come to eat those words.

Raphael provided me with a soundtrack to the next stage of my single life. He had just produced an album for the British songstress Joss Stone. One of the songs, "Bruised but Not Broken," became my anthem in the early days of being on my own. I was down, but not for the count, not by any stretch. I still had fight and fire in me and, I would come to learn, a deep, burning sexuality that just needed a little tinder to set the blaze.

On a cold January night in 2008, I went out on my own, which I never do, but a friend from out of town was DJing at this club. I put on a T-shirt, jeans, and cowboy boots. To my chagrin, when I arrived, I saw that everyone was in tuxes and gowns. I didn't realize it was the after-party for a gala! As I stood scanning the crowd for a familiar face, I was relieved to see another loner who also apparently didn't get the memo about the dress code. Derek was sitting in a booth, wearing a plaid shirt, his arm in a cast. He looked vaguely familiar. I walked up to him and asked, "What the fuck are you doing in a crowded club with a cast on?" And then I realized he was an actor whom I'd just seen in a movie. He was also in a very popular TV show that everyone else in the world but me had seen. He was funny, smart, handsome, and down to earth. We left the club and walked to Madison Square Park, where we sat on a cold wooden bench, the warmth of our breath pluming out of our mouths as we spoke, in a hurry to get to know each other.

He asked countless questions, which was so refreshing after having spent the last twelve years talking mostly about Yan Ming. He was particularly curious about my kids, which was very endearing. Over the next few weeks, we saw each other as much as possible. He would call if he was in the neighborhood just to walk a few blocks together as he was on the way to work. I would ride the train with him just to steal a standing kiss in the bumpy cars.

The first time we were alone in private, he watched as I took my clothes off and said, "Wow, you have a great body." He would continue to tell me so throughout the night. It occurred to me that my ex had never said that to me in the twelve years we'd been together. That's not an indictment, it just wasn't in his culture or character. But damn, it felt good. I realized that I'd been starving for this kind of affirmation.

Early on, Derek said, "I'm pretty sure we're going to sleep together, and I want to let you know that I'm seeing other women." I appreciated his candor and responded in kind.

"Do I strike you as the kind of woman who cares? And I'll assume you want to know if I'm seeing other men?"

He covered his ears and said, "No, no, no. I don't want to know!" This would become a major issue.

The first night we had sex, I had been celibate for fifteen months and was nervous. Once the kids were in bed, I got ready. I put on a simple black camisole and a purple silk ruffled skirt—the abundance of shimmery fabric created a dramatic silhouette. When Derek arrived at the door, he raised his eyebrows and told me I looked beautiful. We sat around watching TV, then started kissing. It wasn't long before the multiple folds of silk were up around my body, and he was inside of me. *This*, I thought, *is fucking. And I want more of it.*

Luckily, the family of one of Jin Long's classmates was moving out of their rent-stabilized apartment. My income had to fall within a certain window and I made it. It was a 750-square-foot two-bedroom apartment on Eighth Street between Avenues C and D, just a five-minute walk to the kids' school. It was a major downgrade in terms of size and neighborhood, but I loved it and it was time to move out.

Chris had advised me to marry a millionaire, which came to resonate deeply with me. Without a doubt, the most stressful part of single motherhood was being the sole breadwinner.

Even with the work that I hustled up, my parents had to send me money every month. Like clockwork, an envelope would arrive on the fifteenth and there would be a money order wrapped in a carefully handwritten note with only a few heartwarming words like, "We hope you're well, Sophia. Love, Mom and Dad." If you had told me that at forty-three my parents would be helping me pay the rent, I would have said you were crazy. But here I was, broke as fuck. I hadn't thought to ask Yan Ming to help support me. The arrangement was simple: I had the kids for four days, he for three, and each of us would pay for everything during those times. Thank God they had to wear uniforms until eighth grade, and the school sold secondhand shirts and pants for only five dollars apiece. I darned socks and bought a sewing machine so that I could hem our pants and patch up the knees that Jin Long inevitably ripped through as he played with his classmates. All this in addition to the shit that we Asian immigrants do, regardless of how much money we have: cleaning and reusing Ziplocs, drying and reusing paper towels, tearing the halves in half, cutting the bottom of the toothpaste tube to squeeze out that last little bit.

There were dozens of tiny sacrifices. Takeout and eating out were things of the past. I cooked three meals a day, seven days a week. I would peer through the windows of restaurants at the laughing, carefree diners and wonder, *Who the fuck are you people and how can you afford to eat out?* Whole Foods and FreshDirect were replaced by Trader Joe's, and the rare times we went to the movies were before noon at the AMC Theatres, when the tickets were half-price and we'd sneak snacks in. Gone were cabs and car services, which made getting around to various social engagements more challenging.

When I was a teen, I whined about a pair of designer jeans my mother wouldn't buy me. She said, "I can hardly wait until you know how hard it is to earn one dollar." It's funny how statements stay with you for no apparent reason until they return to kick you in the ass. Thirty years later, I had less than three hundred dollars in the bank, and I was counting every fucking penny. I had a nest egg from selling an apartment, but I didn't want to touch it because I knew I could do without and might well need it in an emergency. I spoke openly to the kids about money. It was important to instill in my children a sense of how incredibly privileged we were, despite our small sacrifices. Every night, we said a prayer of gratitude: "I'm grateful for bountiful food, clean water, shelter, my health and that of my friends and family, and that I have the best family in the world that loves me so much." My passions were forced to play distant lovers to my immediate financial responsibilities. My primary concern was keeping the kids happy and making them comfortable with our more modest lifestyle.

Now that I was on my own, it also became clear that I had to make the children feel safe. One day, Jian Hong asked if I'd met R. Kelly and what he was like.

"He's not a good person."

"Why?"

"He just isn't."

A few weeks later, R. Kelly apparently came up in conversation at the temple.

"My mommy says that he's not a good person," Jian Hong chimed in. Then, for some reason far beyond my ken, one of Yan Ming's disciples chose to elaborate.

"That's because he pees on little girls."

That statement freaked her out so much that she came home and told me right away. Outraged, I called Yan Ming. He, too, was upset and promised he would deal with the guy.

I assured Jian Hong that Daddy would take care of it, but I wasn't so sure, based on his past behavior. For a few Sundays, Jian Hong would come home and tell me her father hadn't said anything. I stayed my hand.

A few weeks later, the kids went to Yan Ming's temple upstate. This same disciple told my daughter that a dog had pissed in her soup while she wasn't looking.

Okay, time for Mommy to regulate.

The next weekend, I went to the temple during lunchtime. I stepped into the doorway without even removing my shoes. I spotted the disciple and signaled him over. He followed me out into the staircase and I took a deep breath.

"*Amituofo*, Sophia!" he said, greeting me with the Buddhist blessing.

"*Amituofo*. Please tell me it's not true that you told my daughter that R. Kelly pees on little girls."

His face fell immediately in recognition and shame.

"And that you told her that a dog had peed in her soup."

"I—I'm so sorry, Sophia!"

Too little, too late.

"*Have you lost your fucking mind?* This means that you have had two urine-related conversations with my daughter. She's five! She now has the image of a grown man peeing on little girls and has to try and figure out what that means. Don't you ever talk to my daughter again. Don't even look at her. Stay the fuck away from her, or I'll destroy you."

Sometimes, the kids were witness to my wrath. On a trip to Vancouver that summer, the kids and I went to Granville Island, a large public market. As I was about to park, another car tried to take our spot, but I swooped in before he had the chance. When we got out, the driver, a Korean man, and his family were waiting. He was red in the face and started yelling that I'd taken his spot. I got right in his grill and yelled back. His wife dragged him away. When I turned around, my kids were visibly shaken. They thought the man might hit me. I had no idea my actions would have that effect on them. I told them, "Guys, I would never put you or myself in danger. I knew he wouldn't do anything." But the damage was done. Of course, they had a visceral response: If I got hurt, who would be there to protect them?

Since then, I have continually told my children that I will protect them and be there for them, no matter what. Safety is paramount, happiness secondary. When Jian Hong and I speak about this experience now, she's grateful. "Mommy, I'm glad you did what you did. It taught me that I need to stand up for myself!" It was critical that my kids learn to stick up for themselves. I told their teachers, "I know you have a policy about hitting, but you should know that I am the mother who tells her kids to hit back. And if you send them home for the day, I'll pick them up and treat them to ice cream."

When Jin Long was seven, I enrolled him in soccer at Chelsea Piers. There was a white boy in the class who was pushing everyone around. During the break, I told Jin Long, "If that boy comes near you, I want you to kick him as hard as you can." My little angel looked up at me, startled. That's so not in his nature, but he knew Mommy was dead serious. "I am your mother. I don't care what anyone else here says, and if they have something to say, they can say it to me."

He ran back onto the Astroturf and I secretly hoped that the kid would try some shit again. And try he did, but before he could get his hands on my boy, Jin Long kicked him as hard as he could in the shins. The boy burst into tears. When the coach stopped the game, I told him, "I want you to know that I told my son to kick that boy as hard as he could, because I saw him pushing everyone around." The teacher was surprised by my admission but didn't disagree.

Jian Hong, on the other hand, much more like her mother, needed no coaching. There was a boy at preschool who chased her around every day, asking her to be his girlfriend. She used to scramble to the top of the jungle gym to avoid him. One day, she got fed up and punched him square in the face, giving him a nosebleed and causing him to cry. That's my fucking girl. We still laugh about this story. Neither with an iota of shame.

Teaching my kids to advocate for and defend themselves meant they learned to do it on behalf of others as well. They defended the bullied and invited them to their birthday parties to make them feel included. Jian Hong once told me about a boy whom everyone made fun of and how she cheered him on loudly at a track and field event, which made him so happy. My kids are good, kind, just, empathetic people and that's all that really matters. That's my job as a mother. To make good people who take it upon themselves to help others.

I always told my kids, "I am your mother first, not your friend. You will have hundreds of friends in your lifetime but only one mother." Being the bad cop isn't as fun as being the buddy, but I could never abdicate that paramount responsibility as the caretaker. I started yelling at Jin Long about his grades in middle school and didn't stop until he graduated from high school. It was a huge source of anxiety.

I'm so thankful that I continued to train, so that I had a way to work out the stress. And grateful for sex, which I had once thought I no longer needed but now craved more than ever. Twelve years with Yan Ming had quietly eroded my sexual self-confidence. I needed to build back my foundation, dick and mortar.

Derek was particularly interested in how many men I'd been with and asked a number of times. I refused to answer because there is no good answer to that, short of "one." When I told Q-Tip that Derek wanted to know, he said, "You should tell him if you like him, Soph. It'll show him that you care." So I did. A few months after I told him, we were at my place and I was telling him that I'd never been drunk or high. Without an ounce of hesitation, he shot back, "Oh, so you fucked all those men sober?"

Mo-ther-fu-cker. This was precisely why I didn't want to tell him, because he took the number and weaponized it against me. When I had asked him the same question, he had no idea how many women he'd been with and I didn't care. *Hold up, so you want me to give you my precise tally but you don't even keep track?* What kind of fucking patriarchal bullshit is that? For real. I am so sick of women being asked this question and judged for the answer. I hereby announce to the world that my dick index is seventy. I have fucked seventy men. I am not proud of that number, but I swear on everything that is sacred and profane that I'm not fucking ashamed, either. Call me what you will, but know that I don't care. Women should be able to own their sexuality and number without being considered whores. If it's a turnoff for men that women have had multiple lovers, that should be their problem, not ours. *Go take your insecure dicks somewhere else, you bitchass motherfuckers.*

Eventually, I would sleep with someone other than Derek. It started via the wonder of fiber optics. Late one night, I got a call from James, an artist friend whom I'd known for a while. The sexual tension had been mounting between us of late. He was in the studio and apparently needed some inspiration.

"Soph, I bet you're one of those nasty girls who has naked pictures of herself."

Luckily, just months before, I had asked my girl Linda Chinfen to take nudes of me after a friend had showed me a picture of herself peeking out of a bed sheet that she had sent to a man. *How audacious and fun!* Linda set up lights in her room while I undressed and lay on my stomach. She proceeded to take hundreds of nudes of me on the crisp white sheets atop her bed. I had taken tens of thousands of pictures and had so few of me. Always the photographer, never the subject. Now here I was, in my very own photo shoot. It was easy and empowering and the results were beautiful. The intention wasn't to share them with anyone; I wanted to memorialize how my body looked after twenty-two years of kung fu. But once I crossed the Rubicon with James, I would come to take thousands of revealing photos of myself that became indispensable tricks of my trade.

James and I proceeded to have awesome phone sex.

When I told him it was my first time, he didn't believe me. I don't know where it came from, but come it did. We would continue this practice for months late at night, once the kids were asleep, and early in the morning after drop-off. That virgin foray into phone sex opened my eyes to a world of possibilities, straddling the intersection of dick and tech. After that, I explored all virtual media: texting, Skype, BBM, DMs. I got to the point where I would be sexting while grocery shopping at Trader Joe's. Broccoli, onions, "I miss that dick in my mouth," bagels, cheddar, "I want you to suck on my clit," you get the picture. You might say that this little red Corvette can go from zero to sexty in under three seconds.

James and I eventually found ourselves in the same city and had actual sex. I figured I should tell Derek. When he heard the news, he said that I'd promised to tell him before it happened. Now, I know that memories are faulty, mine is no exception, but there is no fucking way I would have agreed to that. Not only because it's none of his fucking business, but also, the impracticality. At exactly which point would I make that call? When I was giving head, was I supposed to pull a dick out of my mouth and say, "Excuse me, I've just gotta shoot someone a text"?

The juggling act between the men, the kids, chairing the School Leadership Team, work, and the gym was no small feat. Single mothers make Cirque du Soleil look like toddler fucking gymnastics. When Jin Long was a baby I would be nursing him while talking business on a cordless headset and preparing dinner. No way could a man do what we do. No goddamn way. The tightrope walk on a unicycle while twirl-ing plates became all the more intense leading up to the re-lease of Raphael's album. I was on the phone and emailing sixteen hours a day and it was energizing. We could feel the anticipation for the album.

For some unknown reason, Raphael asked to be copied on every email I sent to the label. I'd never had an artist ask that of me. They usually wanted to stay well out of the fray. The manager's job was to be the front line. When I told Chris about his request, he said, "That's not a good sign. Don't do it, Soph. He'll take over the conversations and you'll be out." I didn't want to believe him. I believed in the project so pas-sionately and could not imagine not being a part of the team to see it through its cycle.

The album came out in September 2008 and was a huge success. It was critically acclaimed, and a number of the tracks were used multiple times in TV and film. Seeing my hard work pay off was so rewarding. I secured Raphael a perfor-mance on the first season of the long-running series *Live from the Artists Den* through an old friend, Alan Light. The week before Thanksgiving, Michael called me, and I could imme-diately hear reluctance in his voice. He told me that Raphael didn't want me to be part of his team anymore because I was too aggressive. *Wow.* This was the first time I'd been fired. What made it worse was that I considered Raphael a friend. The fact that he didn't do it himself deepened the hurt and humiliation. When I told Chris what had happened, he could have said, "I told you so," but he said, "This music shit is for the birds, Soph. You'll be fine."

I told Michael I didn't think I should go to the taping of *Live from the Artists Den.* He disagreed, telling me, "Soph, you deserve to be there more than anyone else. You got him that show. You walk in there with your head held high, like the princess you are!" Even with those beautiful words of love and support, I couldn't bring myself to go. I was too embarrassed to see everyone and act as if nothing had happened. It was agonizing to be fired, but managing Raphael so closely with Michael taught me a lot about the current state of the major labels and about myself.

Later, someone suggested that I'd been fired because I was a woman. It made sense when I thought about being called "too aggressive." Looking back on how I behaved, there's little to nothing I would have changed. I have been called a bull in a china shop, but that characterization is inextricably linked to my being an Asian woman who is expected to be anything but. I am extremely calculated in my actions and words and sometimes willing to take the risk of offending someone to achieve the desired outcome. And of course, there are times that I overstep.

A friend once told me, "Sophia, the thing with you is that you know that you are always the smartest person in the room, and you want everyone to know it. In the thirty years that I've been negotiating contracts, I've had the leverage 90 percent of the time and knew I was going to get what I wanted, but went along with the back and forth so that the other side never felt stupid." That was a tough lesson for me. That impulse to show how smart I am, though obnoxious, is born of being a small Asian woman who's easily overlooked. As difficult as it can be, I've learned to keep my mouth shut and let others speak until it's the right moment to make my point. There are also occasions when I'm sitting in on meetings as a guest and choose not to proffer an opinion unless I'm asked. One such occasion turned into a job for me.

In February 2009, a friend invited me along to a meeting he was having at a digital agency called Sarkissian Mason. The men at the table discussed building a luxury shopping site. At one point, the owner of the company, Patrick Sarkissian, said, "Why don't we ask the woman in the room? Sophia, what do you think?" I asked some questions before explaining how I shopped and what I looked for in an online store. By the end of the meeting, Patrick invited me to Vegas the next week to meet the clients. I knew nothing about digital retail or building websites, but fuck it, let's go! And just like that, I had another revenue stream.

A few months after I'd started, Patrick told me he was talking to Chris about collaborating on a client. Chris said, "She's really creative" when Patrick mentioned my name. When I first heard that, it felt as if he were reaching for something nice to say, but I should have known better. Chris chose his words carefully, especially when he knew they would have an impact, as these did, on my new boss. I now truly appreciate what he meant. Creativity doesn't always result in art, and my innovative approach to management and hustles *were* creative. I could be creative in ideas for my clients, but also in terms of how to get to a certain destination. Being scrappy and resourceful, in addition to being innovative, was a powerful combination. Thank you, Chris, for seeing something in me before I saw it in myself.

The gig at Sarkissian Mason didn't last long, so it was back to the grind for money. I loved my freedom, but the life of a freelancer is a constant financial roller coaster that has you dreading the first of the month. Hustling so hard for money also left me little time and energy to help the kids with their schoolwork. During fourth-grade orientation, Jin Long's teacher announced solemnly to the parents, "At this point, you shouldn't be helping your kids with their homework anymore. They need to learn to be independent." All the couples looked at each other with concern. I wanted to run victory laps around that classroom with my hands up in the air, yelling, "GOOOAALL!" Remember the show *Are You Smarter Than a 5th Grader?* Well, I'm not smarter than a fucking fourth grader.

Around the same time, Hua Hsu, an amazing writer whom Heesok had hired at Vassar, invited me to be on a panel about race sponsored by the school's Asian American students group. Right before we went into the classroom, Hua said, "Sophia should just do all the talking because she's the only one with any real-world experience here." I was reminded of my New Music Seminar days and how much I enjoyed public speaking. I had spent the last several years finding platforms and outlets for Yan Ming, neglecting my own voice.

While I was amplifying my voice to the public, I was muzzling it with one of my closest friends. Toward the end of 2009, things started to get inexplicably tense between Joan and me. She called out my privilege, which, frankly, probably needed to be checked. But it felt like she was contradicting everything I said, to the point where I was walking on eggshells around her. She had given me constructive criticism in the past, but this felt different. Gone was the gentle brilliance that had guided me for so long. She seemed resentful, even angry, and I didn't know what I had done to bring this on. It was painful because not only had I trusted Joan implicitly to help me read situations and tell me how to navigate them, but also I had learned so much about race and gender from her. She had always made me feel like I was one of us, but now I felt like one of them.

Under the strain, our friendship would fracture completely a year later. I had been insensitive about the death of her dog and, despite my apologies, that was the breaking point for her. After so many years of friendship, I realized that it might be time for this one to draw to a close. We had mutual friends but never found ourselves in the same spaces. It would take something much more weighty than social circumstances to bring us back together.

As I was losing one of my best friends, I gained my best client. I started managing GZA in spring 2011. He became the client that I managed longest and was by far the most gracious, generous, and grateful. For his Bonnaroo performance, he wanted to perform *Liquid Swords*, his first solo album—largely considered the best Wu-Tang solo effort—with a live band, an ambitious endeavor. We teamed up with Grupo Fantasma, a Grammy Award–winning Latin funk band from Austin. The show was incredible.

The next day, when we parted ways at the Austin airport, GZA said, "Thanks, Soph, we did it." The managers out there will be shocked by two of the five words in that brief statement, the first being *thanks*. That might sound crazy, but managing talent is a thankless job because most artists are so narcissistic it's hard for them to say the thing we are all taught to say from childhood. The more powerful word was the simple two-letter first-person plural pronoun *we*. I almost cried because it demonstrated that GZA recognized how much work I had put in and saw me as his partner. Another super-rare thing that GZA said on the regular was "Soph, do I owe you any money?" I'll give you a fucking G if you ever hear that one uttered from an artist's lips.

When GZA and I worked together, he was in his mid-forties. Though he was making plenty of money doing shows, I wanted to give him another revenue stream for when he would inevitably slow down his touring. I got him started on his lecturing career with the hope that his speaking fees would one day surpass and even replace his show fees. As the child of Korean immigrants, the first school I pitched him to, naturally, was Harvard. A friend put me in touch with the Harvard Black Men's Forum. They were thrilled by the idea. I wrote up a press release, had it sent out, and it ended up being featured in *New York* magazine's "The Approval Matrix" as one of the great things going on that week.

When GZA stepped onto the stage at Harvard, he was not the same artist who had performed thousands of times before to massive crowds. He walked up to the podium, looked humbly into the audience that was waiting with bated breath.

Then the master of ceremonies, one of the greatest rappers of all time, quietly uttered three simple words: "I'm really nervous." What followed was an eloquent, poetic talk about his inspiration, love of science, and creative process. He went on to lecture at NYU, Cornell, NASA, Oxford, and many other elite learning institutions. He recently told me that his lecture fees are greater than his show fees. I'm proud that I was able to get his speaking career going, but it took an artist willing to take a risk and make little to no money when he started, in order for it to take off the way it did.

As I watched GZA grow into a public speaker, I found myself yearning to get back to it myself. Luckily, Hua invited me to speak again in March 2012, for the Asian American Writers' Workshop, about the uprisings in LA post–Rodney King. This was the first time I prepared by writing a script for myself. I took a lot of time with it and rehearsed it many times over. My dear friend Elizabeth Méndez Berry came with me and sat in the front row, recording my talk. I loved every minute of it. I posted the video on Facebook and Heesok shared it, saying, "Sophia gives a bravura performance." After I googled *bravura*, I almost cried. He had never voiced such approval of anything I'd ever done. His endorsement fortified my belief that this shouldn't be the last time that I speak publicly. The bug had bitten me for good this time, but it would still take years to fully own this.

This was one of the most difficult periods of my life, but when I surveyed what I was able to achieve during these years, especially how I was able to pick myself up after the end of my marriage, I started to understand how powerful I could be if I combined my passion with my people skills and network and, yes, creativity. It was so rewarding to help an ephemeral idea living in an artist's head transform into a piece of art to be enjoyed by all. I truly believe there's no one out there better than me at helping people tell their stories. It never occurred to me that I would be the artist, and that one day I would aggregate all those skills on my own behalf.

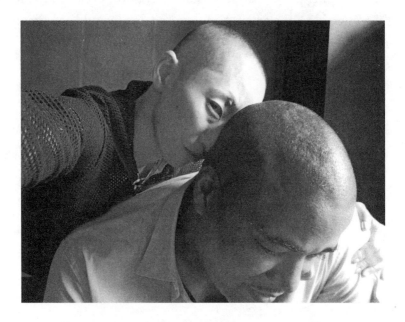

CHAPTER 10
BLINDSIDED

Around 2008, just as I was getting my career at B-Hive off the ground, I started noticing that my father was sleeping an inordinate amount when we went home to visit. I would look at him curled up on the couch and something didn't seem right. He wasn't as energetic with the kids, he didn't cook as much, he didn't join us on all our outings. I told Heesok, "It's like he's dying." Heesok reassured me that he was just getting old. A couple of years later, my parents told us that my father had been diagnosed eight years prior with prostate cancer. Eight years. The delay might surprise you if you don't have Asian parents. Generally, our families don't talk openly about difficult issues, and parents are loath to burden their children. I was upset by the news but not by the time it took my parents to tell us. I can't say I wouldn't do the same. Prostate cancer is one of the more curable cancers, but by the time my father was diagnosed, it had already metastasized.

They chose to tell us because my father's PSA counts were dangerously high. The PSA is the prostate-specific antigen, which is measured to gauge the level of cancer. The first time I went home to see my folks after we'd heard about Dad's illness, I saw a calendar on the dresser in my bedroom. On it my father had marked his PSA numbers every two weeks, whenever he was tested. The numbers got as low as the single digits—four is considered normal range—and as high as the high double digits, which is very scary.

When I told Michael that my father was sick, he told me, "Soph, you need to take your kids to Vancouver to spend as much time with him as possible." He had recently lost his wonderful mother, Evelyn, and understood how meaningful it was for her to spend time with her granddaughters. We took his advice and spent spring break, the month of August, and Christmas in Vancouver. My father, like all grandparents, loved seeing his grandchildren. I scolded the kids once for being too loud around him, and he said, "No, Sophia! I love to hear them laugh and have fun!"

As the years went on, so did the illness. It spread and my father's health declined further. He went through chemo. He lost his beautiful head of hair and his weight dropped dramatically. On a trip to see his oncologist with my mother and Heesok, I told the doctor's assistant, "It's really frustrating that my father won't eat more!"

"Frustrating for whom, Sophia?"

"For us."

"Well, your father has only lost a couple kilos over the last year, and we're not concerned. You might want to think about his quality of life at this point." In other words, "Your father is dying. You might want to stop nagging him." I'll never forget her words. They were so wise. Clearly, she'd seen my behavior countless times before and understood that the patient wants peace in their final weeks, months, or years.

We had set up a bed in the dining room and hung a curtain to create a makeshift bedroom so he wouldn't have to climb the stairs. Toward the end of his life, he suffered dementia. He said something to me about all of his math books that was completely nonsensical, but I loved that even in the twilight of his life, he was still so attached to mathematics. Our house was filled with volumes of incomprehensible mathematics journals. Once he was transferred to the hospital, we would visit him there, and the sight of his grandchildren motivated him to get up and walk around the floor to get some exercise.

On July 12, 2012, I was at a wrap party for the second-season finale of *Project Runway All Stars*, for which I had just produced the fashion show. In the middle of the party, Heesok, who was in Vancouver with my mother and father, called. I couldn't hear a thing above the din. I yelled over the noise that I'd call him back and hung up. When he called right back, I knew what the call was. My father's health had declined precipitously and I had to go home immediately.

I was on a plane the next day and went straight to the hospital. It was a small but clean room with a beautiful view of the mountains. My father was so thin and frail but still somewhat conscious. I spoke to him and told him the kids were great, that they loved him and missed him. I read him passages from Camus's *L'Étranger* and Coelho's *The Alchemist*. On July 16, we were sitting at his bedside. My mother was holding his hand. Everyone was silent and my father was still. At 1:30 p.m., my mother said, "I think Daddy just died." His breathing was so slight, I don't know how she knew it. Yes, I do. That's what happens after a lifetime of love. You feel the last heartbeat of the man you've loved devotedly for over fifty years, because it's your heart too. And a little piece of you leaves with him.

The day of my father's passing, I sent out an email to my closest friends: "At 1:30 p.m. today my father stepped onto the Elysian Fields with grace, peace, and dignity and a merciful lack of pain or discomfort. I love you all dearly. And today of all days I am grateful for and humbled by the love, support, and safety you've all offered me throughout the years." The kids arrived with their auntie Carrie the next day in time for the services. Heesok, the children, and I delivered eulogies. Watching my kids up there, only ten and twelve, speaking in front of a large packed church, made me so proud. They were so calm and self-possessed and delivered beautiful, unadulterated messages of love for my father. Then it was my time to speak:

"Thank you all for coming. We have been overwhelmed by the outpouring of love and support from friends and family. All a testament, of course, to Bomshik Chang. I stand before you today and humbly ask that you bear witness to a daughter's gratitude for the many great gifts that she received from her father.

"Thank you, Dad, for the gift of life.

"Thank you, Dad, for a big brother who has been a true friend and constant mentor.

"Thank you, Dad, for cherishing your wife deeply and wholly, proving that love does conquer all.

"Thank you, Dad, for being a devoted, determined, and disciplined father, informing me as a mother to my two brilliant children.

"Thank you, Dad, for defending the less fortunate or able, arousing my own sense of duty to champion the oppressed.

"Thank you, Dad, for teaching me that being just, fair, and color-blind is not a choice, but an obligation.

"Thank you, Dad, for sharing a deep love of music that led me to my current path.

"Thank you, Dad, for having the courage and strength to overcome adversity, thus opening my heart to the hip-hop artists I've worked with who share the same narrative.

"Thank you, Dad, for believing you could realize your potential, giving me the confidence to foray into worlds unknown.

"Thank you, Dad, for pursuing your passion, mathematics, which inspired me to pursue my aspirations.

"I'd like to leave you with a quote from Paulo Coelho's *The Alchemist* that I read to my father just before he left us to be with the Creator: 'Tell your heart that the fear of suffering is worse than the suffering itself. And that no heart has ever suffered when it goes in search of its dreams, because every second of the search is a second's encounter with God and with eternity.'"

The church was packed. It was heartwarming to see that

my father was so beloved. When we were kids, my folks used to have university students over all the time. My mother would cook for them, and they would drink Crown Royal, and one of them would play the acoustic guitar, and they would sing loudly. It's surely where Heesok and I inherited our love of cooking and hosting. The room was full of these former students and other members of the Korean community. Carrie and her mother had driven up from Washington State for the services. Many of Heesok's and my friends attended as well. They all talked about how hospitable my parents had been to them, and I realized that my parents were unique in this. We hung out at our friends' houses, but none of the parents were as engaged as mine, talking to our friends and cooking for them.

My father was eighty-one when he passed, and despite his grim childhood, he was full of joie de vivre. His oncologist told us that when he was first diagnosed, the prognosis was that he might live another eighteen months to two years. He survived with the illness for thirteen years. Thankfully, my father chose to take a number of experimental drugs, and he benefited greatly from them, even the placebos. Clearly, his will to live was incredibly strong. I'm sure his grandchildren had something to do with that. What I am most grateful for is that he lived to see Jin Long and Jian Hong develop into the people they are now as adults. My mother still tells me that as he was dying he said, "Tell Sophia not to worry about Jin Long, he'll be okay." He knew that I had been stressing about Jin Long's grades. I still find such comfort in those words.

I was met with a deluge of profoundly moving and eloquent words of love from friends. I felt so fortunate to have such an incredible support system. Everyone knew that I didn't grow up surrounded by a big family, and that my immediate family was so important to me. One of the most heartwarming calls I got was from Joan. We had been by each other's sides for every moment, big and small, over the past two decades, and it felt right to hear her voice at this massive juncture. It had been almost three years of us not communicating, and I was sad that it took a tragedy to bring us back together. I knew the next time we spoke, it would be under happier circumstances.

RZA, who had met my father, was so warm and comforting. GZA, with his deep, calm voice, consoled me through the phone as if he were right there in the room with me. When I called Ghost to share the news, I was lying in the twin bed of my childhood, looking up at the cracked, faded, dusty pink paint in the corners of the ceiling.

"Peace!" he said.

"Peace, Ghost," I said weakly.

"Peace, Soph, what's up?" He knew immediately that there was something wrong, because I usually greeted him with something like, "Is this the man of my dreams?"

"My father passed away yesterday," I answered, my voice cracking.

"I know you're sad, Soph, but you can't let him hear you cry, Soph. Because it makes him sad, and he can't let go if he knows you're crying."

"Thanks," I said, only crying harder, "I love you, Ghost."

"Love you too, Soph. You know I'm always there for you. No matter what, if you need me."

The one person I didn't hear from, oddly, was Chris Lighty. He had recently moved into the city. When I went to see his new place he had said, "Soph, I live in Manhattan now, let's go for dinner more." It sounded odd coming from him, because I was always the one to initiate contact. The way he said it almost made it sound as if he was hurt that I hadn't been reaching out to him more.

Once back in New York, I called Chris immediately. For some reason, he hadn't seen the email about my father. We talked on BlackBerry Messenger, his preferred mode of communication, and planned to see each other. His domestic situation had become pretty rocky, and I felt he needed me as much as I needed him. One night a few months prior, we had met at his office. He had an overnight bag and we went for dinner at a nearby sports bar in Chelsea. It was a big, bright restaurant filled with massive flat-screens. We sat and ordered typical sports bar fare: chicken tenders, fries, and so on. Hardly his kind of spot. But it was perfect for this night: quiet, empty, and in the cut.

He told me about a fight he and his wife, Veronica, had gotten into. Sadly, I wasn't surprised. I had seen them together and the energy felt noxious. I noticed that he had started drinking, which I had never seen him do in more than twenty years of friendship. Scott La Rock (rest in peace), his mentor, who only ever partook of orange juice, had taught him to stay sober and levelheaded. It wasn't as if Chris were getting drunk and sloppy, but I feared that he wasn't drinking to loosen up, rather to numb down. I am not here to say that either party was solely at fault. After all, it takes two to tangle. I, of all people, know this.

Chris and I talked about the ways things might get smoothed out, but it felt pretty futile. I know what it feels like when it's too far gone, and I also understand wanting to keep it together, particularly when children are involved. Chris was massively successful and used to beating the odds, but this wasn't about winning, it was about doing it right. He had six children by four women. This was the first woman he had married, that he planned to have a child with, and he was determined to make it work.

To see Chris with his young son, Jaden, his only child with his wife, was heartwarming. I think he looked at Jaden and saw endless hope, which wasn't an emotion common to him. Drive and ambition, yes, but optimism, not so much. I had asked him about his goals on a flight from LA to New York once several years before.

I had just left Yan Ming and the kids with RZA and his family in LA and needed to get back to New York for business. RZA sent me to LAX in a limo, and I felt so sad and alone, leaving my families behind. On the drive to LAX, I thought about how shitty the transcontinental flight would be, crowded in coach. When I approached the Continental counter to check in, who should be standing there but Chris. He asked me where I was going. I told him I was going home but we were flying into different airports.

Without hesitation, he pulled out his American Express Black Card and bought me a first-class ticket on his flight. It had been a while since we'd seen each other, and I relished the thought of six uninterrupted hours with him. When we were on the plane, he told me about some beef that one of his artists was having with another crew. It wasn't just hip-hop diss-you-on-a-track beef, it was bang-bang-shoot-'em-up beef. His offices had been shot up in 2003, and it seemed the feud had escalated from there. I was aghast.

"Chris, when is it enough? You have so much money. My concern about the paper chase is that it's never enough. The more you get, the more you want." I was exasperated and distressed.

"That's not me, Soph. I'm going to do it until I make enough money to take care of the kids. Once I know that they're all set to go to college, I'm out."

"God, I hope so, Chris. This really scares me."

"Don't worry, Soph. I've got this."

I hoisted myself up in the big leather seat, reached across the wide armrest, and curled my scrawny arm around his elbow, cinching it tightly. I rested my prickly, bald head on his big bicep and just lay there silently for a while.

I knew that it wasn't solely about the money for money's sake. Even back in his days of being crime-minded, he told me that he wasn't about the gold chains and fancy cars. He loved the challenge and the power. Now he was driven by his desire to care for his kids. But it felt as if he were on a clock, almost as if he knew he was in some sort of fateful race with time.

At the time of this flight, Jaden hadn't even been born yet. That night in Chelsea, as I listened to him talk about his new family, I could hear how his heart was breaking at the thought of it falling apart. When he started talking about Jaden, his voice changed. I looked up, disquieted by his tone. He dropped his chin and said, "Soph, I've gotta make this work. I can't lose Jaden . . ." And for the first time in the twenty-five years that I'd known him, I saw Chris Lighty cry. I watched just a few tears fall. Maybe it was because of the surreal nature of the moment, maybe it was because his eyes were so big and beautiful, but those teardrops appeared huge, like clear chandelier crystals. I quickly looked down and mechanically started dipping cold fries into the ketchup and eating them.

All I wanted to do was what he had done for me for decades: to shelter him from the storm, to tell him it was all okay, and envelop him so that the outside world couldn't touch him. I told him that everything would be all right, but I didn't know that. I had to find something to say to fill the agonizing silence. I told him there had to be some way to make things better, but I didn't have any suggestions. I wanted nothing more than happiness for this man who meant so much to me, but his life was ever so complicated.

Chris paid and we went to a hotel down the street. He checked in and we went up to the room. It wasn't a fancy hotel, it was something like a Hampton Inn, but it was close to his office and home, where he could have some peace. He was clearly exhausted. He brushed his teeth, changed into a T-shirt and sweats, and got into the crisp queen-size bed. I turned the lights down and sat on the edge of the bed. Chris lay still. Stiller than I'd ever seen him. I held his hand and massaged his big, stubborn forehead until he fell asleep. I let myself out of the room quietly. Just as I was leaving, he said, "Thanks, Soph." It was one of the most intimate moments I'd ever spent with him, and though under unfortunate circumstances, I will cherish it for the rest of my life—because I think I was able to offer him the gift of sanctuary, which he had given to me countless times throughout our friendship.

Some months later, Chris told me that his wife had accused him of being a psychopath. It had clearly upset him.

"You're not a fucking psychopath, Chris. You're not. I don't know a lot about it, but I know enough to know that you're not that!" I hated that someone could make him doubt himself in this way. I couldn't stop thinking about the conversation and emailed him a psychopathy checklist of symptoms with the subject line, "YOU ARE NOT."

He responded: "Hey God bless. Focus on your family and don't worry about me. Your family needs you. I am sorry about your father passing. He is on to a better place."

Something must have happened that afternoon, because he called me the next morning with this message: "Soph, you have to stop emailing me and sending BBMs. Just call me from now on. I don't want to pull you into this shit and for you to be subject to all the negative energy."

"Okay. I want to see you. I need to ask you something and I'd rather do it in person. Can I come by today?"

"Sure, come in the afternoon."

I stopped by in early afternoon after the gym. We sat out in the open area of his office and talked about family and work. After a while he got up. His older son was at the office and they were about to get lunch.

"Soph, come with us to get sandwiches."

As we walked down Sixteenth Street, I told him that I was trying to move into a bigger apartment in my rent-stabilized building. They wouldn't accept my mother as a guarantor because she lived in Canada, so I was wondering if he would mind doing it. It wouldn't involve any money, just a signature. He said he'd get back to me. As we turned the corner and headed west, I noticed that he had talcum powder on his shirt. I hadn't seen it in the office, but outside in the blazing-hot summer sun, I saw the trace of stark white against the solid black of his pristine polo shirt.

"Did you get your head cut today?" I asked, knowing that his barber came to his office two or three times a week to clean up his lines.

"Yeah."

I reached up and lightly dusted the powder off his big shoulder. He didn't even turn his head to see what I was doing. He trusted me like that. He wasn't exactly a warm person and certainly not one for public displays of affection, but he knew I enjoyed and at times needed it, so he wouldn't flinch when I touched him. Grimace perhaps, but never flinch. As we got to the Panera Bread on Union Square East, he turned to me and said, "Come by and see me tomorrow, Soph."

"Okay." I grabbed him around the chest and held him tightly. "I love you, Chris. Thanks for everything."

"See ya, Soph."

I watched him and his son go into Panera, then I walked down Union Square East, my head a little higher, my stride a little longer, my resolve a little stronger, as it always was after I saw Chris. He always gave me a shot of confidence and a sense of invulnerability. I thought it was odd that he asked me to come by again the next day, because we rarely saw each other two days in a row, but I was happy that I'd see him again so soon.

The very next day, August 30, 2012, was a typically hot and muggy New York City summer day. I was having lunch with Elizabeth Méndez Berry, at Angelica Kitchen, the East Village vegan fixture. I planned on going to see Chris after lunch. I was wrestling with the menu, disheartened by the choices, when I saw that Joan was calling. I ignored the call because I thought it could be a mistake, since we hadn't yet re-established contact even after my father's passing. She called again, then sent a text: "Soph, please call me." I excused myself and went outside.

"Hey, Joan, are you okay?"

"It's Chris, Soph, he's in the hospital. He shot himself in the head."

I went numb. "What?"

"Tip called me. He's in a hospital in the Bronx."

"Can we go see him?"

"No, not yet. I'll let you know when I hear back from Tip."

I went back inside and told Elizabeth. We finished lunch and I went to the gym, waiting to hear more. Joan called and said that a mutual acquaintance had posted "RIP Chris Lighty" on Facebook. I called that person immediately. "Hey,

I heard that you posted 'RIP Chris Lighty' on your Facebook page. Will you please take it down?"

"Why should I?"

"Because I know that Chris wouldn't want it up on a Facebook page."

"Well, I'm not going to take it down because it's true," he said smugly.

I hung up.

My head was reeling, my heart crashing. I was contending with two emotions: the first was anguish, the second was rage at this dumb motherfucker playing Chris's death as some sort of credibility card, as people do in the race to show that they've heard the bad news first and want to announce it to the world. I also knew that Chris didn't even like this guy. I called Michael and GZA and Janet, whom I'd worked with decades before at Jive, to tell them. While I was talking to Janet, I started to break down. I finished my workout, showered, and went home in a daze.

On the morning of September 5, I woke up and checked the weather as I do every other day. Sunny with some clouds, high of eighty-one. But unlike every other summer day, I didn't mindlessly throw on shorts, a tank top, and sneakers to head to the gym. I took my time with each element of my outfit: a black Vivienne Tam crochet dress, black patent leather Prada stilettos, and of course, my Gucci fedora. I took a car up the East Side to the Frank E. Campbell Funeral Chapel, where I met Bethann Hardison and Janet. The streets were packed. When they let us in, the hallways and room were packed. Like so many shows he had been a part of, it was standing room only. Mona Scott, who had worked with Chris and went on to create the hugely successful *Love & Hip Hop* TV franchise, spotted us and escorted us to the front of the line.

As we approached the casket, my heart started to drop. Thank God Bethann and Janet were on either side of me, because my body crumpled when I saw Chris lying there in his dark suit, asleep for eternity. In that split second, I suddenly had the agonizing realization that I would never hug him again, never cry on his shoulder again, never hear his laugh again, and it broke me. I burst into tears and my knees gave way. Bethann and Janet each grabbed an elbow and supported me down the aisle. Mona seated me with the family. When I saw Jaden, I lost it all over again. He was only five, so young and innocent, and probably barely aware of what was going on.

Afterward Bethann, Janet, Joan, and I walked over to E.A.T. on Madison. We sat outside and didn't exchange many words. Anything that had transpired between Joan and me melted away and seemed meaningless compared to the love we shared for Chris and each other. One of Chris's parting gifts was reuniting us.

I was so glad my mother was staying with the kids and me at that time. I was a mess. She was so sympathetic. One night, I stood in front of the hallway closet for some inexplicable reason and crumpled to the floor, sobbing. My mother said to my kids, "Your mom is very sad. She lost a really good friend." I asked her if she understood why it was hitting me so much harder than my father's death, and she said, "Of course, he was so young! Daddy was eighty!"

I talked to a number of mutual friends in the wake of Chris's death. Many asked, "How did he seem? Did you notice anything?" because I had seen him less than twenty-four hours prior. If there were signs, I didn't read them. In the past, when he had revealed something troubling, I would probe, but he would quickly change the subject. I don't think he wanted me to see the depths of his despair. I wonder if I didn't push hard enough. But D-Nice, who was very close to Chris, said, "Soph, he gave some to you, some to me, some to other people."

I know all this, but I still hang on to guilt. How did I not see any of the stress that must have been weighing him down so heavily? Why didn't he tell me? I fear that I burdened him unfairly; I so needed him to be my superhero that he must have felt he couldn't disappoint me. And I realize that I was only one of probably scores of people who counted on him the way I did. Big as his shoulders were, how could any one human being support such a heavy load? Believe me, this is not easy for me to talk about. It blows a cold clean hole right back through my heart every time. I do so in the hopes of starting a broader and deeper conversation around the issue of mental health. Perhaps this will encourage someone who's listening to seek help or reach out to a loved one who may be struggling with depression.

Within six weeks, I had lost two of the most important men in my life. But the impacts of their deaths were so dramatically different. My father's passing was a long time coming; we had years to prepare. By the time he left, his quality of life was so drastically diminished that it was almost a relief.

It was like watching a slow steam train approach from the horizon, like a Turner oil painting. We had time to get to the tracks, stand, and wave as it passed lazily by. When Chris died, I felt as if I were blindsided by a bullet train and didn't even realize that I was on the tracks.

What I am grateful for is that I took every opportunity to tell Chris earnestly, explicitly, and vividly how much and why I loved him. I had sent him a note via BlackBerry Messenger on May 13, 2010, just a few days after his forty-second birthday:

"I hope you see yourself now as clearly as I've always seen you: Brilliant, enigmatic, caring, generous, loving, protective, intuitive, sympathetic, empathetic, savvy, insightful, incisive, strong, honest, loyal, ferocious, fearless, bold, forthright, kind, charismatic, funny, charming, laconic, bullish, confident, unflinching, arrogant, analytical . . ."

"I am trying," he responded.

"And above all: GOOD. Truly, inexorably, fundamentally GOOD. Don't ever let someone make you doubt that, Chris. It's at your very core and ultimately motivates you, regardless of whatever else is going on. I will never let you forget. Because I know it."

"Thanks!" he exclaimed.

"No, thanks, Chris, it's what I am bound to you to do. It really really hurts me to see you doubt yourself. Remember today and every day that no matter what you do or where you go. That this little girl with a big big heart loves you with all her might."

I believe it is a primal human need to be loved and a deep

desire to be told that you are loved. The tragic truth is that many of us wait until we're standing at a podium in front of a flower-covered casket to express these sentiments. I implore you to bookmark this page, call someone important to you, and tell them how utterly you love them.

I'll wait.

CHAPTER 11
DOORS OPEN

When I became single, I suddenly had a number of close friends offering me dating advice. Ironically, none of them would be considered stellar in the field themselves.

Before he departed, Chris had said, "Make the next one a millionaire, Soph." In the meantime, he said, "You've done twelve years hard time. Go be Q-Tip. Go fuck whoever you want."

Tip had advice of his own: "Soph, you might want to grow your hair back, you've been rocking that Caesar for a minute now."

When I told Raphael what they had said, he laughed. "Soph, my advice to you is to not let either of those guys be your love coaches. Look, it's not gonna be easy for you to find a man because you're too hard."

"What are you talking about?"

"You're this little woman but have a huge personality. You boss people around, and you're strong as shit."

"So what? That doesn't mean I'm hard!"

"Yes, it does."

Frustrated, I cut the conversation short. Lemme call the man who's known and loved me for years. Who knows that I'm as soft and sweet as cotton candy. He'll make this right, I thought.

"Peace, Soph," Meth's gruff voice said.

"Peace, BFF, I am so mad!" I fumed.

"Why, what happened, Sophie?" he asked, instantly worried.

"I just got off the phone with Raphael, and he had the nerve to tell me that I'm going to have trouble finding another man because I'm too hard! Can you believe it? He just doesn't know me like you do! He hasn't been around me enough!"

No response.

I pulled back the phone to see if we'd been disconnected. "Meth . . . ?"

Two more seconds of excruciating silence followed. Then a deep, deliberate intake of breath, like a long, slow pull on a blunt.

"Well . . . you is kinda hard, Sophie . . ."

"What? What are you talking about? I'm not hard! You've held me so many times and made me feel better! You've seen me cry. You know who I am!"

"Yeah, Sophie, all of that is true, and I know that, but you do be acting kinda hard a lot of the time, so maybe Raphael's right. Maybe a man won't see you like I do."

I thought I'd learned the lesson to let my guard down, to let the soft balance out the hard, like in Taiji. Twenty years before, I had had a similar talk with my friend Benny Medina. It was a picture-perfect Los Angeles day. I drank in the sun, chin up to the blue sky, and let the wind hit my face, my right arm dangling out of his shiny black vintage 450SL drop-top. As we made our way through West Hollywood, the conversation turned to relationships.

"So, what are you looking for in a man, Sophia?"

"Someone who will take care of me and make me feel safe. I run shit and pit-bull all day, Benny, but when I get home, I wanna hang up the Superwoman cape at the door, curl up on my man's lap like a kitten, and have him hold me and say 'It's okay, baby.'"

Silence. I looked across for a response, but his mouth was agape.

"What?"

"I can't believe that's what you're looking for; I never would have guessed it."

I had earned my reputation as an independent, no-nonsense kind of woman who took care of everyone else, and I guess I didn't let anyone see that I, too, wanted to be cared for. If I wanted the relationship I was describing, I'd have to allow myself to be emotionally naked.

One warm fall day in 2012, not long after Chris's passing, my old friend Dominique Trenier (rest in peace) called and said he wanted D'Angelo to train with Yan Ming. No matter what I was feeling about Yan Ming personally, I would never tell someone not to train with him. He gave me D's number and asked me to talk to him about it. I looked at the digits and dialed. The phone rang a couple of times.

"Peace," a voice said, low and soft.

"Peace, D, it's Sophia Chang. Dom asked me to call you."

"Yeah, he told me you'd be calling."

As I lay on my back on my queen-size bed, looking at the sun shining down on Alphabet City, we talked about training before the conversation turned to other topics: loss, Ol' Dirty Bastard, when we'd met before (which I didn't remember, shockingly), music, divine vessels, family, hometowns, church, and so much more. I rolled onto my stomach, propped myself up on my elbows, and looked in the huge mirror that stays by my bed. I studied myself because I wanted to remember how I felt during that conversation.

Back in 1999, when the world gasped at the naked wonder of D'Angelo's body, his palpable sexuality and unmistakable falsetto, Sophia Chang was seven months pregnant. Tasting his brown sugar couldn't have been further from my mind. Of course, I saw the video for "Untitled" and was duly impressed. But I wasn't devouring music as I had before. I hadn't grown up on the rich tradition of R&B that would have given me context to prepare for the stunning arrival of D'Angelo—a man who sang like an angel in a heavenly choir but rocked cornrows like a straight thug. I didn't fall in love with the naked, sweaty, perfectly sculpted D'Angelo. I fell in love with Michael Archer thirteen years and several pounds later. I was entranced and intrigued not by the myth but by the man who revealed himself as being sensitive, empathetic, caring, as well as incredibly funny, phenomenally smart, and deeply intellectually curious.

I remember that first conversation, or rather, how it made me feel (pun intended), as clear as the chords of a Hammond B-3 organ ringing through church on a Sunday morning. There were two things Michael Archer said to me that stood out in particular. The first was "Sophia, I'm a God-fearing man." The second was "I love you," which he said three times in those wondrous ninety minutes. It wasn't the "I love you" of budding romance, but the discovery of a deep, soulful connection. And though I felt the same, I didn't say it. I didn't need to because he knew it.

Our conversations were about so many things: politics, film, TV shows, and, often, music. I would tell him what I was listening to and I even made him a mixtape, actually a mix CD. One of the songs on there was the Rolling Stones' "Beast of Burden." D talked about the fact that most people focused on Keith Richards's lead guitar riff, but that it was Ron Wood's rhythm strums that were the soul of the song. I had been listening to the song for thirty-five years and never heard it like that and never will again.

Of the many privileges I enjoy from working with talent—free weed, ample pussy, and VIP access being none of them—the greatest is hearing them perform just for me. Whether it's Meth rapping a cappella the lyrics he's going to use in Jim Jarmusch's film *Paterson*, or Raphael Saadiq leaning close to my ear in a noisy restaurant to sing the Isleys' version of

"Hello, It's Me" as he hears the original Todd Rundgren version for the first time. But the most magical of these moments happened late at night as I lay in bed. Long past midnight, D'Angelo woke me out of my deep slumber and we started talking about music again and I told him that I had been listening to one of my favorite songs of all time, "Never Too Much" by Luther Vandross. He said he loved the song too. Then he—I gasp just thinking about it—sang me the song from the second verse through the last chorus and every single ad lib. Flawlessly. And hearing D'Angelo croon his way through "Never Too Much" was almost too much. Go listen now and imagine D singing it.

The universe had kept D'Angelo and me separated for decades, now to unite us forever. We can go without talking for months, but we are never apart. He is one of the most expressive people I know and is constantly commending me about things that I don't see in myself. We're friends in a way that we were never lovers, and I think that's for the best. This love is, as Luther Vandross would say, so amazing always and forever.

D'Angelo was put into my life to remind me how it felt to be vulnerable and fall in love, even though we chose to be friends rather than lovers. His gentle spirit, magnificent capacity to love, and sultry tenor pulled back my defenses and compelled me to tune in and listen to my heart. After years of skirting commitment, I was prepared to commit my heart to one man again, with his assistance. There is a special kind of growth that I only achieve when I'm in love and have the emotional intrepidity to allow myself to be truly open. I wasn't looking, but I wasn't blocking anymore either. I've never gone out in search of love. When I have opened my heart to the universe and fully humbled myself before her bounty, she has granted me the gift of love. Question was, now that my heart had been opened, who would step inside?

Just a month after I'd encountered the quiet storm of D'Angelo, there was news of a hurricane headed our way. In my twenty-five years in New York, I'd survived snowstorms, heat waves, and blackouts, but no hurricanes. *How bad could it get?* Two days before Halloween, Hurricane Sandy made landfall and it was catastrophic. The lights went out that night. I put on a brave face for the kids, but for the first time while living in New York, I was truly scared. The building's front door was secured by an electronic buzzer that was no longer working. I pictured midnight marauders coming in to pillage. We lived on the third floor, but I'd seen our super scale the patios up to our floor one day when I was stuck inside because the lock had malfunctioned.

I stepped into the eerily pitch-dark hallway, using my cell phone as a flashlight. I had stood in that exact spot thousands of times before, but never in utter blackness. It now seemed completely foreign. As I moved toward the elevator, I heard an odd sound. As I got closer, I realized it was gushing water, as if there were a waterfall directly behind the doors. I thought if they'd opened, a wall of blood would come cascading out, like in *The Shining*. I rushed back into the apartment, locked and chained the door, lit a candle, and put a ten-inch chef's knife by my bedside. All I could think of was keeping the kids safe. That was one of the longest nights of my life. I barely slept.

The next day, I managed to call Joan on my super's cell. All the major servers were down in the bottom half of Manhattan, but somehow his MetroPCS flip phone was working. God bless him. His eyes were blood red; he hadn't slept or rested at all. Apparently, the noise I heard in the elevator was the water rushing into the basement and flooding the shaft. The kids and I packed some clothes and headed uptown. Lower Manhattan looked postapocalyptic—hundreds of people with huge backpacks and suitcases migrating uptown. We kept walking farther west and north until we finally caught a cab. The Upper West Side looked completely normal. We were so relieved to get to Joan's. We crammed into her studio apartment with her and her son Sule, who was a close friend of the kids, and had a wonderful time cooking and watching movies. It was like a camping trip.

When we were finally able to come back home, we had to throw everything out of the fridge and freezer. That was a huge loss, particularly because among the bounty were three of my mother's famous homemade apple pies. Once we'd settled in, I decided to splurge. I bought flounder fillets as a way to treat the kids and celebrate our return with a special meal. I prepped the fillets their favorite way, just like my mom had taught me: dipped in egg and lightly breaded in flour. They smelled delicious as they sizzled in the mix of butter and olive oil. Just as they had gotten to the perfect golden brown on one side, I knocked the frying pan clean off the stove. My shiny, stainless All-Clad twelve-inch sauté pan that Heesok had bought me for Christmas spun in the air like a fucking ninja star, and the fish splattered all over the floor that Jin Long had just mopped. The kids froze, their eyes wide. All that food and money and effort wasted. I looked at our delicious dinner creating a mess on the newly cleaned hardwood, and dropped to my knees, thoroughly defeated.

"I'm so sick of being off my game. I'm so sick of not being able to take you out for dinner and having to cook every meal," I said, crying.

The kids immediately knelt down, hugged me, and started cleaning.

"What more can we do, Mommy? You already do so much," Jian Hong said. "Do you wanna go for pizza tomorrow night, Mommy? I'll pay!" She was ten. She was willing to spend the money she'd saved up from every birthday card her grandparents had sent her to give me a break. In a flash, my kids turned into caretakers, and I was so proud of them.

This was a low point. Sitting on the floor, crying over spilt fish.

For Christmas, Heesok gave me a small plastic MUJI box filled with twelve envelopes, each labeled with a month of the year and containing a crisp fifty-dollar bill. He called it "The Flounder Fund." He had perfectly embodied the idea that my friend Bethann Hardison, legendary model manager and fashion activist, once told me: "*Family* is a verb."

As we welcomed in the New Year, Michael, who always epitomized the concept of family, presented me with yet another great opportunity. Q-Tip had asked him to be his manager, to which Michael's immediate response was: "On one condition: I get to bring Soph with me."

That's some ride-or-die shit right there. Michael knew that I would be a valuable addition to the team, but he was also looking out for his mentee and her family. Like RZA and GZA, everyone was a Tribe fan, and there was no door that Tip's name couldn't open. However, I didn't have the freedom to knock on as many doors as I wanted because his management comprised a team of four, which limited my purview and commission. Working with Michael was always a dream, but the complications and duplication of efforts were frustrating in this scenario.

The top of 2013 also signaled a shift in my heart that had been catalyzed by D'Angelo. Exactly six years after I'd announced to my shrink my marriage was over, I told myself that I was open to love again. I had enjoyed more than enough paramours to reconstitute my ego and wondered who would be able to pull Excalibur out of the stone and tame this feral filly. I imagined that he would be around fifty, divorced, with kids, like me. I knew it wouldn't make sense to date someone who wanted children. My uterus was permanently closed for business.

I wasn't sure where I would meet my prince, as my social life was still pretty anemic. The one consistent pulse was going to see Q-Tip DJ every week at Output in Williamsburg, just a quick ride over the bridge. I would make sure everything was straight, then dance for hours, often by myself. Kung fu requires discipline and focus. The Sophia Chang who emerges through martial arts is a fearsome warrior. Dancing is the opposite for me—I pay no attention to form, only to rhythm. The Sophia Chang who is released through dance is a liberated lover. Both are forms of meditation and vital components of my being, identity, and self-care.

Likely because my spirit and body are so free when I'm dancing, I've never had trouble meeting men in clubs. I think it's also much easier because I'm not emitting the energy that says I want to get married or have children. Having those milestones behind me changed the dating landscape dramatically. Because I wasn't looking for anything serious, I sashayed with a lot of younger men, who tend to like being with older women because we know our bodies better and say what we want.

I had a lot of good, but not amazing, sex, because it takes time for me to build the trust and create the interbody dynamic that is fully satisfying. And the added component of being in love always deepens the pleasure. But all these men helped me start to see myself as a desirous and desirable woman. I felt empowered to stretch myself sexually and explore new territory. I'm hardly saying I'm some supernatural lover. I think fucking is a water-level sport; I'm only as good as my partner. I'm sure there are men out there who would say I was an underwhelming lover, and that would be true in many cases, because the chemistry wasn't there. However, I will say that when the circumstances are right, I do go above and beyond the call of booty.

One of the great things about getting older is being able to have candid conversations about coitus. My demands are simple: respect and discretion. I have other rules of engagement. I don't fuck with other women's men. It's not a moral thing, it's a messy thing. I don't judge what anyone else does, but I can't stand drama. The thing about me and my girls is that fucking us is never just about pussy. We're the whole package: beauty, confidence, wisdom, and brilliance. Meaning that we don't just linger in your loins, we stay on your minds too. That's a dangerous cocktail for a married man.

Before engaging too deeply, I tell men, "I don't care who you're fucking as long as you're being safe and you keep it out of my house." I also ask these three preemptive questions: "Do you have a wife? Do you have a girlfriend? Is there someone who thinks you're her man?" The final one is important, because men might think they're not attached but have led some poor woman to believe that she is the one. The questions don't guarantee the truth, but at least I've asked and made my own intentions and values clear. At some point, I learned to ask a fourth: "Do you have a pregnant ex?" Because I walked into this situation . . . twice. Not once, twice. Yo, men are foul. I was ready for a good one.

On November 14, 2013, I attended a friend's birthday party at a swank hotel penthouse on the Upper East Side with my friend J.Period. The invitation said "formal," which seemed odd for a birthday party, but I complied, having no shortage of gear to suit the occasion. I was in black from the top down: my Gucci brim, a silk halter top, a floor-length silk skirt, a fur-collared, satin-embossed jacket, and short boots. The room was full of hip-hop alumni—it was like a high school reunion. I met a couple of cute men and exchanged numbers before J. and I cut out to see Q-Tip DJ in Meatpacking.

When we got back to the party, I noticed some newcomers. One in particular caught my eye. He was sitting slouched on the corner of the couch in a sloppy red beanie, leather jacket, and jeans. Apparently, he hadn't been briefed on the dress code. Despite the hat pulled low over his face and his recumbent posture, I could see that he was handsome, tall, and lean. Just my type. He spotted me making my entrance and watched me hold court. He then stood up, strode over to me, and introduced himself. He got points right there for having cojones.

His name was William. We started talking and I told him that it was really pretty outside, so we went upstairs to the roof deck. We stood looking out at the city in the cold fall air, and it already felt romantic and sexy and grown. Eventually, he asked for my number. He called the next day and said, "I'd like to see you this weekend." Not "What are you doing this weekend?" which I think is some bitch shit that men do to preempt rejection. Look, if you're going to ask me out, walk a straight line, don't take the circuitous route, trying to figure out if I'm busy, or worse, hope that I ask you first. Neither William nor I was interested in games—we never waited for a certain amount of time to respond to a text or didn't call even when we wanted to talk to each other.

We planned to see each other a few days later. I watched as William walked toward me on Eighth Street from Avenue C. I drank in every step: he wore a Gaultier black leather motorcycle jacket and black jeans. He had a confidence and ease in his gait. We went around the corner for dinner. Afterward, he walked me home and kissed me in front of my building. His lips were soft and his hands strong. He held my waist, and I could feel his fingers on the small of my back. I was not going to leave this kiss on the sidewalk, so I invited him upstairs, but it would be a while before we had sex. Usually I wasted no time in getting into bed because that was often all I was looking for, but there was more here. I wanted to wait. One of the things that I loved about William was that he would never push; he always let me set the pace.

After that first date, he asked me what else I wanted to do. I told him I had never walked over the Brooklyn Bridge in the twenty-six years that I'd lived in New York. William called the next day and announced that he had made a plan—we would walk over the bridge to Brooklyn and take a car back. That's what a man does when he wants to send a signal to a woman. When he wants her to know that he's listening and wants to please her. He picked me up and we walked over the bridge. It was a cold, clear day, and we stopped halfway up, like all the tourists, to take a picture. This nascent bond felt substantial, real, like it had a future.

Over the next few weeks, we saw each other once or twice a week and always ended up in my bed. We engaged in lots of sextracurricular activities, but not actual intercourse. I was still seeing a few other men but becoming less interested in anyone else as I became more attached to William. *Shit, did I just say* attached?

I started falling. Hard. And I was straight shook. This would be only my third serious relationship in almost fifty years. He was younger, handsome, charming, and out a lot because he worked in nightlife. I was scared to ask if we were together and exclusive. I kept putting off the conversation, but every time we saw each other, I got in deeper. I had built up so much suspense around the answer that just asking the question felt like a dive off a tall cliff without knowing if there was a net to catch me.

Around mid-December, I started wondering if we would spend New Year's Eve together. It had been years since I'd kissed a man at the stroke of midnight and, more than anything, I wanted to kiss William to bring in 2014. I was ready but not confident enough to ask him. Finally, he asked me what my plans were and invited me to see him DJ at a hotel in Midtown. They had provided him with a room for the night. I wondered if there would be any conspicuously pretty women vying for his attention. Would I walk in to see him chatting up a pretty young thing? I got to the door and took a deep breath as I entered. I saw William before he saw me and let out a sigh of relief. He was focused on his music, looking terribly handsome in a suit and tie. He looked up and a big smile spread across his beautiful lips. I hung out with him at the DJ booth and met some of his friends.

When the countdown to 2014 started, I was standing right next to William. I would not miss this moment for the world. *Ten-nine-eight-seven*, down to *one* when he grabbed me around the waist with both hands and planted a hard, warm kiss on my lips. He kissed me as if to say, *I'm here. I'm here for you and only you.* I closed my eyes and let myself experience this moment for all of its weight. I hoped that I was reading the signals right, but there was only one way to know for sure. Ask.

Shortly after midnight, I went up to his room at the hotel and got into bed. I fell asleep waiting for William. I was awakened by a gentle kiss on my forehead. I looked up, and he said he was going to shower. When he emerged from the shower, I was wide awake with anticipation and excitement. I knew tonight would be the night we would make love for the first time. He climbed into bed next to me, smelling perfectly fresh and completely edible. He leaned over and kissed me, and we fell into each other's bodies as we had done several times before. But this time it was different. I would finally let him in.

I rolled on my back and opened my legs. "Do you have a condom?"

Of course he did. Even in that moment I wondered, *Does he carry one around all the time in case he's going to get a quick fuck?* The thought melted when he kissed me again and I closed my eyes. I opened them to see that he was hovering over me, looking at me. It's time. When he finally did push inside of me, I uttered a long, low gasp that rose from the depths of my heart and soul. I love the breathless moment right before penetration with any man, but with William, it was all the more excruciatingly delicious because I wanted him so badly, and we had taken our time. All the kisses and touches and foreplay led to this one incredible moment that lasted only a second but that I would remember forever.

This first time, and every one thereafter, was easy, organic, and profound. Not only because William's dick game was on point, but also because the richness of the experience was deepened by how much I liked him. As we lay in bed, I finally worked up the nerve to ask him about the elephant in the room. I couldn't even look him in the eye so I waited until he had turned away momentarily.

"Hey, I have to ask: Are you seeing anyone else?"

He turned around and looked straight at me. "No, are you?"

I can't describe my sense of relief.

"No. I'm so glad you aren't because if you were, I would have to leave because I like you too much and I'm in really deep."

Just moments after the end of the year that had started with me saying that I was open to love again, here was William, and we loved each other so hard. He was thoughtful, patient, generous, calm, calming, intuitive, and attentive. He took care of me in a way I hadn't known—perhaps in a way I hadn't allowed. In some ways, being with William was the diametric opposite of my relationship with Yan Ming, who had been the sole focus of my universe before the children arrived. Another striking difference was that William and I never, ever fought. Can you imagine Sophia Chang never fighting? Me neither. This was partly because William was so centered and steady, and partly because I had matured to the point that I didn't blitz headstrong into arguments as I had in previous relationships. There were times I would have welcomed a fight, but he never took the bait. He had an amazing ability to diffuse tension. William taught me to let go.

We had a conversation very early about children. I had announced my policy of not having the baby should I get pregnant. William admitted then that he wanted to have children. I told him I didn't want to be the woman who stopped him. "Sophia, I'm a grown man. I can make my own decisions," he said.

We spent so much time together during the days and

on the weekends when I didn't have the kids. But it wasn't enough. We wanted to be together all the time. That meant he had to meet my kids. The only man who had met my children before was Derek, and that was only once we'd stopped seeing each other. When William met the children, it was uneventful. The kids were now thirteen and fifteen, and it didn't take as much explaining as it would've if they'd been much younger. The fact that they were older also meant that they were more independent and didn't spend that much time around him.

William eventually moved in, though he always kept his own place. Like with Yan Ming, he met everyone in my life and they all loved him. I deleted a bunch of men's numbers from my phone and ignored the wolves at the gate. I was all his.

Right before my first Valentine's Day with William, Michael surprised me with another work opportunity. Universal Music Group was looking for someone to run A&R Administration and Operations. I would oversee all the album budgets on Republic, Def Jam, and Island and work closely with the legal team to secure the necessary clearances to release an album. Budgeting was far from my passion, but the job would provide me with a steady paycheck and great health insurance for the family.

Having had no experience in this area, without Michael's backing I never would have been considered for the position. Despite my own doubts, Michael's faith in me was unshakable. He taught me to trust others' experience and authority if they want to hire me, despite my reservations. Sheryl Sandberg writes about impostor syndrome in *Lean In*, and I am very familiar with this beast. I too have vacillated between being super confident about my qualifications and fearful that someone will expose me as a fraud. I certainly felt this way when I took the job at Jive, leaning more toward feeling like a fake.

Before the interview, I asked Michael what to say about my children, because the music business fully expects people to work long days, nights, and weekends, and I was not down. "All you can do is be up front and honest about it, Soph," he said. During the interview I said, "If this is a job that requires late hours and extensive traveling, you've got the wrong person. I have to be home to spend time with my children. That's more important to me than anything." I also told them I'd never done A&R admin before, but they assured me I'd have a staff and it was my job to oversee the department.

It had been a long time since I'd been in a corporate interview, but I knew what would resonate. They saw a confident, smart, level-headed adult who was up to the challenge. I focused on my strengths rather than my lack of experience. They understood that my vast and varied experience could counter the corporate calcification that sets in with lifers who have become too comfortable with the status quo. Their main issue was that many of the projects were going over budget, and they described the dysfunction at the different labels.

"Do you have children?" I asked.

"Yes."

"Then you'll understand what I mean when I say you have a discipline problem." They looked at each other and smiled. In that moment, I knew I had the job. When, and only when,

I had signed the employment agreement, I called my mother to tell her I had a steady corporate job with a good salary. Not only did I hear her sigh of relief, I'm pretty sure I felt it on my face from across the continent.

Calling my mother with the news was easy; calling GZA to tell him I wouldn't be managing him anymore was agonizing. He didn't make it hard; I did.

"Peace, Jus, I have something to tell you."

"Okay, Soph. Is everything all right?"

"Yes and no. I just got a job offer from Universal and I'm going to take it. The conversations have been going on for a while, but I didn't want to say anything until everything was confirmed. It's a great opportunity for me and the family. I'm so sorry to have to stop managing you, but they won't let me keep any of my clients."

"Oh, okay. That's good, Soph. I'm happy for you."

"I want to thank you for letting me manage you. It's been such an honor and I loved working with you. I love you so much."

"Love you too, Soph."

On my first day at Universal, my staff was brought into my boss's office and I was introduced as the new head of the department. I found out later that none of them saw it coming. They were not at all happy about it, particularly the woman who was the acting head of the department. I don't blame them. It was a clumsy way to introduce me. That afternoon, I sat individually with each member of my team and assured them that I was not hired to clean house and that their jobs were not in jeopardy. I told them my intention was to help them the best I could to optimize their efforts. I asked them to tell me what their workload consisted of, what they would change if they could, and what I could do to make it better. I had an open mind and walked in with a trusting attitude, which was terrifically naïve.

My friends warned me it would be political. I had no fucking idea just how political. I always contend the greatest frailty of any organization, large or small, is poor communication. Universal was no exception. People kept others in the dark because they were either careless or territorial, which resulted in duplication of efforts and confusion. At the opposite end of the spectrum were others who copied everyone and their mothers on emails in an effort to cover their asses, wasting precious time.

One of my key motivations to do more public speaking came from what I observed within the label system: it was full of dissatisfied women—from women in their early twenties who were underpaid, overworked, and underappreciated, to women in their midthirties and older who were well paid, overworked, and underappreciated, but with the added indignity of watching their dreams of motherhood become more and more distant with each passing day. It became clear that my experience, particularly as a working mother, could be valuable. After having been so faithfully mentored by Michael, and understanding the impact he had on my life, I was happy to put my energy into helping others.

Though there were many hushed conversations about these concerns behind closed doors, there was no open discourse, which is needed to achieve a shift in any culture.

So I founded the East Coast branch of the Universal Music Women's Network. It was fantastic to assemble women of different ages, backgrounds, and ranks to discuss the issues that impacted us all.

I was also taken aback by the racism I encountered. It surprised me, considering the progressive nature of the business and the fact that hip-hop and R&B were such dominant genres and huge sources of revenue by this time. One day my colleague, a white woman, and I were talking about Amber, a black woman I had recently hired. She told me Amber would be a "good fit" for Def Jam.

"But she's a rock girl, not a hip-hop head," I said. "How would she be a good fit?" Despite understanding exactly what the subtext was—that because Amber was black, she would work well with the other black folks and black artists at Def Jam—I wanted to push her.

"She just would."

"How so?"

"She just would, it's cultural," she said.

The language of racism, and all prejudice for that matter, is often highly codified. She had made an assumption about Amber and erased the expertise Amber had in other areas of music as well as her professional ambitions.

Just over a year after I'd started at Universal, one of my staff came into my office and closed the door. "Sophia, I've been hearing some things. You need to watch your back." She was one of the few people who looked out for me in that snake pit, and I believed her.

I told my friend Maria that the knives were out.

"Soph, you'd better buy an apartment while you still have a job; otherwise you'll never get a mortgage!" That was all it took. She was right: I was making enough money that I could handle a modest down payment, and a letter of employment from a global music corporation would go a long way. I started looking immediately and bought the first apartment I saw, a big two-bedroom on the Lower East Side.

Things at work started to get a little crazy. There were a couple of women who clearly had it in for me. They were telling my superiors straight lies about me. Michael went to see my boss, who said the carping had become untenable. Michael could read the writing on the wall and recommended a perfect solution on the spot. He suggested that I switch from working for all the labels to one in particular, where he knew the president was a big fan of mine. If it hadn't been for him, I would've been fired.

Things at work were settled, my kids were growing into gorgeous humans, I was a new homeowner, and I was deeply in love. What a fantastic way to mark my fiftieth year. I love celebrating my birthday, and this was a big one. William planned the dinner. He had a relationship with the restaurant, and we got a huge private dining room. We got dressed together, but he left before me because he wanted to be there to greet the guests. Michelle and Byron had flown out from LA and were staying with us. One of my friends, Gabe, whom I hadn't seen in a while, grabbed me to say: "Okay, did you order him from a catalogue?" William wore a navy suit and I wore my favorite piece: a forest-green first-season Alaïa dress. My favorite people in the world were in that room.

As I had done on my fortieth, I went around the table and toasted my twenty closest friends, telling them why they were all there. I chose to toast William last. I talked about how he had helped me redefine love and find myself after a long marriage and two children. And then, this time, I let them toast me. Many of them talked about the extraordinary and diverse group of friends who had assembled to celebrate with me.

After dinner, we went over to Number 8, Amy Sacco's post–Bungalow 8 spot. RZA hosted, and DJ Scratch and D-Nice, my two favorite DJs, spun. It was a magical night and I felt very, very loved. Watching William do for me what I had done for countless others for decades made me love him even more, and my friends had a new level of respect and affection for him. At one point, I wanted to get air and he walked me outside. Those few minutes in the New York City spring evening with the man I loved so deeply, holding me tightly and telling me through every part of his body that he loved me, was nothing short of perfect. William, in fact, rarely said those three words. He had told me very early that he wouldn't say it often, and I was fine with it, because he walked the walk so hard.

One night, we were planning on going for dinner. As usual, I was in producer mode and tried to figure out where to eat. He said, "Let me take care of it, Sophia." I honestly don't think I had ever heard those words before. It meant relinquishing control and power, but I needed that lesson. And he chose the perfect spot. It resulted in a more profound love and, as anachronistic and patriarchal as it sounds, I was happy to let the man be a man. Especially in the bedroom.

At fifty, I was having the best sex of my life.

CHAPTER 12
LETTING GO

As we rounded into fall of 2015, I was beckoned into the president's office mere moments after I had finished mastering an album, which I had A&R'd and delivered on time and under budget. I strolled in expecting a hearty pat on the back, just like in fifth grade when I got asked to stay behind to talk to my teacher. When I walked in and saw the head of HR, I was about to joke, "Am I getting fired?" Then I realized, *Oh, shit, Sophia, you're getting fired!* I was greeted with warm but sheepish smiles and told that they were letting me go because they were restructuring. I would be paid out of my contract, which gave me a full six months to find something else. Numb, I thanked them for the opportunity to work with them and walked out. Despite the murmurings, I hadn't seen it coming that soon.

I went into my office, closed the door, and called William.

He stopped what he was doing to come straight to me. We packed up my stuff and left the office. I went home and sent a gracious thank-you email to everyone whom I'd worked with at the company and separately to everyone outside the company. I was surprised and disappointed but not hurt. Michael had taught me not to take things personally. By this point, I recognized that the people I worked with were not my family. That's a corporate mindfuck that they employ to squeeze every last cell of work out of you. I knew they didn't give a shit about me; they were beholden to larger mandates that all had to do with the bottom line.

William urged me to take the next six months to work on my blog and my memoir. People had been telling me for years that I should write a book, and I knew that it was in my future, but I was a serial hustler. I went from gig to gig, and my immigrant work ethic would not allow me to sit back and collect a check. I figured I could work and write at the same time. I'd been multitasking for years; this shouldn't be so hard. Michael liked to say, "Soph's a heat-seeking missile. Point her in the right direction, and she'll get there faster than anyone else can." My life had taken many different paths, mostly by my own hand. The night I got fired, I texted Steve, a business acquaintance who ran a small label and management company. "I got fired today, let's make money together," I said. Within a week, he hired me as his general manager. I would make all calls on spending, operations, hiring, and firing. "No sacred cows," he said. I had heard this at Universal as well. Steve told me there was a woman named Jane whom I'd have to fire, because despite being thorough and organized, she was widely despised by both the staff and the artists.

In the first marketing meeting, I went around the table asking each of the staff members for updates on our projects. I started with Jane. I asked about one of our artists, G Herbo, who was slated to perform at the Red Bull Music Festival in Cali. She responded, "He's not going to go to LA until we move his mother out of the hood." She actually smirked and rolled her eyes. The second she uttered the words, I thought, *Bitch, you're fired.*

What was so galling was that Jane clearly didn't care. Herbo was concerned because his mother, father, and younger sister still lived on the notorious East Side of Chicago. How did I know? Because I had asked. Because I'd listened to his music and wanted to know what experiences, at the tender age of twenty, could have informed his art with such violence, rage, and pain. He told me about walking his little sister to kindergarten and witnessing a point-blank gun killing up close. Naturally, she was traumatized. "The crazy thing, Sophie, is it didn't even phase me. I'd already seen so many murders by then." He had been thirteen. Jane had never asked him why he was so worried about his family, yet she was perfectly happy to make a living off his music, tag along on tour, stunt in the VIP, and smoke blunts backstage.

The president was the one to fire Jane, but I was there, coaching him through it. There were a number of others who needed to be cut loose, but they were his boys and he wouldn't let me fire them, despite the promise that I could run the company the way I wanted to. I ended up leaving because I realized that I couldn't be effective if I wasn't fully empowered. A paycheck is not worth that frustration.

William told me I wouldn't be happy until I was running my own thing, but I ignored him and kept jumping into new ventures. The travel and day jobs put a strain on my relationship with William, because our schedules were diametrically opposed. Even with us living together, it was hard to find time. I worked when the sun was up, he when it was down, and that left little time for us to see each other. By the time he got home late at night, I was asleep and had to be up early to get the kids to school. I started to feel as if he was checking out, and we chose to take a break in early summer.

As we neared the fall, William and I got together to figure out what we were doing. We rode bikes down the FDR, around the bottom of the island, and up to a restaurant on the West Side. It felt sweet and romantic, and I just knew he was going to tell me that his desire to be with me was stronger than the challenges we were facing at that time. We took pictures in the warm sunset, and it felt so good to lean into William's body again. When we sat down to dinner, I told him how much I loved him and what I had learned from being with him. It took a second for him to respond. I thought he was trying to figure out how to say that he loved me like the moon loves the sun, and that he'd decided that we should get married, as we'd talked about. Instead, I got these six words: "Being with you taught me patience."

After I'd opened up to him in a moment of such uncertainty, his statement shot through me like a cold blade. I got up, leaned over, and said, "Put my keys in the mail." I got on a bike and rode home, hoping the whole way that he would chase me, but he wasn't that man and this wasn't a rom-com. I got into bed and, in a fit of sadness and frustration, reached out to all the boys I'd been ignoring since getting together with William. I needed to fill this hole, so to speak.

About a week later, William came to get his stuff. Gathering all his clothes, folding them up neatly, and stacking them on my dining room table was a heartbreaking exercise. I felt numb. It was perfectly cordial, but that's highly imperfect and excruciating when you still love someone. When he hugged me goodbye, I thought, *I'm smelling him for the last time. I'm feeling the gentle pressure of his strong hands on the small of my back for the last time. And I'm feeling the warm touch of his soft lips on my forehead for the last time.* He walked out the door, as he had done hundreds of times before, and I locked it behind him, as I had done hundreds of times before, and in the minute that I knew it would take the slow elevator to get to my floor, I hoped again for a Hollywood moment. For William to knock on the door, for me to open it, fall into his arms, for no words to need to be spoken. I stood by the dining room table, waiting to hear his footsteps come back to me. Even after I heard the elevator ding and the doors close, I thought he might come back. He didn't.

For the next couple of weeks, I had Sia's "Chandelier" on repeat. Not sure what the song meant to her, but for me, it was a promise to myself that I was going to live the fuck out of life. For now, though, I would embrace my sadness. I sat in the bathtub, hugging my knees to my chest, hot water

cascading over me, and belted out the lyrics to the song between breathless sobs.

It would be several months before we spoke again, and it
wasn't to wish each other Merry Christmas or Happy Birthday. A woman I had recently befriended in LA texted me
while I was at the gym. She was hoping to get coffee and
asked if I was still in town.

"No, is everything okay?" I texted back.

She responded with a cryptic text and asked if we could
get dinner the next time I was in town. Apparently, we had
"shared history" that she seemed anxious to talk about it.
"Shared history"? *Oh, you mean we fucked the same guy.*

I responded, "I don't give a fuck." This was a sophomoric
conversation that could not be less interesting, particularly
since I didn't know her like that.

I continued my workout but something stopped me mid-
kick and my step faltered. *FUCK, what if it's William?* My
mind started racing at a velocity and in a direction that only
begot dread: he had spent a lot of time in LA, they were both
in music, they could have easily found themselves in the same
rooms . . . I took a deep breath and typed the next words:
"Who was it?"

It seemed as if it took her an eternity to respond. My blood
ran like mercury through my veins; I could barely breathe.
When I finally got the response, I felt a sense of relief the
likes of which I don't recall feeling in years. It was Derek.

I thought about it later and decided I wanted to talk to
William about it. He called me back the next day. Again, I
was at the gym doing kung fu.

"Hey, thanks for calling," I said.

"Are you at the gym?"

"Yes."

"I still know your schedule."

That simple statement already started to break me down.

"I was calling because I had an interesting experience . . ."

When I got to the point in the story where I asked her who it was, he said, "Who was it?" I could hear him smiling.

"It wasn't you." But he knew that before I even answered.

"Sophia, I told you that when I was with you, I was never with anyone else."

"Neither was I. But it made me realize that I would be really upset if I saw you again. So I wanted to make a deal with you: since it's entirely possible that we'll end up in the same room, can we please do each other the courtesy of warning the other if we think that's a possibility? Especially if we're going to be there with a date?"

"Well, that won't be necessary because I moved to Cali. I couldn't stand the thought of running into you on the East Side."

And boom, there it was: I started to cry. Leaning on the rolling metal box that housed the gym stereo, I watched as my tears dropped onto my phone.

"Oh, you did? When?" My voice was breaking.

"Not long after we broke up."

"Oh."

"How are the kids?"

"You know what, William? I'm not ready for this. I can't do small talk. It's too painful to hear your voice."

"Okay, Sophia. Take care."

"You too."

I hung up the phone and thought about Chris. Until that moment, I had only ever thought about how the grief for someone who's passed away can blindside you. But this exchange showed me that the loss of love can lurk in the corners of my heart, which, thank God, still beats with ferocity and abandon.

Even though it was clear that I still loved William, I didn't allow myself to wallow in sadness and linger in the past. It's not in my nature, and it's a luxury that single mothers simply don't have. The kids were now fourteen and sixteen, on the express train to college.

I had a friend, who is no longer a friend, who told me it was stupid to take Jin Long to see MIT because he would never get in. That is one of the cruelest things anyone has ever said to me. I told Jin Long after we'd visited schools that I didn't want him to feel the pressure to get into one, I wanted him to see what was out there. When it came time for him to apply to colleges, I got really stressed out, because he didn't seem to feel the urgency as much as I did. I never insisted my kids get straight As, but I wanted more than anything for them to live up to their potential, which Jin Long was not doing. I didn't know what to do because he didn't want my help. I called my girlfriend Nikki, whose son is fifteen days younger than Jin Long and one of his closest friends.

"Sophia, let him do it himself," she said. "Our sons are about to be eighteen; it's time that we let them grow up. I moved here from Korea by myself at fifteen; they should be able to do their own college applications. Let him go and he'll surprise you."

This was one of the most difficult lessons in faith that I had encountered. I am a manager and a producer. Taking care of every aspect of a business or project is in my blood, so walking away from the biggest step in my son's life to date was incredibly difficult. But Nikki had never steered me wrong. So I did as she said. I let go. As a result, with the exception of filling out the financial aid forms, Jin Long applied to almost twenty schools on his own. When the first acceptance letter came, he texted me a picture of the email and wrote, "I couldn't have done it without you."

Colleges also became a major part of my life. I went back to school, in a way. Adam Mitchell, a student at MIT, asked me to come speak. I did my first lecture there in the fall of 2016 and loved it. The room was filled with young, eager minds, mostly children of immigrants from Asia and South Asia. Speaking to and engaging with them told me, once and for all, that this was what I was meant to do. During the lecture, I showed a slide of my kids and said that my son would be applying to MIT.

I came back to Boston a couple of months later and spoke at a number of other schools. When I shared my vision with my friends, they all told me that I had to write a book in order to secure bigger speaking gigs. I told myself again that I could develop and write while working.

When I left the weed company in the spring of 2016, I jumped right into running Pro Era Records for my dear friend Joey BadAss, the Brooklyn hip-hop artist. I told him

I would do it as long as I was simultaneously working on my book. After five months, it became apparent that I couldn't maintain the balance between work and writing. Running a small label was something I could do in my sleep, whereas writing was like sticking hot needles in my eyes. I knew I had to stop taking jobs in order to commit myself to the book. It took every immigrant iota of willpower to walk away from a steady paycheck.

Joey and I met in Bryant Park to discuss my resignation. It was a beautiful, warm, sunny Friday afternoon—the kind that makes you fall back in love with New York and forgive her all her sins. I sat waiting for him at one of the metal tables on the south side of the park. I looked around at the people, the beautiful hustle and bustle of the city I call home. I saw Joey bounding across the street, his dreads bobbing high atop his tall, lithe frame. We hugged and when we sat down, I said, "I love you and the guys and I love this job, but I can't stay. I told you when I started that I would only do this job as long as I was still writing. Unfortunately, my book became my sidepiece."

"I love you too, Soph, and I understand. You told all of us that. I'm just sorry it has to end now."

"How long do you want me to stay?" I asked, almost hoping he'd say a number of months.

"Soph, can you give me two weeks?" Joey said.

I panicked slightly. "Do you think that's enough?" I didn't want things to fall apart and took the quick turnaround personally. Maybe he didn't think I was that important to the organization? "I can give you until the end of the year, if you want."

He placed his right fingertips down gingerly on the table, his hand and wrist raised high above them.

"I can't cage you, Soph, you're a butterfly. You need to be free."

I knew he was right. I am a free spirit who needs to fly toward her destination, unknown though the outcome may be. It wasn't that he didn't value my work, it was that he valued my dreams more than my utility to him. In short, he loved me enough to let me go.

Around this time, Joan texted me a flyer from NYU, where William would be lecturing the next day. It was hard for me to look at it, but I was happy he was lecturing. I knew he'd be great at it. The next day, I thought of him as I rode a bike past his old place on the way to the dentist. On the way home, as I rode down the FDR, I saw him running toward me. We both slowed down and stopped at a bench.

"I talked you into existence," he said, smiling. "I was just running down the FDR by your place and thought I should come see you."

"You always were witchy that way."

This conversation didn't feel like the last one. It was easier, but I barely looked him in the eye, and my body language told him to keep a respectful distance. We engaged in small talk and he told me about his lecture. For some stupid reason, I acted like I didn't know.

"I'm DJing on Saturday night if you want to come by."

"I'd rather fuck you than see you in public."

Ah, she opens the door.

This might sound counterintuitive, but it had been a full

year since we'd broken up, and I felt I had enough emotional distance to engage with him again. And I really missed fucking him.

"We can make that happen," he answered, boldly stepping toward me, pulling me in close, and clapping his right hand firmly on my ass.

I went home, exhilarated and nervous. As Joan would say, "Well, Soph, I think you've gotta stop asking for shit because you keep getting it." I called Michelle and Joan and they cautioned me against seeing him. I wasn't sure if they were right, but I knew I wanted to see him, to feel him inside of me again, to experience once more that unique connection that intersected with love, respect, and sexual chemistry.

When he walked in the door late that night, he looked around and commented on everything that had changed in the apartment, then went straight to the bedroom. He took a shower, as he always did before he got into my bed, and climbed under the covers, naked. *Je frissonais de désir.* I was shuddering with desire. The second he kissed me lightly and pulled me into him, the months that had separated us melted away. He remembered every inch of my body, and I his.

Jian Hong once told me she was sad because she had no memories of her father and me happy together. That's some hard shit to hear, but I got to offer my children an example of a healthy, loving partnership with William. I am grateful for the two and a half glorious years we spent loving each other.

William and I still see each other when he's in New York or I'm in Cali. We catch up, have amazing sex, and don't talk much in between. I never thought I'd be able to do this, but it's part of maturing. Eventually, each of us will fall in love with someone else, and we'll be truly happy for each other. I find myself again wondering what the next man will look like. What I am certain of is that he will have to know how to take care of me, as William did. I still feel his hands and hear his words and those are gifts. His gentle pushes to get me to write helped me arrive at this keyboard where I type now.

By 2018, it had become clear that I needed to move my mother out of our childhood home. It was a modest 2,500 square feet but three floors, and it was nerve-wracking to think of our mother navigating those stairs alone. She started to get scared by the noises the old house would make at night. Since my father's death, we had talked about moving her into a condo, but Heesok suggested assisted living, seeing as she would eventually end up in such a facility. She was eighty-five when we started the conversation. Better to move once than twice, and better to do it, as her doctor said, when she could, as opposed to when she had to. Because he was on an academic schedule, Heesok was able to spend months at a time in Vancouver with our mother and took her to see some facilities. My mother complained that the most upscale one was "too white." Which I thought was fucking hilarious. We settled on a beautiful place on the UBC campus, where she had spent decades of her life working.

Moving my mother out of the house was one of the most challenging things I've ever done. Imagine moving forty years of life. Now imagine that the person who lives there is an Asian immigrant who has been through two wars. My mother never met a takeout container, jar, or plastic bag she didn't deem worthy of keeping. I have to resist doing it myself. Then there was the nice stuff that we never used. The good plates and cutlery. And how about the fancy cake service that Heesok and I had never seen and she didn't even remember? We gave a bunch of stuff away to friends and donated the rest. It took countless garbage bags and trips to Goodwill.

I am grateful that my mother kept every one of my report cards. One summer when I wasn't in Vancouver, Heesok showed my high school report cards to my kids and said, "If your mother ever nags you about your grades, tell her you've seen these." They thought that was the funniest shit in the world, and the three of them laugh about it to this day. I was a B-average student, and most of the comments were along the lines of "Sophia talks too much in class."

I spent the first few days of cleaning out the house seething with anger, because I had been saying since my father passed that we should start getting rid of stuff. It had never been so tense between my mother and me—and that includes when I was a teenager. I was so angry and judgmental of every little useless thing she wanted to keep, which, in retrospect, was rude and insensitive. At one point I called my girlfriend Tanya and told her I couldn't take my mother anymore. She said, "Soph, your mother is eighty-five and she's moving her whole life into a new place. Maybe you could have a little more patience." I said, "Fuck you, Tanya!" Just kidding. Of course I stuck it out, but I had a really hard time letting go of my resentment. The emotional underpinning of all of this, of course, was my mother's mortality and by extension, my own. We were moving her into the house where she would live until she died.

On top of all that, selling the house was extremely unnerving. The Vancouver housing market has long been considered the largest real estate bubble in the world, but by the time we decided to sell, the air was leaking out of that bubble. After waiting for months, we ended up selling below ask, but it was still exponentially more than what my folks had paid for it forty years prior. When I told friends that we had moved my mother, they said we were lucky she went willingly.

I asked Heesok recently, "Do you think Mom is happy?"

He laughed and said, "I don't know how to answer that question. And I don't think she'd know how to answer that question."

I don't think my parents ever thought about their happiness. Their lives were such a struggle from the gate, and once they made the big move to Vancouver, it was all about providing for their children. They gave me the extravagance of pondering and seeking my happiness daily. Of finding my passion and pursuing it throughout my whole life. I never wondered if they were happy. I never asked who they were as people beyond being my parents. I knew what they enjoyed and disliked but never asked about their dreams, their disappointments, their internal lives.

My mother and father survived two wars and emerged champions. I can only hope to embody a small part of their grit, courage, and unyielding belief that on the other side of today's difficulty, there is a better tomorrow. After almost drowning, being caught by the North Korean police, escaping from the Japanese, almost freezing to death (which my father described as "the most pleasant sensation right before you're about to die"), and being closely acquainted with misery and death, they managed to live happy, beautiful lives full of fun, laughter, music, food, and friends.

Just a couple of months after we moved my mother, Jin Long was off to college. That spring, I went with Jian Hong and Heesok to attend the ceremony for an academic award he had received for his first term. I was so proud. As we pulled up to the front of the campus, I turned my head and looked at the large, green lawn, the fountains, and the 1970s modern architecture. It suddenly struck me that this was Jin Long's home now. I said quietly, "I can't believe my son lives here." I had to get out of the car because my tears were suffocating me. I took deep breaths and calmed myself down. I didn't want him to have to greet me as I wept. When we sat down at the Korean restaurant that Jin Long had picked out, I asked him to sit next to me. I hugged him and buried my face in his back. I could not stop crying. I watched as he and Jian Hong laughed and talked and teased each other like the best friends they are.

Just after he started his sophomore year, Jin Long invited Jian Hong and me upstate to go apple picking. He was so excited to host us. He chose the orchard and sent restaurant suggestions. When we got off the train, we met him in the supermarket down the street and he had the whole day mapped. I didn't try to intervene because he had it covered. Until this point, I had always planned our outings, and it was a spectacular role reversal. My boy is a man. An incredible man.

And my daughter an incredible young woman. They giggled and took pictures of each other among the trees. Seeing them together is the best thing in the world.

One of the silver linings of separating from Yan Ming was that it drew my kids closer together. Jin Long has protected his little sister from the day she was born, when he brought her that red teddy bear at the hospital. Once, when they were very young, I yelled at Jian Hong for something and told her she couldn't have any chocolate. Jin Long promptly took her into their room, where he shared his chocolate with her. That's my son. Jian Hong is more like her mother. She is articulate, curious, focused, disciplined, competitive, and mature beyond her years. She has a hot temper and a mean streak. My children are both kind, just, sensitive, progressive, outspoken, defenders of underdogs, funny, and so, so much smarter than their mother. In short, they are good people, and that's the best gift I can offer the world.

CHAPTER 13
A COMING-OF-AGE STORY

As I sat down to write my memoir, I thought about the first and only time I heard my father cry. On Christmas morning 1994, shortly after we'd finished opening presents, Heesok, his girlfriend visiting from New York, an old friend from the neighborhood, and I were sitting in the living room when there was an unexpected knock at the door. Who could be stopping by Christmas morning? I opened it to see my aunt's brother, head down, brow furrowed. He asked to see my parents, who were in the kitchen. He rushed past me, without as much as a hello, closing the door behind him. Heesok and I exchanged a look. Less than a minute later, I heard a sound like I'd never heard: a wail of grief from my father that pierced my heart. And then sobbing. I had never seen my father cry, let alone break down completely. After some minutes, my aunt's brother emerged, red-eyed, and left again without saying a word, closing the front door quietly behind him.

Our parents came out and told us that Heeyon, son of my father's younger brother, Yunshik, God rest his soul, had committed suicide that morning. My uncle was a sociology professor who did his graduate studies at Princeton and followed my father to Vancouver. They moved into a house a mere eleven blocks away and had two children: an older son and younger daughter, just like our family. With the rest of our family in Korea either estranged or incommunicado, it was wonderful to have immediate family so close. My father took to Heeyon as soon as he was born. He adored him. He was so happy and gentle with him. More so, frankly, than I remember him being with us—behavior I wouldn't see again until my own son was born. My father was devastated. I had a trip to Hawaii planned with Sonya that conflicted with the funeral, but my parents insisted I keep my plans.

While in Hawaii, Sonya and I visited the Black Rock Beach in Maui, which boasts a sixteen-foot-high cliff that people dive or jump off. Understand this: I am not a thrill seeker. I don't fuck with skydiving, bungee jumping, or hang gliding and have a near moral opposition to it because, as Maria told me when she got back from a trip to Cambodia, "Soph, having been to the Killing Fields and seen what the Cambodians went through under the Khmer Rouge, I find it offensive that people would pay to come that close to death."

Sonya, on the other hand, loved a thrill and was far more daring than me. After watching a bunch of people jump, she said, "C'mon, Soph, let's go!"

"No, thanks. You go. I'll watch."

"Oh, c'mon, Soph, you only live once!"

Her excitement was contagious. We climbed up to the cliff and she pushed me forward. I walked along the rocky precipice, the uneven porous black rock hurting my feet. When I reached the edge, I stood for what seemed like minutes, trying to muster up the courage to jump. I looked down at the limpid water—it always looks higher from above—and saw the rocks clearly beneath the surface. I started telling myself it was too dangerous, that I could cut myself on the rocks, even though everyone else jumping came out unscathed. A line was forming behind us. I was about to turn back when my legs started to shake, my knees wobbling back and forth. I had never felt fear manifest so physically. I looked out at the perfect cerulean Hawaiian sky and thought about Heeyon. I thought that he would never see this nor have this opportunity to take this crazy jump into the pristine blue waters of Maui. And so I jumped. For him. I wanted to live, for him. All these years later, and I have so many other departed souls to live for: my father, my uncle, who helped fill in the blanks of my father's childhood before he passed, A Son, Chris, Sonya.

And part of that living is sharing my story.

"Tell your story. Tell your story. Tell your story. Tell your story."

On March 29, 2016, Quest Green paced the stage of the Apollo Theater in a pristine white collarless linen shirt repeating this phrase with a heartbreak-laced exigency as he presided over the celebration of Phife Dawg of A Tribe Called Quest, who had passed the week prior. Hip-hop royalty was present. D'Angelo sang "You've Got a Friend," which brought tears to my eyes. But these three simple words—*tell your story*—resonated the most deeply with me personally. I took it to mean that we should continue to share our narratives as a way to honor Phife, seeing as he was no longer able to do so for himself.

My friends had been telling me for years that I should write a book, but I simply couldn't wrap my head around it because it sounded like an exercise in narcissism. What would I talk about, my glamourous life hanging out with famous people? No fucking way. Let someone else write that book. Then a couple of things happened around 2013. First, Sheryl Sandberg's *Lean In* came out, and though it was filled with some nuggets of wisdom, it did not really speak to me as a woman of color. Second, taking on the mentees at Universal Music Group showed me how my story helped others. Then, in June 2017, a film that I'm producing about Chrissie Hynde got accepted into the LA Film Festival Fast Track program, which gives filmmakers the opportunity to pitch to several buyers in a couple of days. It's like speed dating; each team has fifteen minutes. Michelle Sy, Eliza Lee, our screenwriter, and I decided to give a sixty-second résumé at the beginning. When I'd finished telling my minute-long story, the vast majority of the buyers said, "I hope the movie is about *her*." By the end of the day, I was convinced that I had to tell my story.

During a recent interview I did with the wonderful Indian comedian and writer Hari Kondabolu, he said almost wistfully, "My only wish was that I knew you existed when I was fourteen. It would have been wonderful to know that this music that me and my friends listened to, that was our soundtrack in New York City, that there was an Asian person that was contributing to the movement and we had a place."

My heart hurt when I heard that because I understood that keeping myself invisible, though I may have been satisfying my desire for anonymity, was a selfish choice because I could have been an inspiration to a young brown teenager in Queens who would have loved to see himself in the culture that helped shape his identity. And who knows how many others? But it's never too late.

Having crossed the Rubicon out of obscurity in order to tell my story, I understand that there is a myriad of manners in which to share myself with the world. And now that I have made this decision, it no longer seems like an option, but rather a mandate. Everything I do from here on will involve me as a raging raconteuse of subversion. And I see that the reason I am the best facilitator of storytellers I know is because I myself am a storyteller.

The current chapter of my life is proclaiming to be the Baddest Bitch in the Room. The concept came to me more than a decade ago when I attended the second annual Black Girls Rock! awards show. The organization was founded by DJ-turned-philanthropist Beverly Bond to celebrate and empower magical black girls. That night, I was in the company of three such exceptional creatures: Bethann Hardison, Joan, and Sam Martin, my friend at HBO who had bought my screenplay. When we left the event, I ran down the stairs in front of the others to capture a picture of those three women gliding down the staircase like royalty. Bethann with her closely cropped salt-and-pepper hair, wearing a brightly colored African print dress; Joan in a sage raw-silk empire-waist dress; and Sam in a fawn-colored Barney's cotton dress. As I took photo after photo, it occurred to me that my girls were the Baddest Bitches in the Room.

It may sound competitive, but it isn't. It's not about looking antagonistically at other women, but claiming our power and beauty as women who are almost exclusively of color and over forty and fifty in a world where we are given little to no indication that we are powerful and beautiful. There could be prettier, richer, younger, more accomplished women in the room, but those aren't the qualities that grant membership into the Baddest Bitch Club. It's the extraordinary aggregate of our strengths that constitutes our power. And part of being the Baddest Bitch in the Room is owning it. If you truly believe it, that energy emanates when you walk into a room. My hope is that someday every woman will feel as mightily about herself as we do.

I enter every space as if I'm six feet tall. I am heightened by my confidence, desire to stand out, and unique style, which I've spent a lifetime honing as a response to feeling invisible. I am aware of the genetic privilege I enjoy: my father's razor-sharp cheekbones and my mother's hummingbird metabolism. And I know that this playing field is not level, that "beauty is capital," as Joan would say. As a woman, I use every tool in my arsenal to get my foot in the door and a seat at the table. But here's the hitch: once I'm there, my goal is to have everyone saying, "Fuck, she's smart," as opposed to "Damn, she's hot." Furthermore, I haven't kicked down doors to let them close behind me, I keep them open and bring my folks in with me. That's how we do.

Many men have told me that they were initially scared to talk to me. They should be. My confidence serves as a filter.

If you're too shook to approach me or think I'm out of your league, you're probably right, because you lost the second you doubted yourself. Having been the little Asian girl who was bullied, I delight in the idea that I scare people. And if you had told the scrawny ten-year-old who was embarrassed to do push-ups in front of her gym class that she would be considered physically formidable and at her most powerful at fifty-five, she would have called you crazy. I've reached the point where training is as integral a part of my life as eating and sleeping, such that it's harder *not* to do it than to do it. I have to take care of myself so I'm in the best shape possible for my kids and the others in my life for whom I wage tiny battles every day.

But I didn't get here on my own.

I wouldn't have the moxie or muscle or the motivation to do what I do if I wasn't embraced, emboldened, and empowered by the motherfucking village that raised me. My ride-or-dies stand by me when I'm faltering, embrace me when I'm hurting, toss me onto their shoulders when I'm celebrating, talk me off the ledge when I'm about to lose my shit, and pull me aside when I'm fucking up. They are my pillars, my shields, and my mirrors, who challenge me every day to be a better person.

And I discovered what it truly means when I say "My name is Sophia Chang and I was raised by Wu-Tang." The Clan provided me with life-changing firsts: Method Man was the first to call me family and open my imagination to what family could look like, ODB was the first person to hire me as a manager, and RZA was the first to empower me as a general manager. If it wasn't for Wu-Tang, I wouldn't have discovered the power and beauty of my Asian heritage, I wouldn't have trained kung fu, I wouldn't have met the man who would become my mighty love, and, most important, I wouldn't have these two extraordinary children who are my greatest legacy.

As I have transitioned from manager to creative, it has been so touching to see how my artist friends, particularly my former clients to whom I was in service, have embraced this new version of Sophia Chang. They have all been remarkably supportive, gracious, and magnanimous. None of them seemed surprised or concerned that I might reveal any of their confidences, because they trusted me and knew that I would still keep their best interests at heart, even in telling my own story.

My mother's response to me writing a memoir was probably relief because it was the first time in more than thirty years that she could tell her friends what the fuck her daughter did. Heesok is a no-brainer: he's a professor. Me? I honestly don't think there was any time before this that my mother could give any detail about what I actually did for a living. And that's to be expected, for God's sake: she was born in North Korea in 1932 and knew only the traditional occupations. What is the most important is that she never stopped believing in me and always supported me in whatever endeavor.

Everything, that is, short of my sexual exploits. The only discomfort I had during the process of writing was in telling my mother my dick index. Like the jump off the cliff in Maui, I had to work up my courage to take this leap. On the last day of my last trip to Vancouver, right before the memoir was published, I told my mother about men asking women how many men they'd been with.

"Why do they ask that? That's nonsense! It's none of their

business!" She totally understood why the question was sexist and preposterous.

"Well, Mom, in order to start a conversation around how sexist I think this is, I say in my book how many men I've been with."

I saw my mother pause.

"Do you want to know the number?" I asked.

I saw my mother stop moving. "I don't know, do I?"

"Well, Mom, I want you to hear it from me. I don't want you to hear it from one of your friends, so I want to tell you."

I saw my mother take a deep breath.

"The number is seventy."

I saw my mother's head turn sharply toward me.

"I don't believe it. Is that even possible?"

"Yes, Mom."

"What did the kids say?"

The kids didn't care at all. They laughed when I told them because to them, it was such a nothing. Much more important, they are happy for me.

"Mommy, we're so proud of you. It's your turn."

In less than a year, those children, those stunning humans, will both be gone. The nest will be empty when Jian Hong goes to college and I have no idea how I will feel. She has lived with me full-time for the past two years and I hear about school and her friends every day. When Jin Long went to college, I didn't miss him terribly because he had been staying with his father almost exclusively, so I barely saw him, and Jian Hong was still around. When she leaves I think it'll be bittersweet. I'll be happy not to wake up bleary-eyed at 6:30 in the morning, but I'll miss kissing her lightly as she walks out the door, so beautiful, poised, and stylish; I'll miss her coming through the door after school and racing up to her so that she can lay her head on my stomach as she sits on the bench by the door to take a beat after removing her shoes; I'll miss her lying on top of my back as I lie on my stomach as if she's still a small child, but she's a giant teenager; I'll miss her reading me her essays and sharing her impassioned stories about what she's learning. After June, these quotidian habits will become memories that I will hug closely to me as I sit and miss both my children as they enter adulthood.

Perhaps in the interim, I will fall in love so I won't feel so alone. For now, I am single. At the top of 2019, as at the opening of 2013, I told myself that I was open to love again. Not chasing, but not skirting anymore either. Since my breakup with William, a number of men from my past, well, let's call it what it is, a good portion of my dick index, has re-entered my orbit. But the one who never left my heart, even if we hadn't spoken for months, is D'Angelo.

In the first minutes of my fifty-third birthday, as I lay in bed, William called to wish me a happy one. His voice warm and tender and full of smiles, as always. In the final minutes of my birthday, the phone rang again as I lay in bed. I smiled and rushed to answer.

"Peace."

"Peace. Happy birthday, Sophia. I had to call you on your birthday, but I'm not gonna sing to you." He laughed his deep throaty laugh.

"Okay," I laughed back.

I was good with D'Angelo not singing "Happy Birthday" to me because I still had Luther.

That birthday call was a mix of personal and business. Once we'd talked and laughed and asked each other when was the last time we spoke to Raphael Saadiq, I asked if I could read him the passage about him from my book. As I read, I was a little flustered because he is intensely private and I thought this wasn't going to work for him. When I was done, I babbled nervously.

"Are you okay with that? I'm only going to say it if you're okay with it. Are you okay with being in my book?"

And he said, as only D can say, "I'd be honored."

Then he laced me with another badge of honor. "You're a great writer, Sophia."

A year later, I spent my fifty-fourth birthday in Paris with my friend Danielle Belton. As it so happened, who was performing in Paris, on my birthday, but Wu-Tang Clan! I love it when the universe gives me such gifts. That was one of the most memorable birthdays of my life—to be back in Paris for the first time in twelve years, with Danielle, who had never been out of the country, and spend it with the Clan. After the show we went back to the bar at the Hotel Lutétia where the guys were staying and spent hours with GZA, RZA, and Ghost. At one point RZA went over to the shiny grand piano and started playing and singing. I pulled up right next to him and watched as he played effortlessly, a self-taught pianist, as opposed to me, for whom each keystroke was a chore and every lesson an exercise in trying to stay awake. He played and he sang and we talked in between. Happy birthday to me indeed.

At around 2:00 a.m., GZA and Ghost escorted Danielle and me to our Uber, and Ghost shot the driver a smile that said, *Take care of these girls. Because if you don't, I'll fuck you up.* Twenty-six years after yelling at the other subway riders in Times Square, he was still issuing warnings to the people in my immediate proximity. Danielle and I went back to our hosts' home, high on the evening we'd just had. As soon as we got in, we dove into the fridge to retrieve the mocha éclairs we'd bought earlier from a local patisserie. As I shoved the buttery pastry and sweet cream into my mouth, my phone rang with a 929 area code. Where the fuck is that? But something told me to answer. This had better not be one of those damn robocalls.

"Hello?" I said, suspiciously.

"Peace, Beloved."

Ah, those two words. That voice. This man. I rushed to the pullout couch and lay down because it seems I'm always lying down when I talk to D'Angelo.

"Peace, Michael. It's my birthday."

"Wow, really? I didn't know."

But he must have, at some level. It had been exactly a year since we'd spoken. It was still May 17 in New York and as usual, his timing was uncanny. We are bound that way.

Even though D and I have spent time together only a handful of occasions and our communication ebbs and flows, our love is a constant that envelops me like cashmere, that I bathe in like a hot spring, and drink like hot spiced apple cider. Like my love with Meth, it is truly sui generis. I can't name it and I don't feel the need to. It is simply enough that it is and will always be.

In July 2009 the Clan did Rock the Bells at Jones Beach. When I saw Meth I jumped into his arms as usual and he hugged me tightly but pulled me back, looked me dead in the eye, and said sternly, "Sophie, I need you to fall back today." Which was his way of saying, "Sophie, I know you're usually glued to me, but today you should keep some distance from me." Oh, okay, shit's about to go down.

I didn't even question him. He had never said anything like that to me. Later that afternoon my girls and I were backstage and I saw the Clan and their boys approaching en masse. It's like a river rushing into a canyon and you'd better get the fuck out of the way. Someone with a video camera started shooting footage and one of the guys threw a water bottle at him. Suddenly there was another crew approaching from the opposite direction and I saw a familiar look in Popa Wu's eyes. I grabbed my girls and we barricaded ourselves in a nearby room. Even with the door closed it was pretty scary because we could hear the roar of the fight right on the other side of it and bodies were banging into the door. When everything had died down we went outside and the guys asked if I was okay.

I don't know exactly who was involved in the altercation, but I do know that only a fool would ignore the truism that Wu-Tang Clan Ain't Nuthin ta Fuck Wit—they roll crazy deep, have no problem throwing down, and have a long history of bringing da ruckus. After their set I watched as Meth got into his black SUV with tinted windows. I ran up to make sure everything was okay. He said, "All good, Sophie. I'm getting outta here." I went in for a final hug. As his SUV pulled out and I turned around, I realized that there was a crowd watching us.

In June 2017, I went to see the Clan at Governors Ball and after the show I saw Meth surrounded by fans backstage. I ran up, pushed my way through the crowd, and grabbed him from behind, wrapping my arms around his big chest, holding him with all my strength. Without hesitation he said, "I know this has to be Sophie." I told him I was writing my book and there would be a whole chapter dedicated to him. I told him what I wanted to talk about and he remembered every moment and every conversation. When we were done talking, I pulled back and once again saw the huge crowd who had been patiently waiting for us to finish, standing there, just staring at us.

I am deeply, hopelessly, and boundlessly in love with my friend Meth. I've never felt this way about a man before and am sure I never will again. I have plenty of platonic male friends with whom I'm emotionally and spiritually intimate and we might even hold hands and give each other massages, but with Meth it's all that and it's romantic but not sexual at all. I really don't know how to explain it. I would say it's confusing, but it's not, because we're very clear on how we feel about each other. It's simply unnamable. It's singular and beautiful and could only exist between us because of our unique characters and chemistry.

I didn't think it was possible to love Meth more deeply than I had since that day he defended me in the studio, but I did. In the wake of my separation from Yan Ming, I was drawn to how caring, thoughtful, affectionate, demonstrative, and gentle he was with me. He had always been all these things but took particular care of me at this time; the hugs were longer, the gestures grander, the *I love you, Sophie*s louder. I was starving for that kind of tenderness and attention after stumbling out of twelve years with someone who had affection deficit disorder. What's extraordinary is that Meth didn't shower me with love because he suddenly found me more compelling, he did it because his intuition and sensitivity told him that I needed it, even when I didn't realize it myself.

At this stage in my life, my friendships have taken on many forms, no one alike, and in examining my relationships for this memoir, I got to discover the depth, beauty, and complexity of them and piece together this unimaginable kaleidoscopic tapestry that is my life. My family. People asked if it was a cathartic experience, to which I said no, because that implies that I had something like trauma to purge. I would say the process had the opposite effect: rather than expelling my experiences, I embraced them. Revisiting even the shitty moments was an opportunity for me to appreciate the richness of my life, loves, and experiences. What I am most grateful for is that I learned more about my parents and told their stories.

We hear about second acts in life, and I feel fortunate that I've had many: from music to kung fu to motherhood and marriage, back to music, to film, and now to writing, public speaking, and TV. My path, though unpredictable, is a reflection of my never-ending pursuit of self, to discover what it means to be Sophia Chang: a woman, Asian, mother, lover, friend, hustler.

I don't know what the next phase of my life will bring, but I am excited to find yet another adventure, and I am sure that I will dive in with gusto and panache and enjoy the hell out of it. What I am categorically certain of right now is that it's my turn. After decades of helping extraordinarily talented men tell their stories, I realize it took me so long to tell my own because I believed myself smaller and less important, that my role was limited to support.

Well, the butterfly has emerged from her cocoon and is spreading her wings. What I am asking of the world is simply to imagine that I exist. I have been thinking a lot about visibility and erasure. I believe that any of us who live on the margins have been effaced to some degree. Some more than others, of course. It's as if the dominant culture has a huge and redoubtable brush that systematically, fastidiously, and efficiently paints over us like a new coat on the slats of a white picket fence. And what that means is that we have to fight to be seen. You may not like what you see, but you will see me, motherfucker. My very being is an act of defiance. Think about it: I am a fifty-five-year-old Asian single mother of two who is out here announcing to the world in no uncertain terms, with not an iota of compunction, that I am THE BADDEST BITCH IN THE ROOM. And I think that's fucking radical. I am not allowing the dominant culture to tell me who I am; I am defining myself and telling the world who I am.

ACKNOWLEDGMENTS

My father, Bomshik Chang, rest in peace, and my mother, Tongsook Chang, who always allowed me to chase my dreams, who taught me to love and fight and endure everything with grace, panache, and a hearty laugh.

My brother, Heesok, who has made me laugh and guided me with his unearthly wisdom from the day I was born and whose editing of only the first two pages of the manuscript changed the bones of it.

My son, Jin Long, and my daughter, Jian Hong, for being the inspiration and motivation behind everything I do.

Father of my children, Shi Yan Ming, who taught me the greatest spiritual lessons of my lfe and helped turn my body into a Temple.

My uncle Yunshik Chang (God rest his soul), who filled in the blanks about my father who had already passed when I started writing.

My mentor Michael Ostin who has advised me with love and compassion in all matters personal and professional for over thirty years.

Godfather of my children, and one of my closest friends, RZA, who has supported me for twenty-six years.

Wu-Tang Clan, who claimed me, saw me, protected me, and loved me in a way I'd never known.

My agent, Marya Whitney, who fought for what I believed in and told me I was a writer from the gate.

My editor, Mensah Demary, who gently and effectively helped me tell this story in an even deeper fashion.

My Catapult team, who have been so impassioned and engaged from the first meeting.

My readers: Darnell Moore, Elizabeth Mendez Berry, Hua Hsu, Joan Morgan, Kevin Bruyneel, Kiese Laymon, Marcelle Karp, Maria Ma, Tiffany Liao, Treva Lindsey who loved me enough to be honest with me.

My closest friends: Michelle Sy, who helped me shape the story, who's my home away from home, and is there for me every day to talk me through the good and the bad. And Danielle Belton, who never stopped telling me how amazing my story was and uplifts me in every way she can.

ME, who inspires and pushes me to be a better person every fucking day.

SOPHIA CHANG is a Korean Canadian music business matriarchitect who was the first Asian woman in hip-hop. She worked with Paul Simon and managed Ol' Dirty Bastard, RZA, GZA, Q-Tip, A Tribe Called Quest, Raphael Saadiq, and D'Angelo. In 1995, Chang left music to be trained in kung fu and manage a Shaolin monk who became her partner and the father of her two children. She also produced runway shows, worked at a digital agency, and is developing TV and film properties.